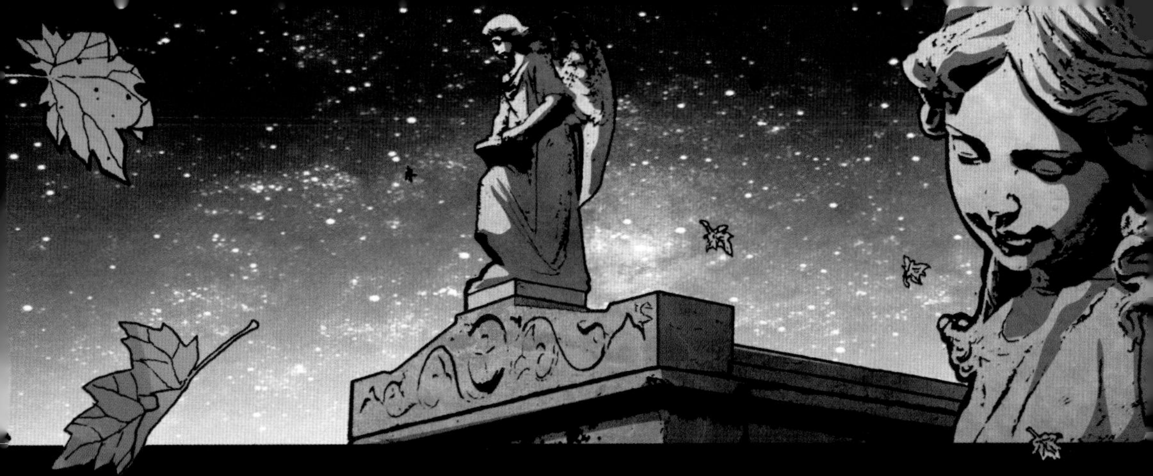

Cemetery Girl

BOOK TWO: INHERITANCE

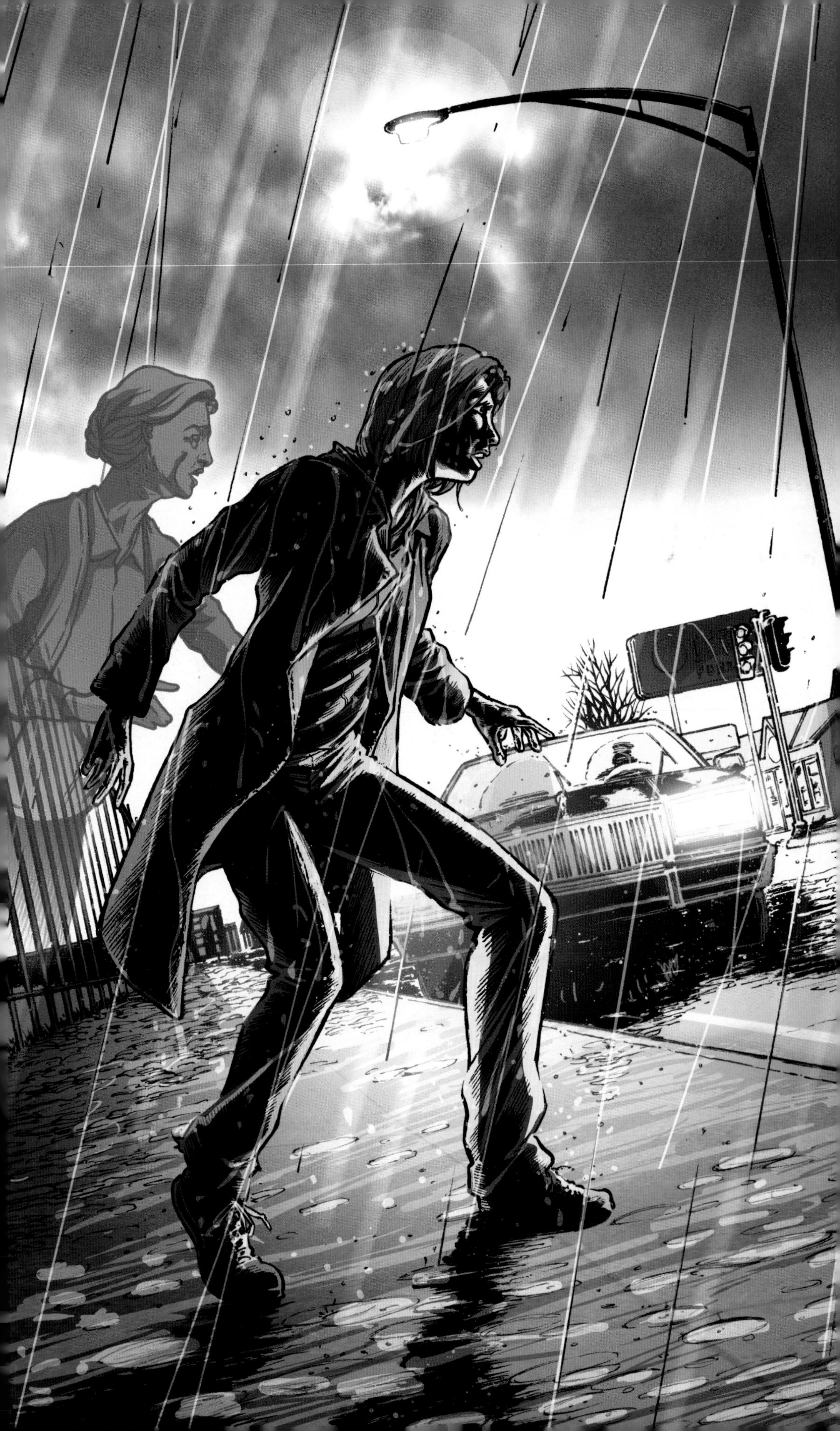

CHARLAINE HARRIS

CHRISTOPHER GOLDEN

CEMETERY GIRL

BOOK TWO: INHERITANCE

ART BY **DON KRAMER**

COLORS BY **DANIELE RUDONI**

LETTERS BY **JACOB BASCLE**

An imprint of Penguin Random House LLC
375 Hudson Street, New York, New York 10014

This book is an original publication of Penguin Random House LLC.

Library of Congress Cataloging-in-Publication Data

Harris, Charlaine.
Cemetery girl. Book two, Inheritance / by Charlaine Harris & Christopher Golden.
pages cm — (Cemetery girl ; book 2)
ISBN 978-0-425-25667-1 (hardcover)
1. Cemeteries—Comic books, strips, etc. 2. Young women—Comic books, strips, etc. 3. Graphic novels. I. Golden, Christopher. II. Title. III. Title: Inheritance.
PN6727.H3757C47 2015
741.5'973—dc23
2015006665

FIRST EDITION: October 2015

PRINTED IN CHINA

10   9   8   7   6   5   4   3   2   1

Cover illustration by Don Kramer.
Cover design by Jason Gill.
Cover colors by Daniele Rudoni.

Penguin
Random
House

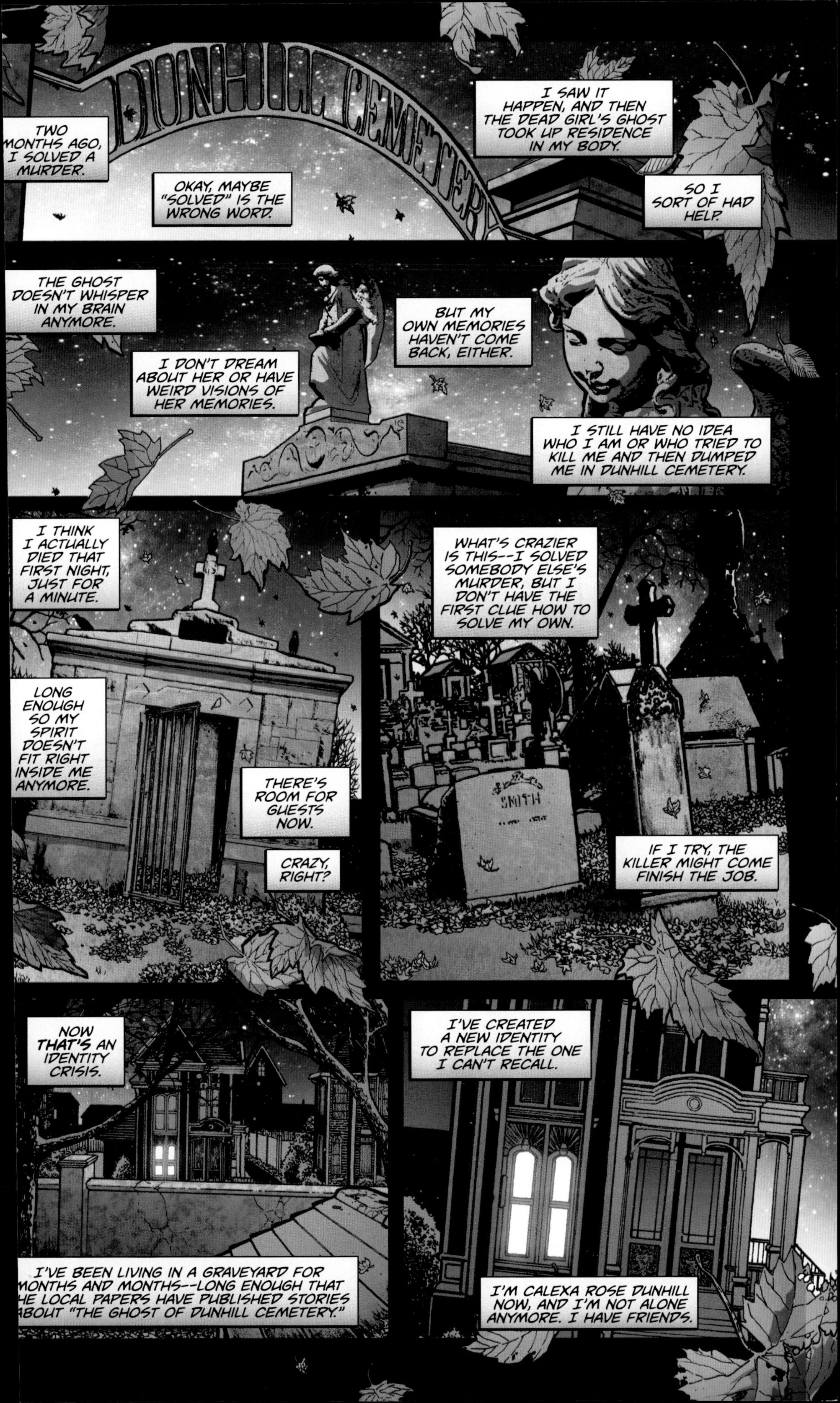

DUNHILL CEMETERY
TWO MONTHS AGO, I SOLVED A MURDER.
OKAY, MAYBE "SOLVED" IS THE WRONG WORD.
I SAW IT HAPPEN, AND THEN THE DEAD GIRL'S GHOST TOOK UP RESIDENCE IN MY BODY.
SO I SORT OF HAD HELP.
THE GHOST DOESN'T WHISPER IN MY BRAIN ANYMORE.
I DON'T DREAM ABOUT HER OR HAVE WEIRD VISIONS OF HER MEMORIES.
BUT MY OWN MEMORIES HAVEN'T COME BACK, EITHER.
I STILL HAVE NO IDEA WHO I AM OR WHO TRIED TO KILL ME AND THEN DUMPED ME IN DUNHILL CEMETERY.
I THINK I ACTUALLY DIED THAT FIRST NIGHT, JUST FOR A MINUTE.
LONG ENOUGH SO MY SPIRIT DOESN'T FIT RIGHT INSIDE ME ANYMORE.
THERE'S ROOM FOR GUESTS NOW.
CRAZY, RIGHT?
WHAT'S CRAZIER IS THIS--I SOLVED SOMEBODY ELSE'S MURDER, BUT I DON'T HAVE THE FIRST CLUE HOW TO SOLVE MY OWN.
SMITH
IF I TRY, THE KILLER MIGHT COME FINISH THE JOB.
NOW **THAT'S** AN IDENTITY CRISIS.
I'VE BEEN LIVING IN A GRAVEYARD FOR MONTHS AND MONTHS--LONG ENOUGH THAT THE LOCAL PAPERS HAVE PUBLISHED STORIES ABOUT "THE GHOST OF DUNHILL CEMETERY."
I'VE CREATED A NEW IDENTITY TO REPLACE THE ONE I CAN'T RECALL.
I'M CALEXA ROSE DUNHILL NOW, AND I'M NOT ALONE ANYMORE. I HAVE FRIENDS.

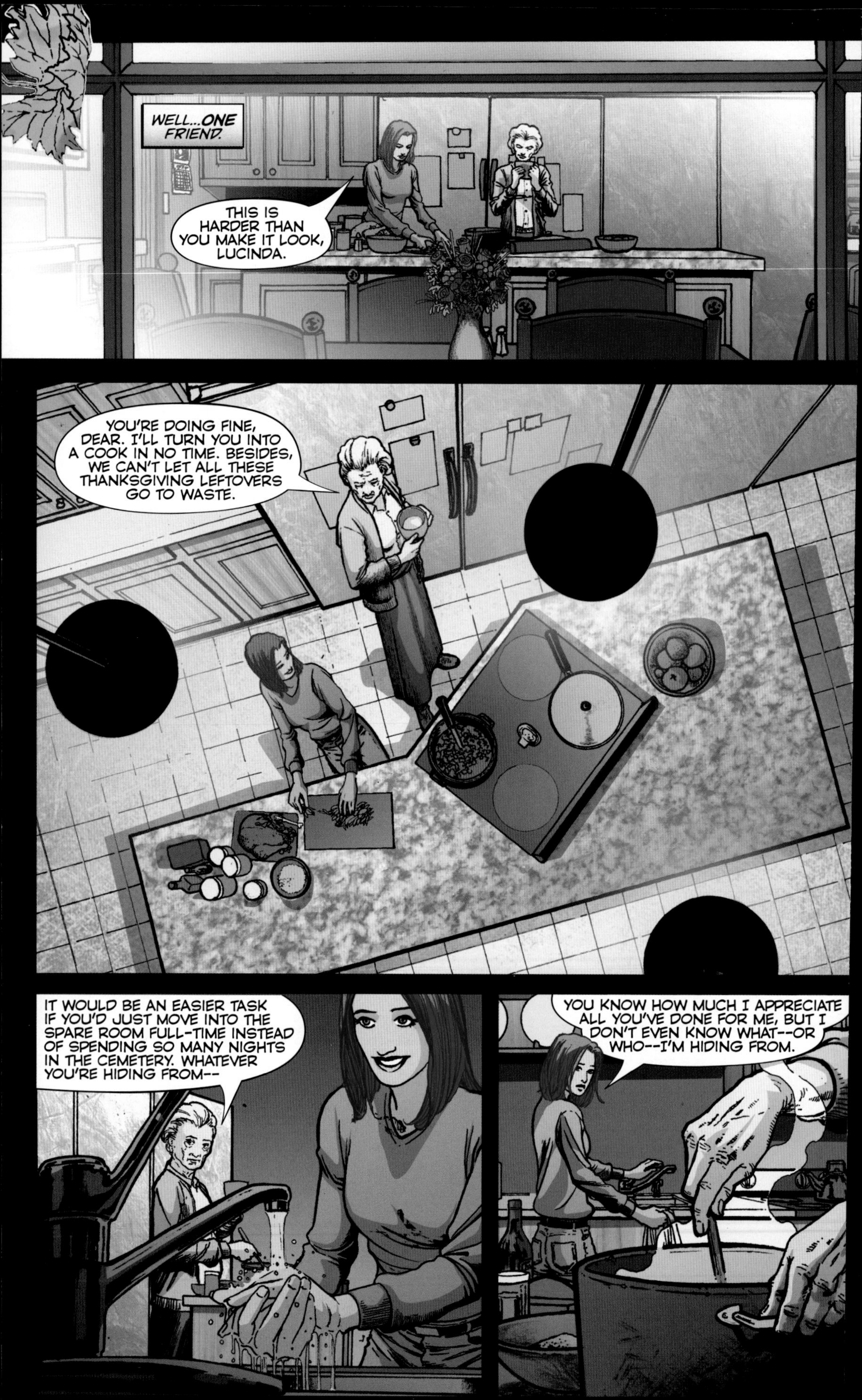
WELL...ONE FRIEND.
THIS IS HARDER THAN YOU MAKE IT LOOK, LUCINDA.
YOU'RE DOING FINE, DEAR. I'LL TURN YOU INTO A COOK IN NO TIME. BESIDES, WE CAN'T LET ALL THESE THANKSGIVING LEFTOVERS GO TO WASTE.
IT WOULD BE AN EASIER TASK IF YOU'D JUST MOVE INTO THE SPARE ROOM FULL-TIME INSTEAD OF SPENDING SO MANY NIGHTS IN THE CEMETERY. WHATEVER YOU'RE HIDING FROM--
YOU KNOW HOW MUCH I APPRECIATE ALL YOU'VE DONE FOR ME, BUT I DON'T EVEN KNOW WHAT--OR WHO--I'M HIDING FROM.

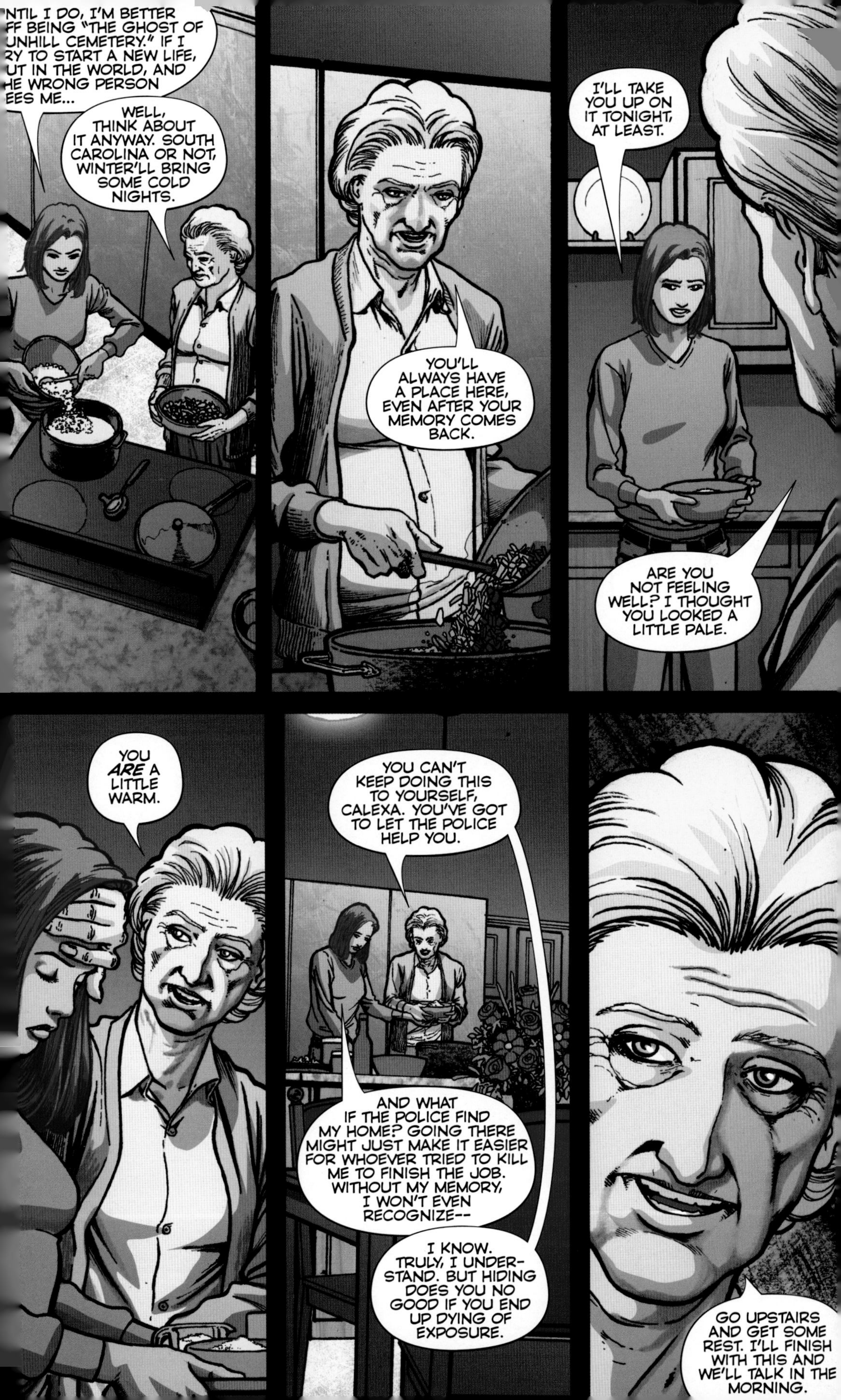
NTIL I DO, I'M BETTER FF BEING "THE GHOST OF UNHILL CEMETERY." IF I RY TO START A NEW LIFE, UT IN THE WORLD, AND HE WRONG PERSON EES ME...
WELL, THINK ABOUT IT ANYWAY. SOUTH CAROLINA OR NOT, WINTER'LL BRING SOME COLD NIGHTS.
YOU'LL ALWAYS HAVE A PLACE HERE, EVEN AFTER YOUR MEMORY COMES BACK.
I'LL TAKE YOU UP ON IT TONIGHT, AT LEAST.
ARE YOU NOT FEELING WELL? I THOUGHT YOU LOOKED A LITTLE PALE.
YOU *ARE* A LITTLE WARM.
YOU CAN'T KEEP DOING THIS TO YOURSELF, CALEXA. YOU'VE GOT TO LET THE POLICE HELP YOU.
AND WHAT IF THE POLICE FIND MY HOME? GOING THERE MIGHT JUST MAKE IT EASIER FOR WHOEVER TRIED TO KILL ME TO FINISH THE JOB. WITHOUT MY MEMORY, I WON'T EVEN RECOGNIZE--
I KNOW. TRULY, I UNDER-STAND. BUT HIDING DOES YOU NO GOOD IF YOU END UP DYING OF EXPOSURE.
GO UPSTAIRS AND GET SOME REST. I'LL FINISH WITH THIS AND WE'LL TALK IN THE MORNING.

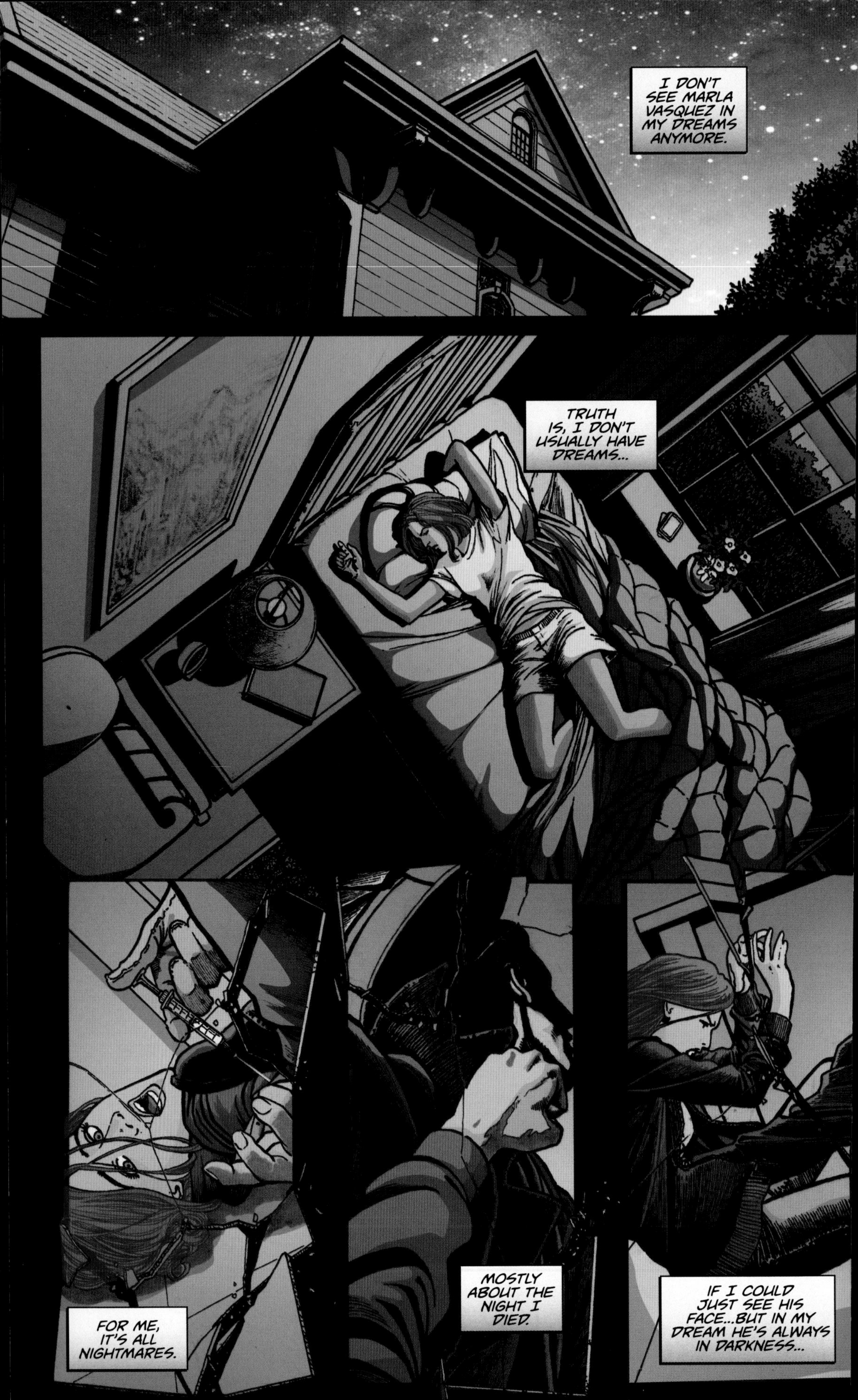
I DON'T SEE MARLA VASQUEZ IN MY DREAMS ANYMORE.
TRUTH IS, I DON'T USUALLY HAVE DREAMS...
FOR ME, IT'S ALL NIGHTMARES.
MOSTLY ABOUT THE NIGHT I DIED.
IF I COULD JUST SEE HIS FACE...BUT IN MY DREAM HE'S ALWAYS IN DARKNESS...

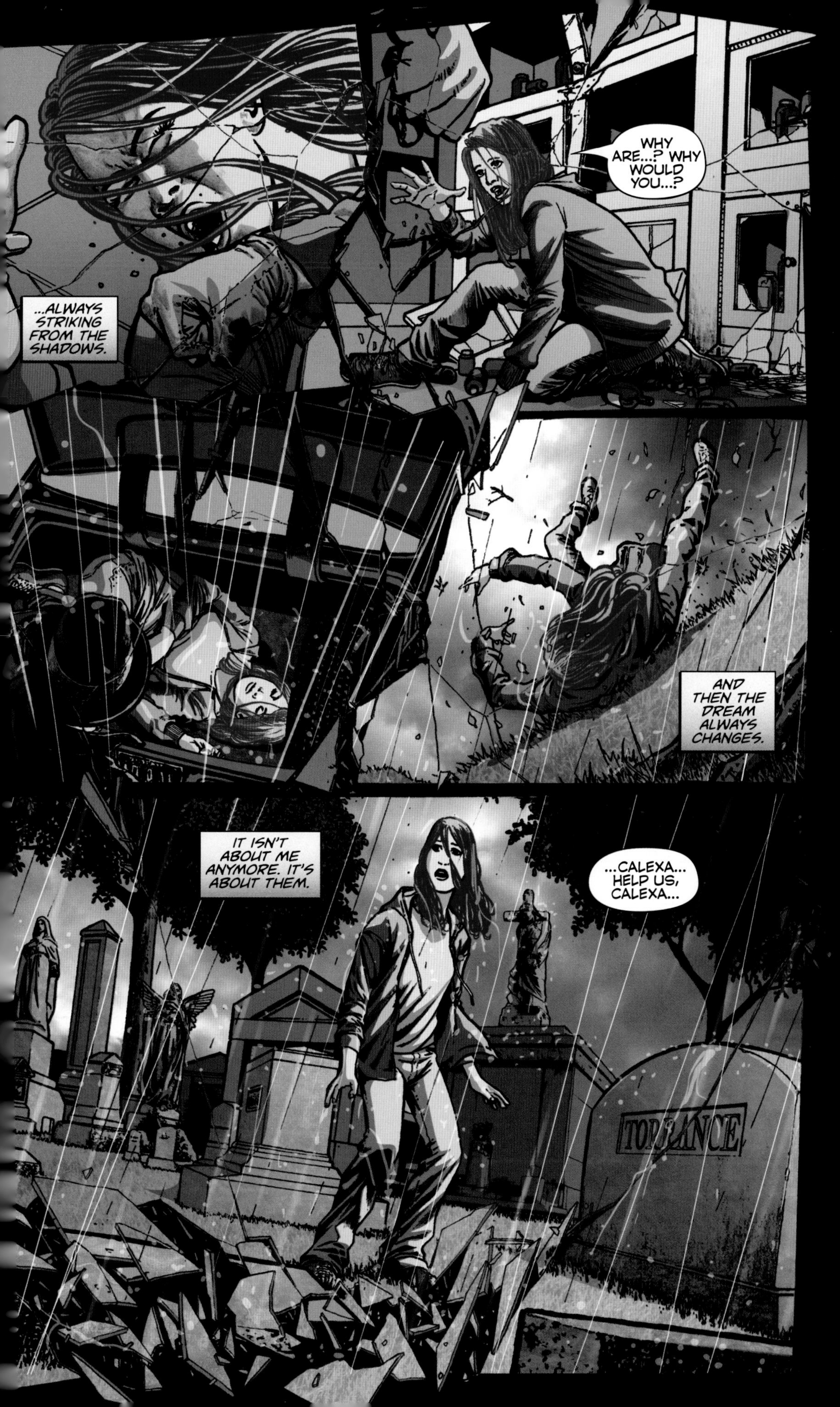
WHY ARE...? WHY WOULD YOU...?
...ALWAYS STRIKING FROM THE SHADOWS.
AND THEN THE DREAM ALWAYS CHANGES.
IT ISN'T ABOUT ME ANYMORE. IT'S ABOUT THEM.
...CALEXA... HELP US, CALEXA...
TORRANCE

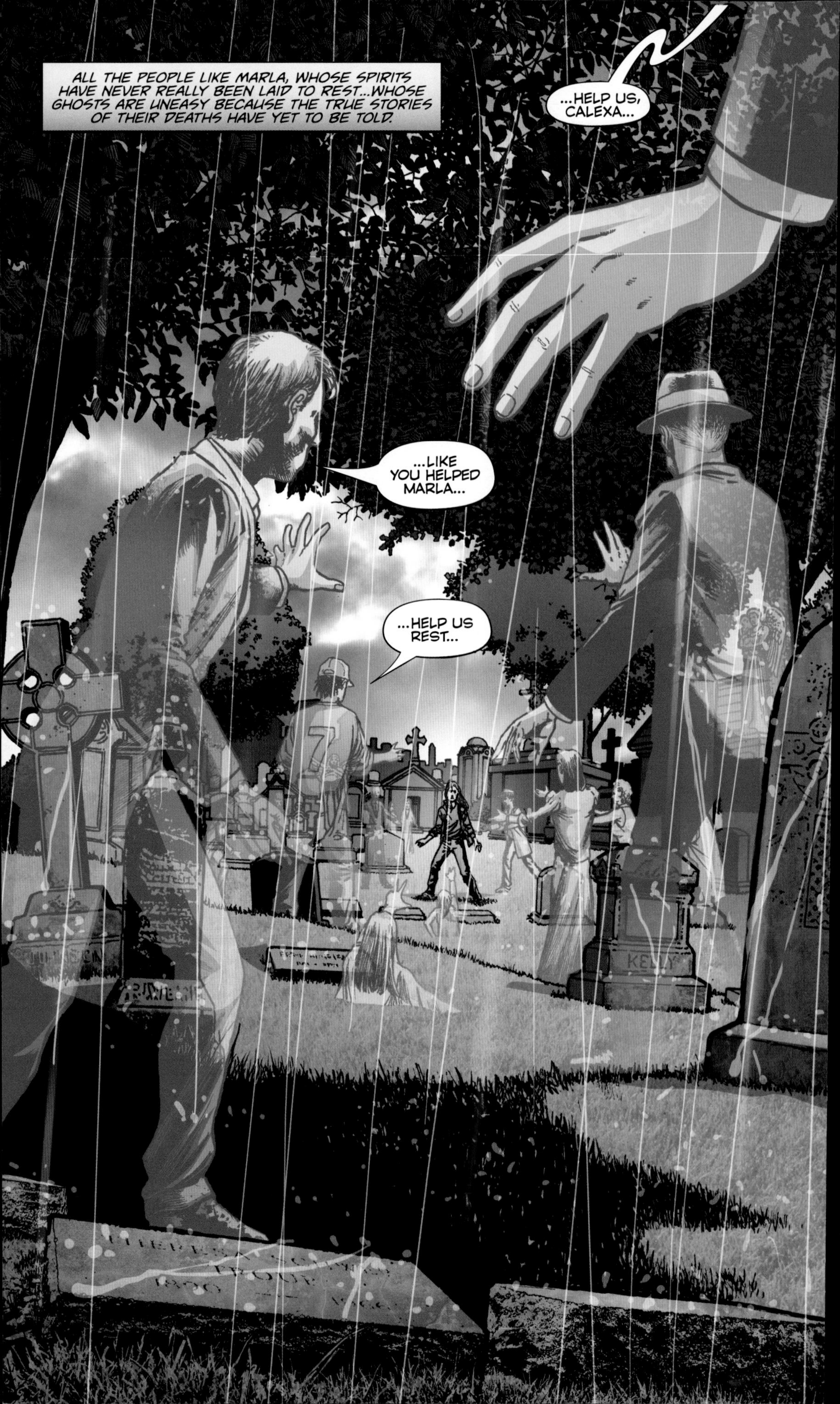
ALL THE PEOPLE LIKE MARLA, WHOSE SPIRITS HAVE NEVER REALLY BEEN LAID TO REST...WHOSE GHOSTS ARE UNEASY BECAUSE THE TRUE STORIES OF THEIR DEATHS HAVE YET TO BE TOLD.
...HELP US, CALEXA...
...LIKE YOU HELPED MARLA...
...HELP US REST...
KELLY

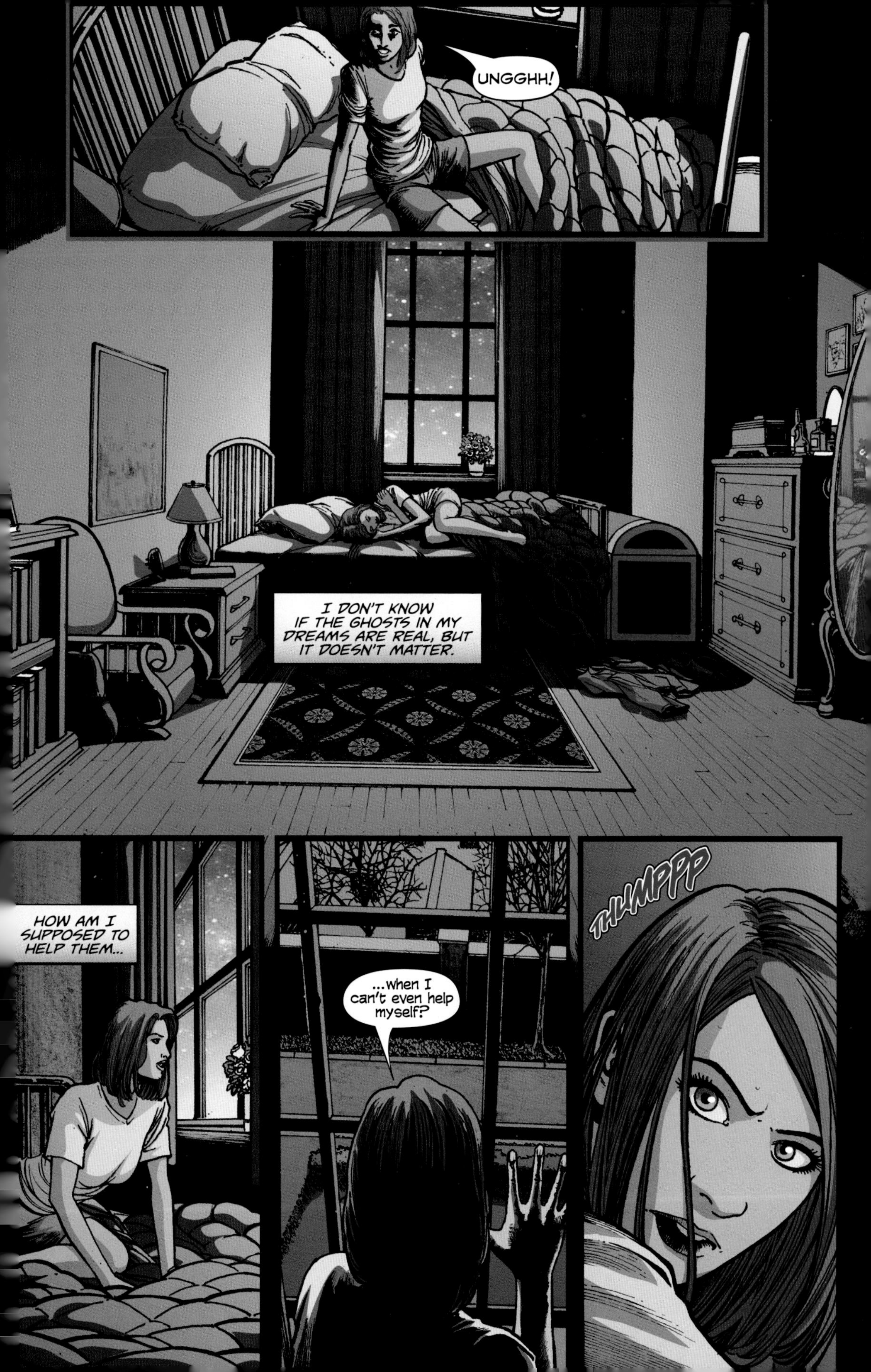
UNGGHH!
I DON'T KNOW IF THE GHOSTS IN MY DREAMS ARE REAL, BUT IT DOESN'T MATTER.
HOW AM I SUPPOSED TO HELP THEM...
...when I can't even help myself?
THUMPPP

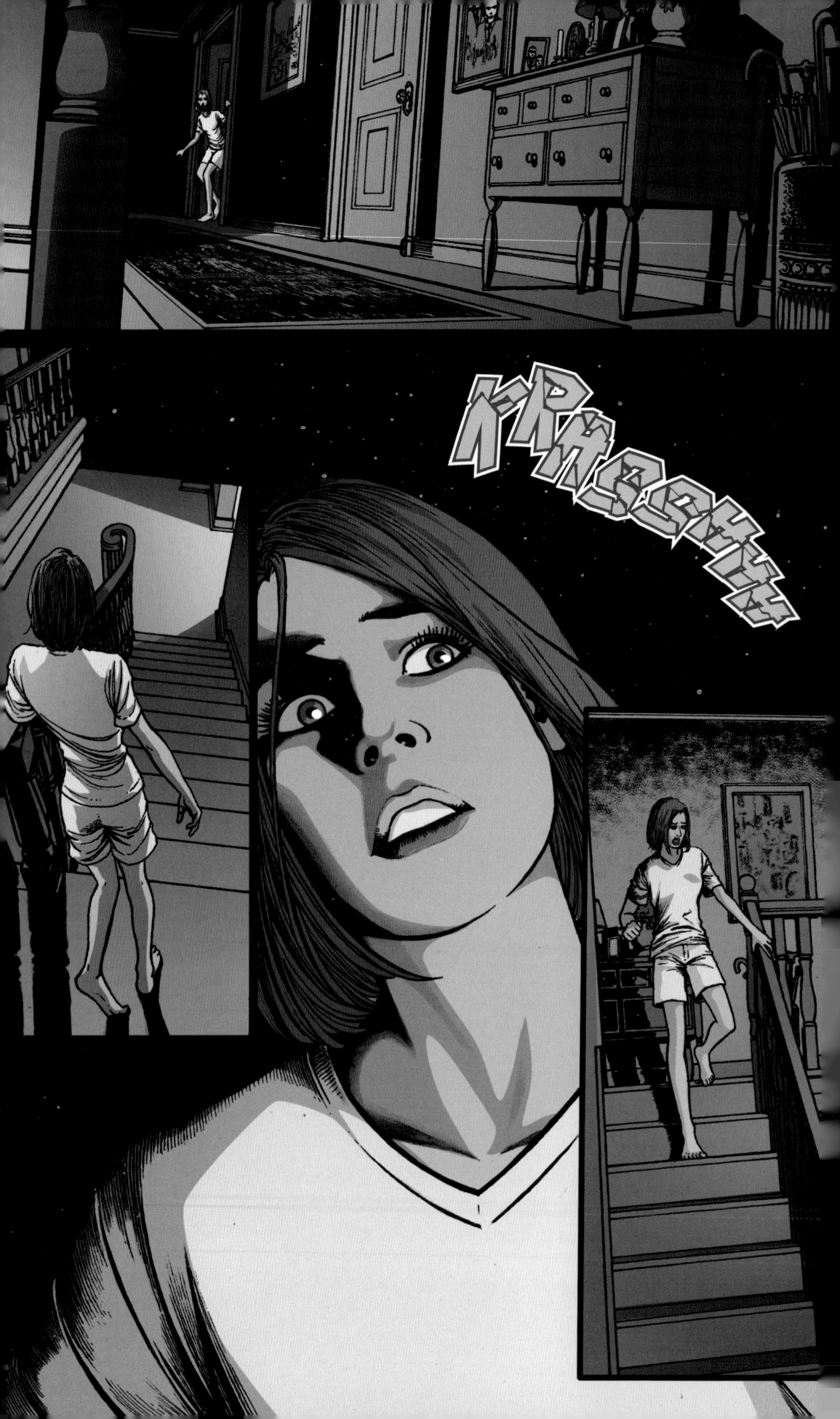
KRASSHHH

CREEEEEAKK

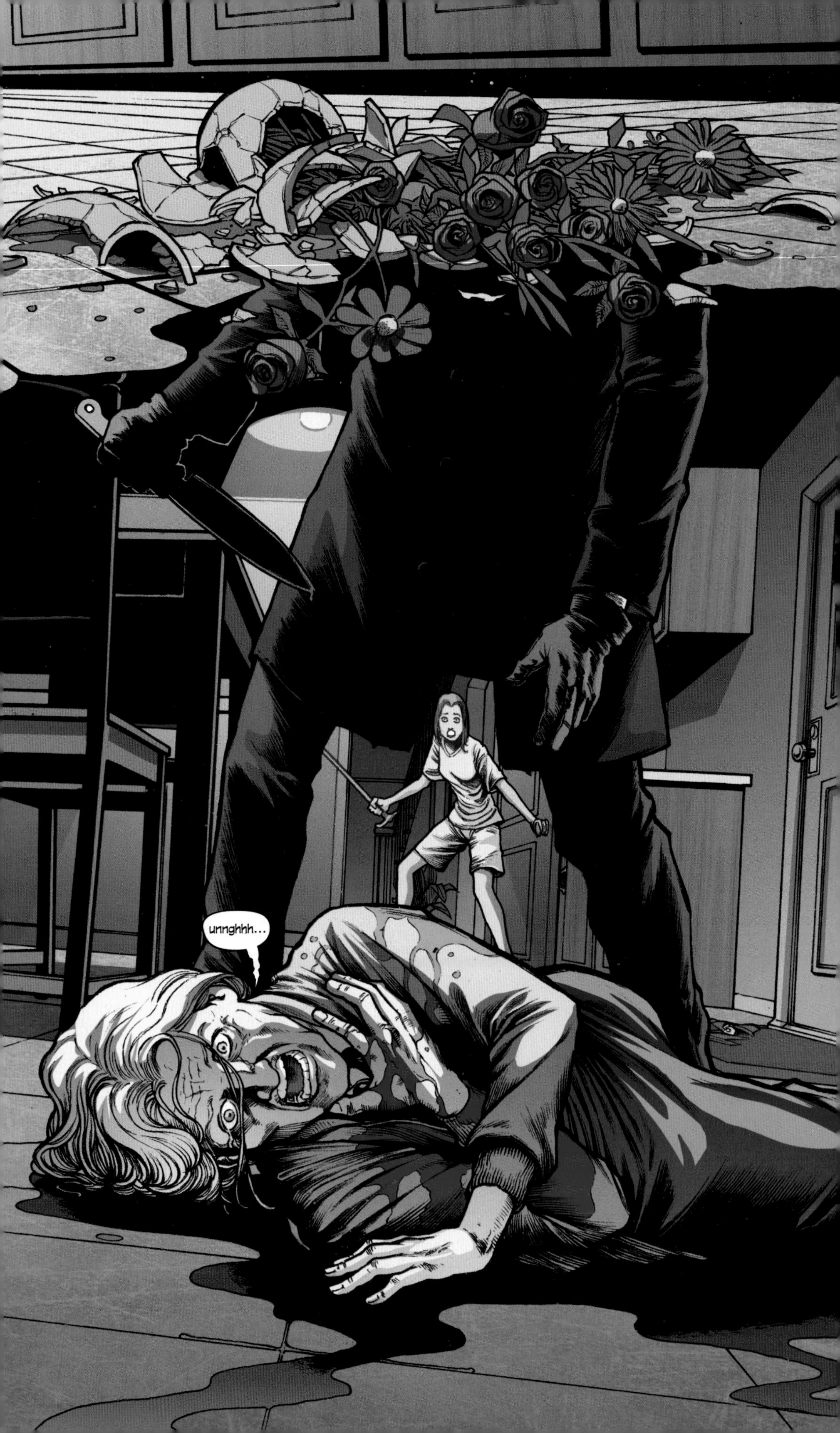
unnghhh...

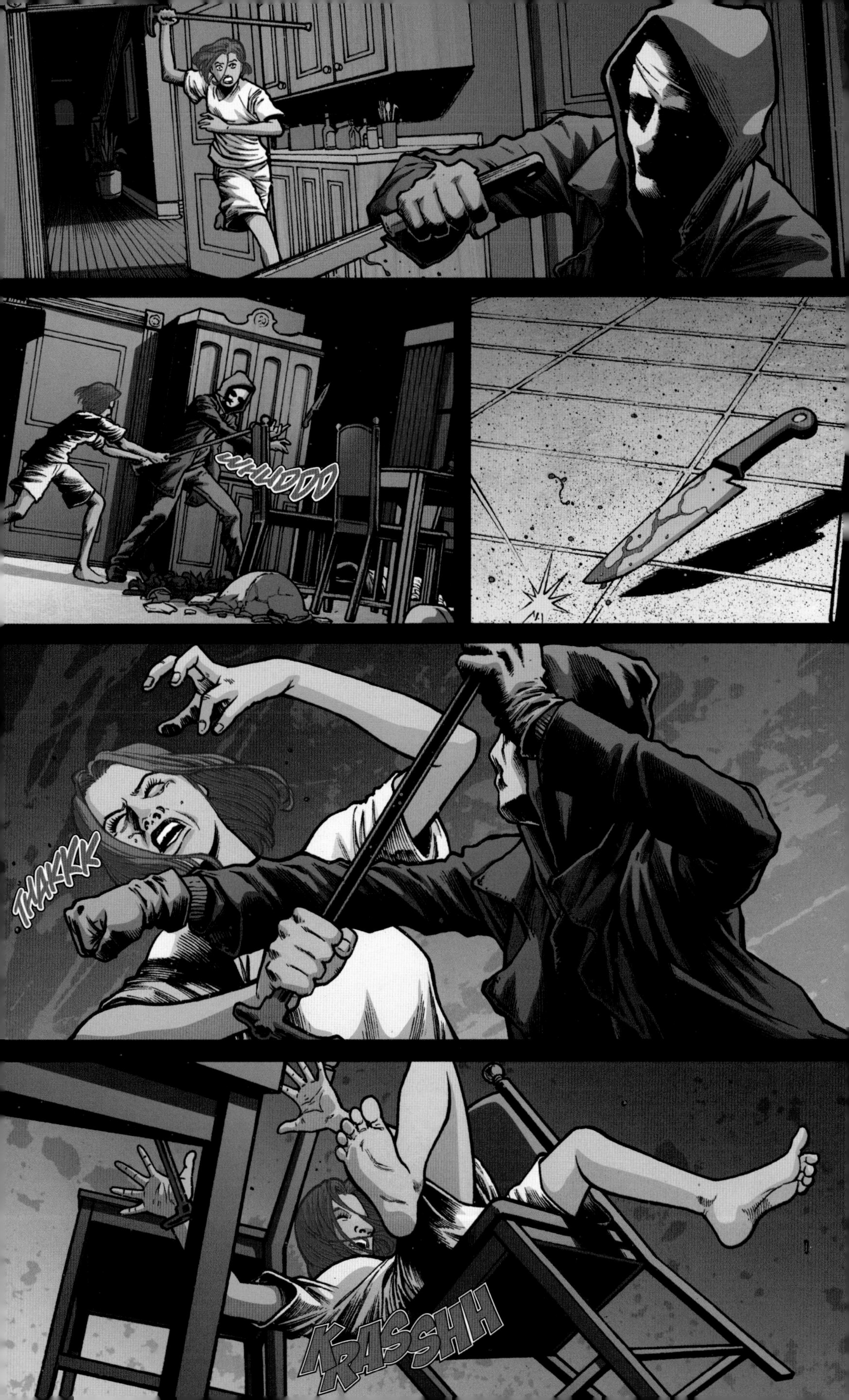
WHUDDD
THAKKK
KRASSHH

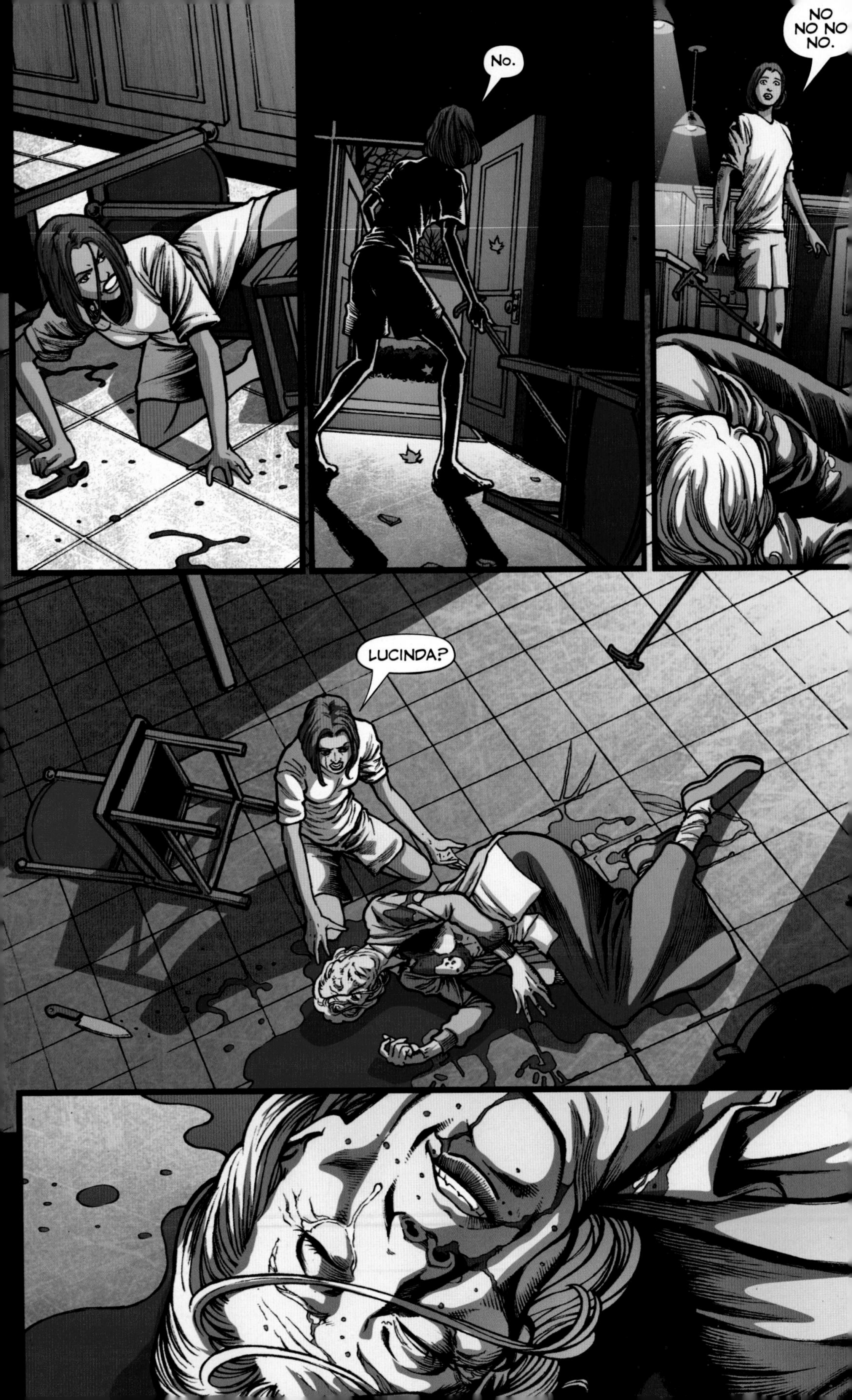
No.
NO
NO NO NO
NO.
LUCINDA?

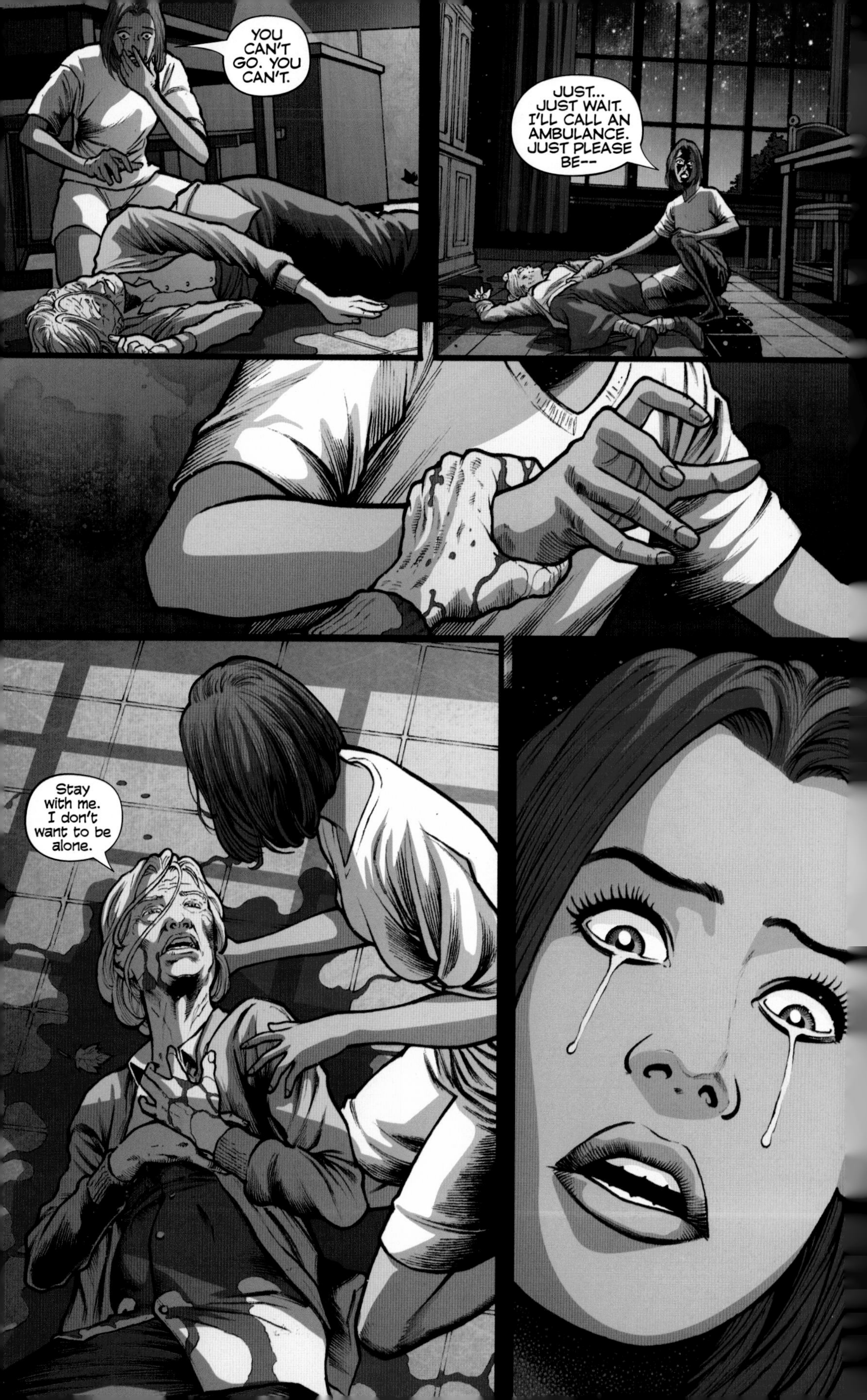
YOU CAN'T GO. YOU CAN'T.
JUST... JUST WAIT. I'LL CALL AN AMBULANCE. JUST PLEASE BE--
Stay with me. I don't want to be alone.

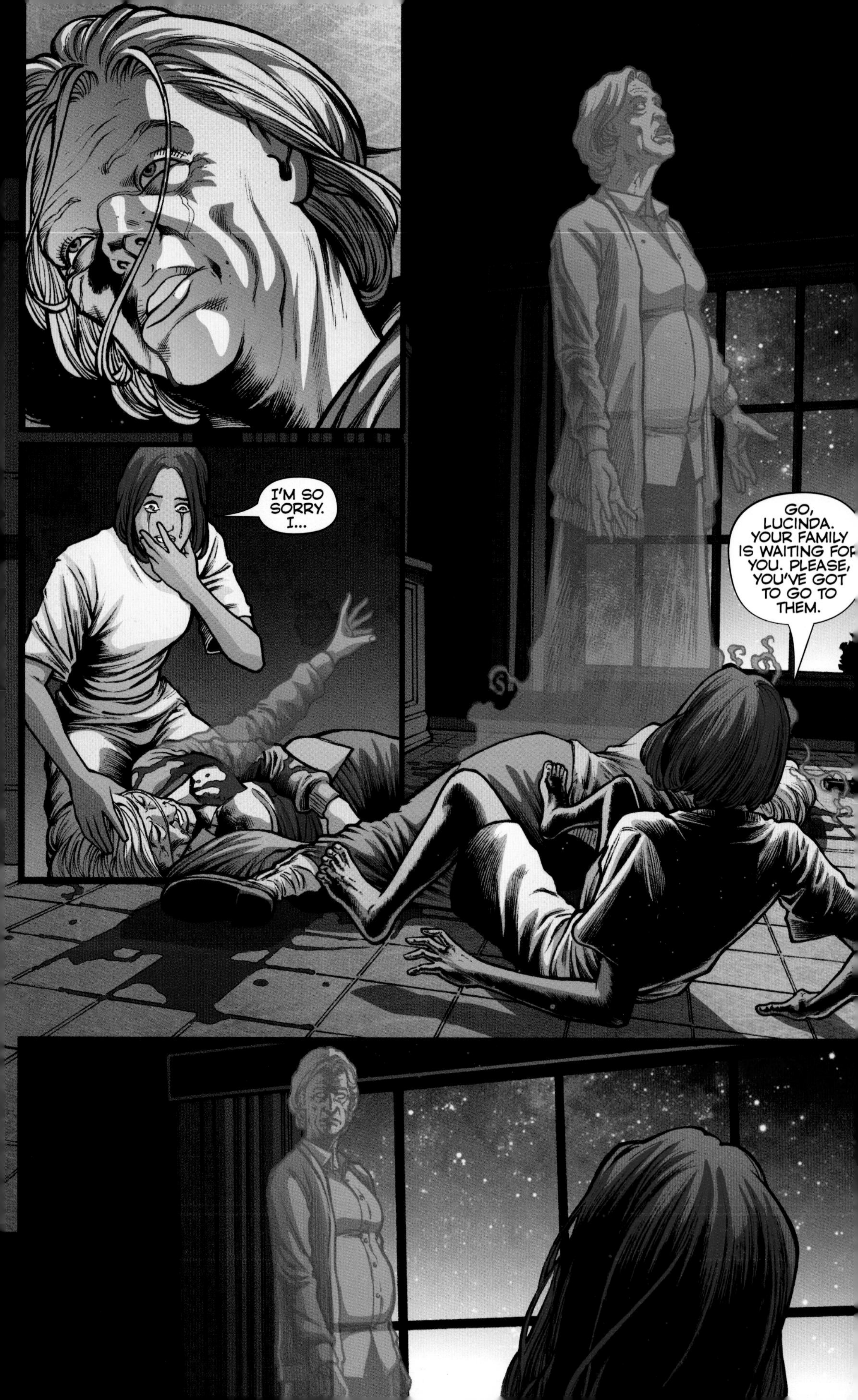
I'M SO SORRY. I...
GO, LUCINDA. YOUR FAMILY IS WAITING FOR YOU. PLEASE, YOU'VE GOT TO GO TO THEM.

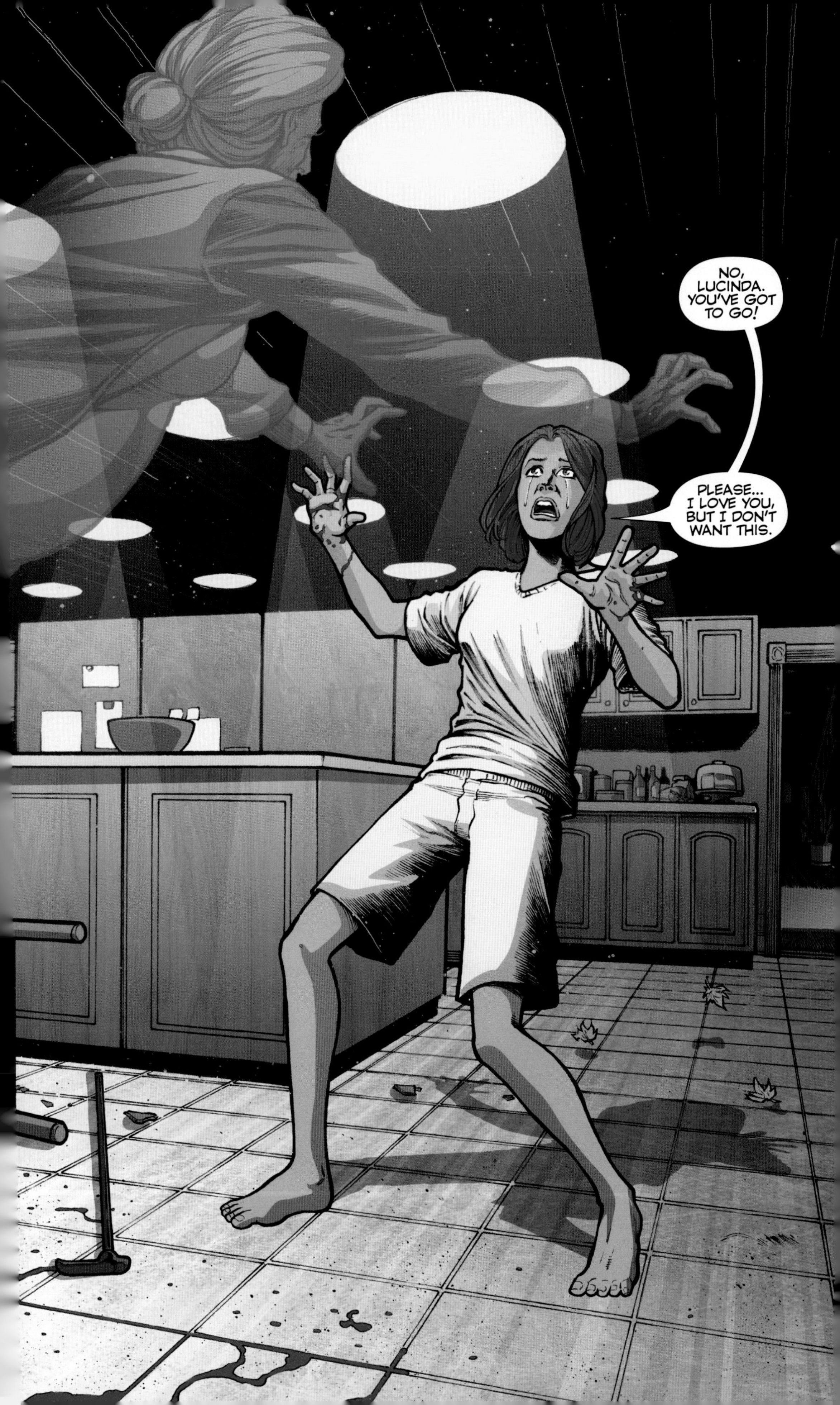
NO, LUCINDA. YOU'VE GOT TO GO!
PLEASE... I LOVE YOU, BUT I DON'T WANT THIS.

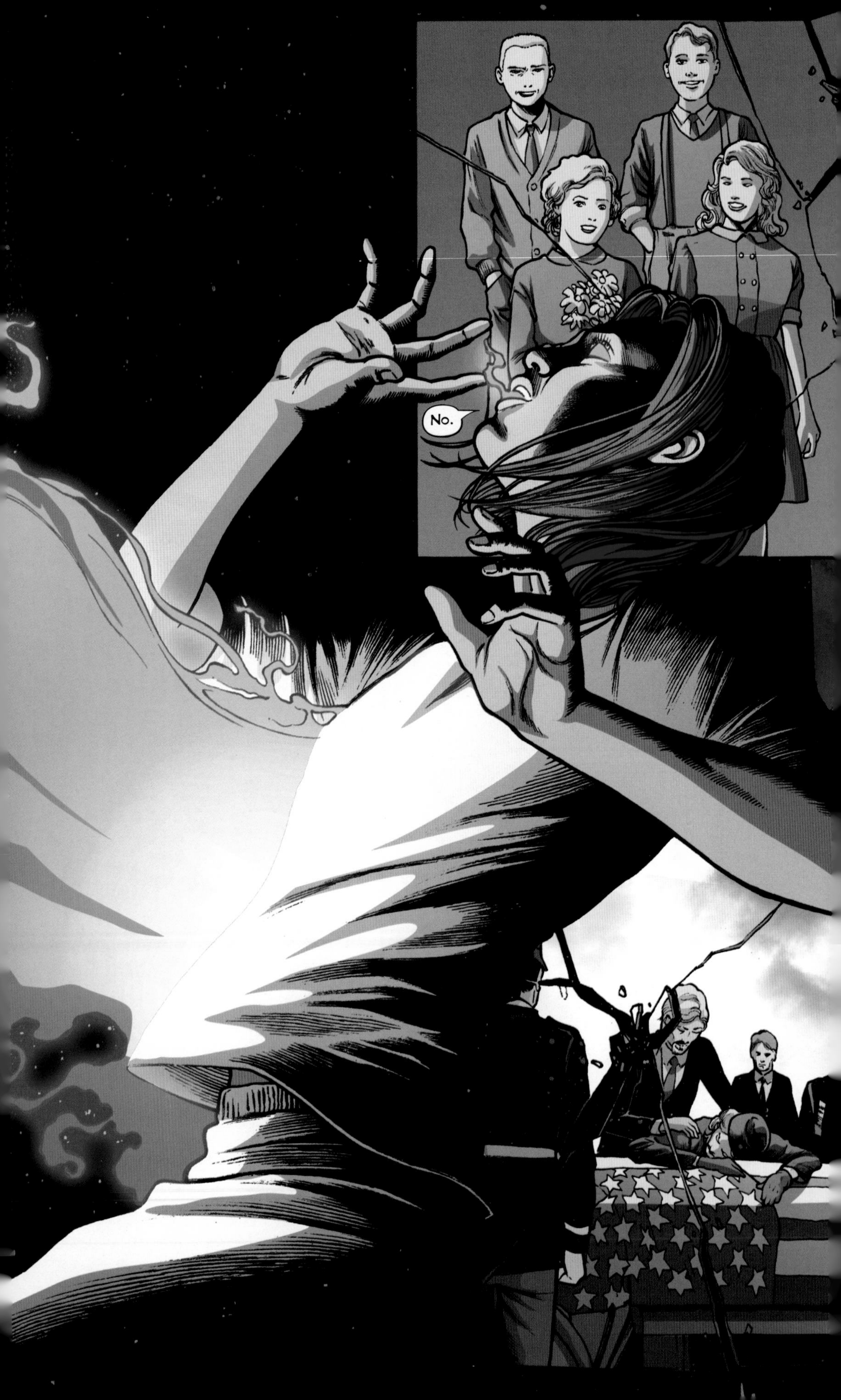
No.

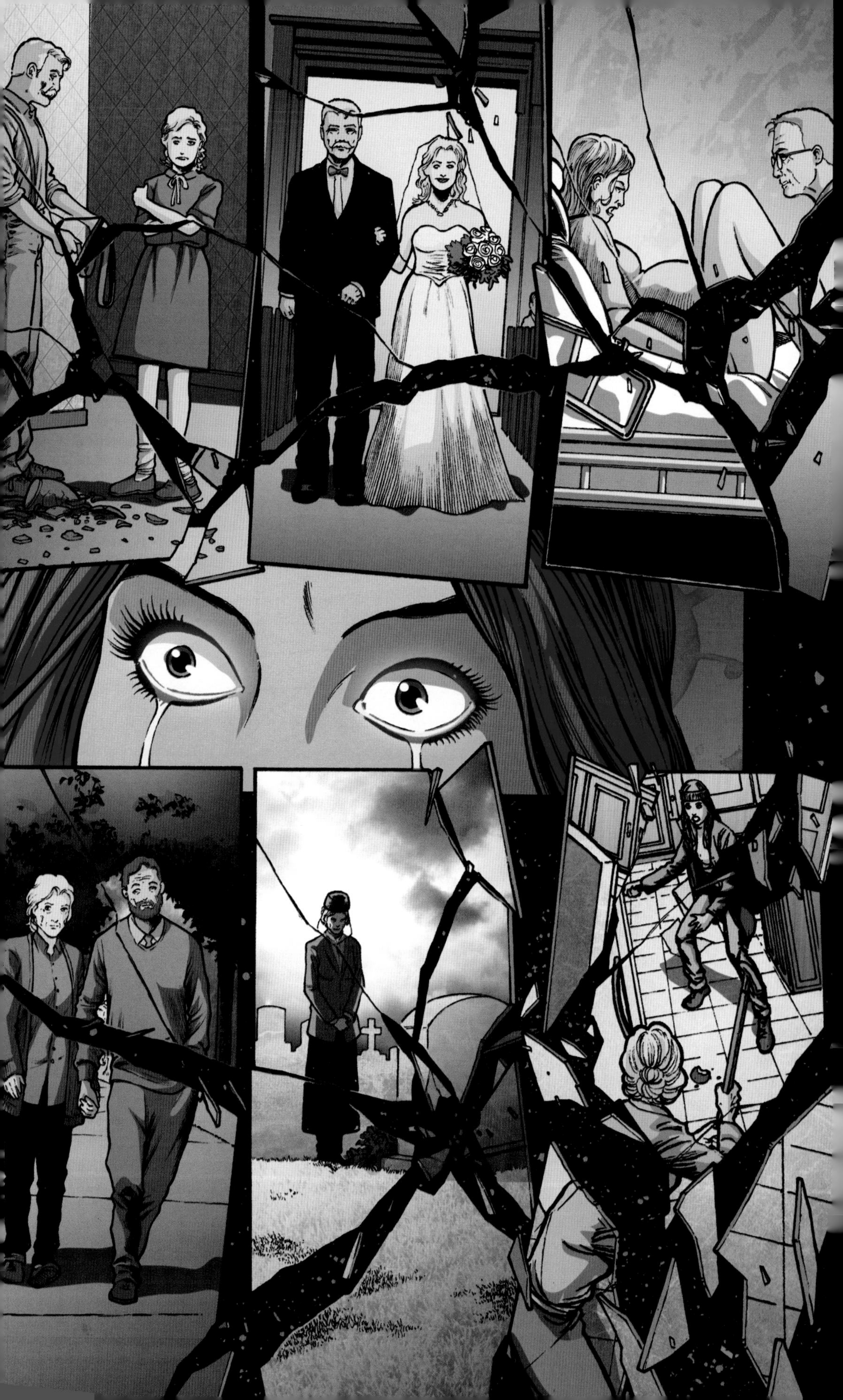

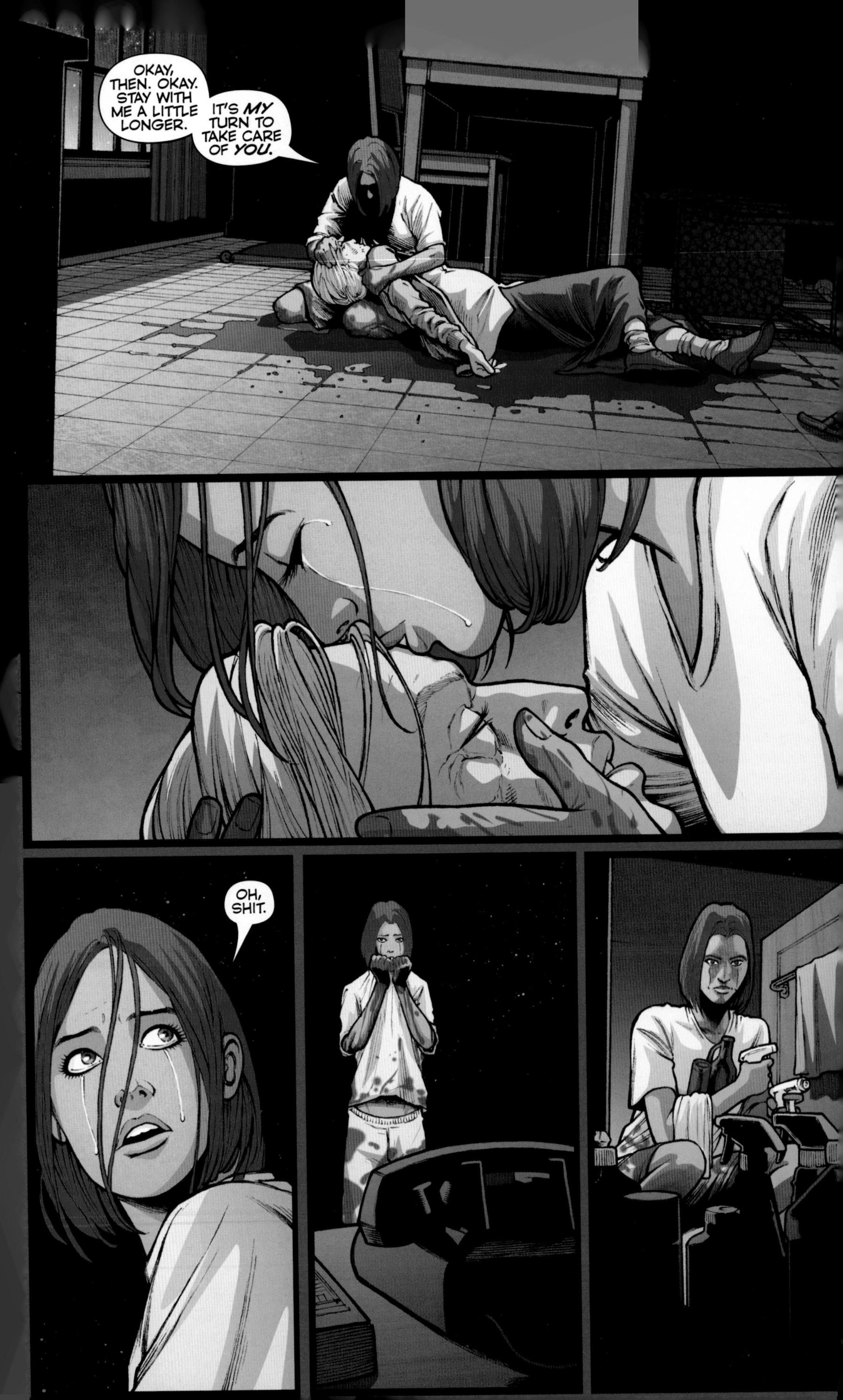
OKAY, THEN. OKAY. STAY WITH ME A LITTLE LONGER.
IT'S *MY* TURN TO TAKE CARE OF *YOU*.
OH, SHIT.

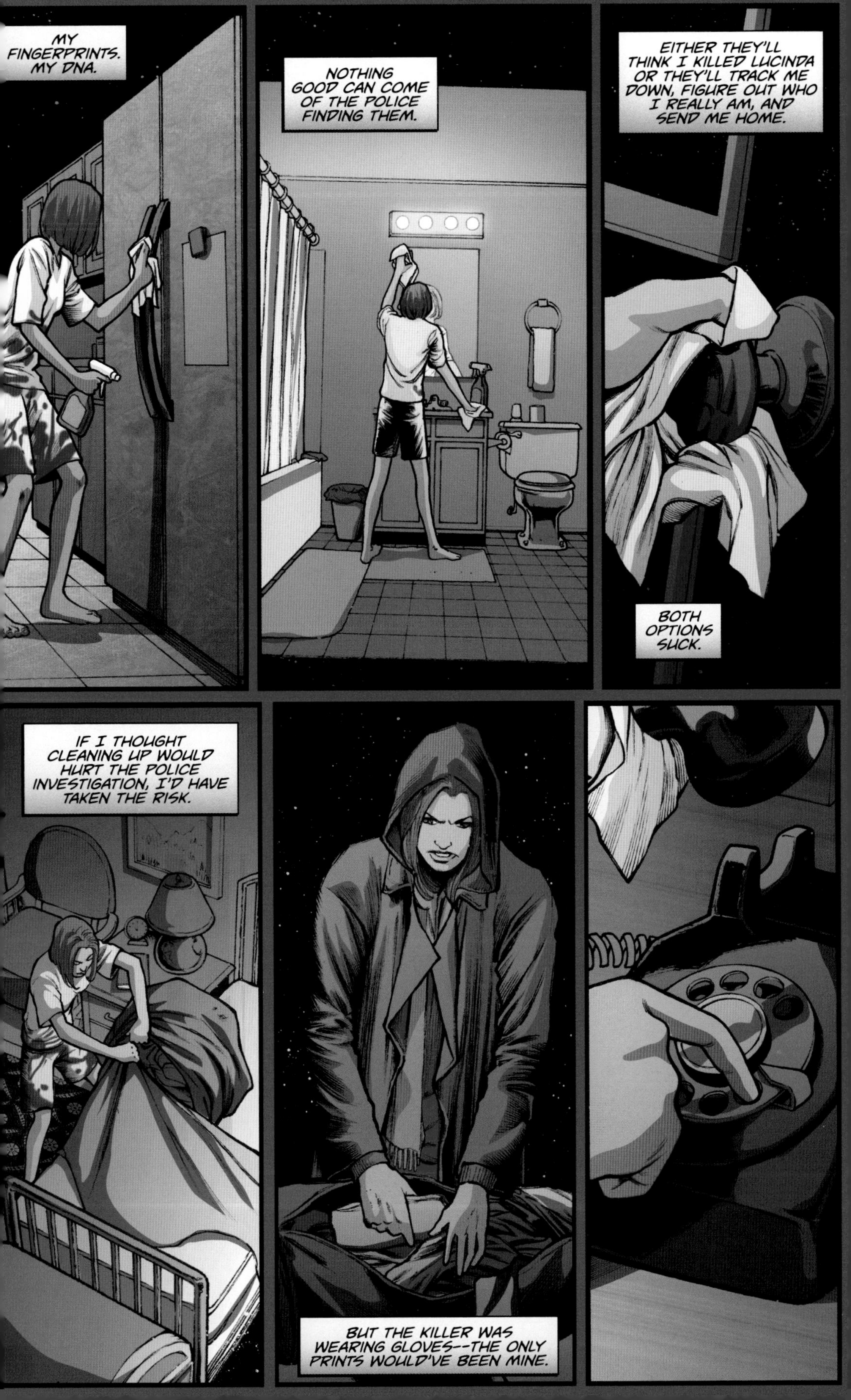
MY FINGERPRINTS. MY DNA.
NOTHING GOOD CAN COME OF THE POLICE FINDING THEM.
EITHER THEY'LL THINK I KILLED LUCINDA OR THEY'LL TRACK ME DOWN, FIGURE OUT WHO I REALLY AM, AND SEND ME HOME.
BOTH OPTIONS SUCK.
IF I THOUGHT CLEANING UP WOULD HURT THE POLICE INVESTIGATION, I'D HAVE TAKEN THE RISK.
BUT THE KILLER WAS WEARING GLOVES--THE ONLY PRINTS WOULD'VE BEEN MINE.

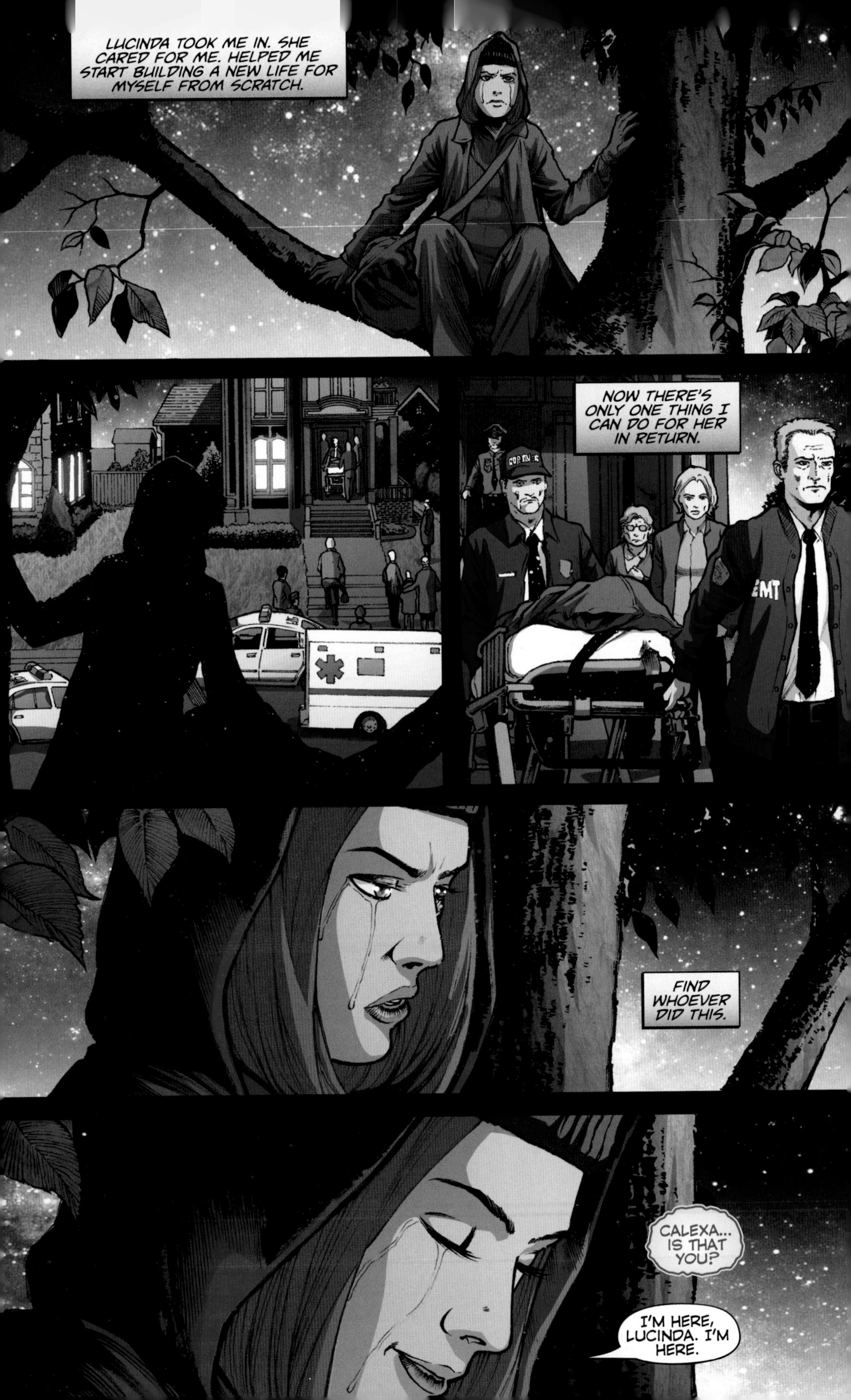
LUCINDA TOOK ME IN. SHE CARED FOR ME. HELPED ME START BUILDING A NEW LIFE FOR MYSELF FROM SCRATCH.
NOW THERE'S ONLY ONE THING I CAN DO FOR HER IN RETURN.
EMT
FIND WHOEVER DID THIS.
CALEXA... IS THAT YOU?
I'M HERE, LUCINDA. I'M HERE.

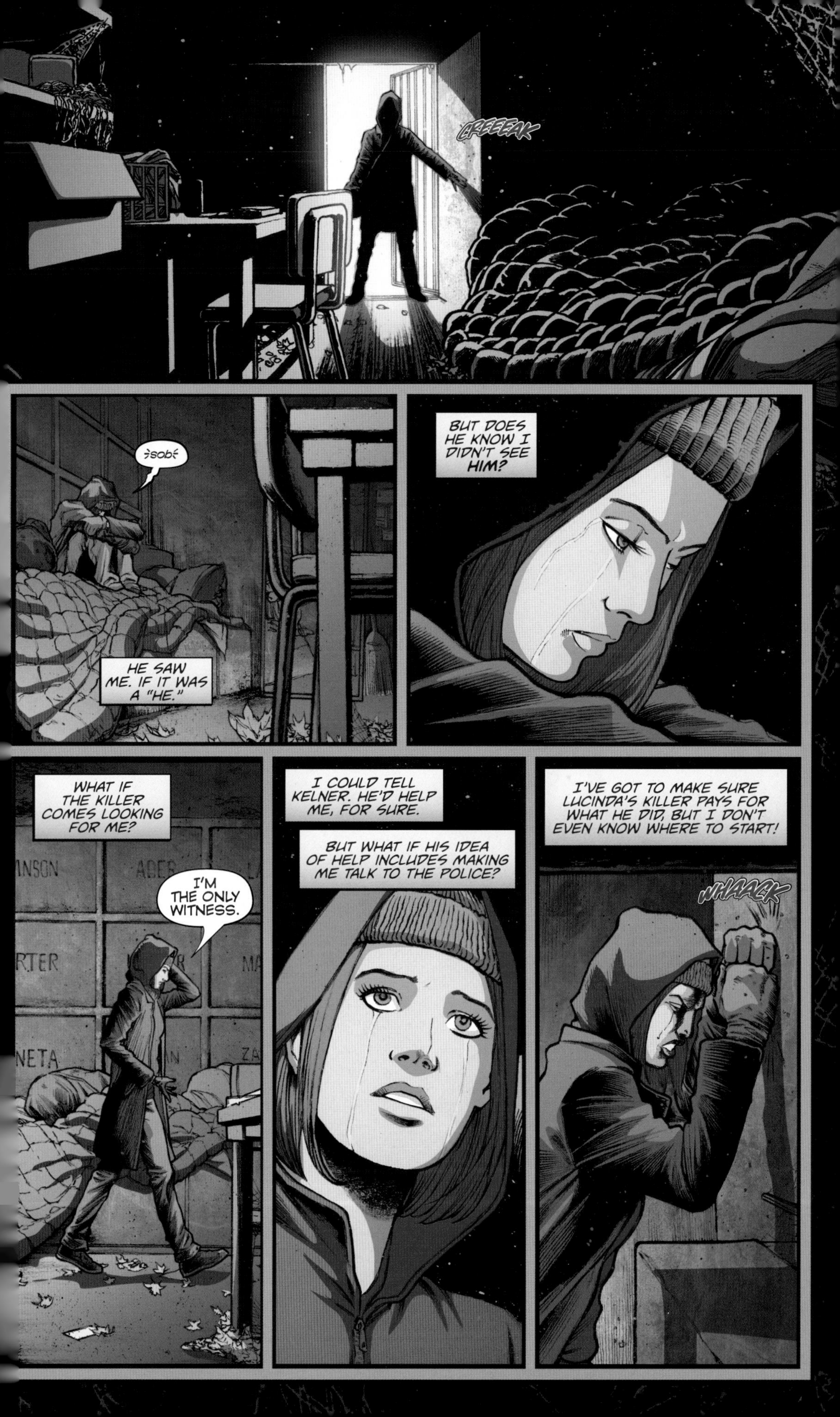
CREEEAK
SOB
HE SAW ME. IF IT WAS A "HE."
BUT DOES HE KNOW I DIDN'T SEE HIM?
WHAT IF THE KILLER COMES LOOKING FOR ME?
I'M THE ONLY WITNESS.
I COULD TELL KELNER. HE'D HELP ME, FOR SURE.
BUT WHAT IF HIS IDEA OF HELP INCLUDES MAKING ME TALK TO THE POLICE?
I'VE GOT TO MAKE SURE LUCINDA'S KILLER PAYS FOR WHAT HE DID, BUT I DON'T EVEN KNOW WHERE TO START!
WHAAACK

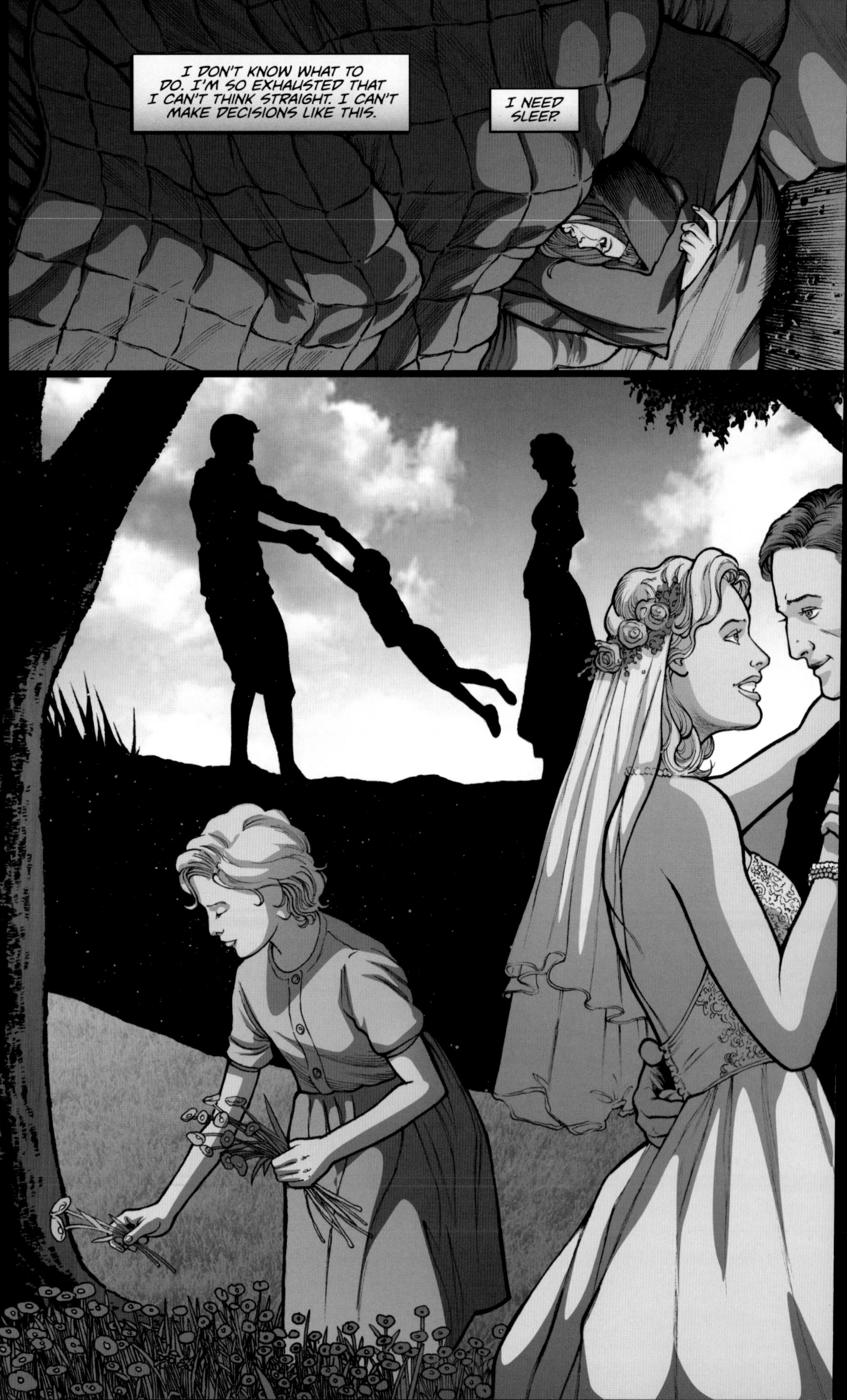
I DON'T KNOW WHAT TO DO. I'M SO EXHAUSTED THAT I CAN'T THINK STRAIGHT. I CAN'T MAKE DECISIONS LIKE THIS.
I NEED SLEEP.

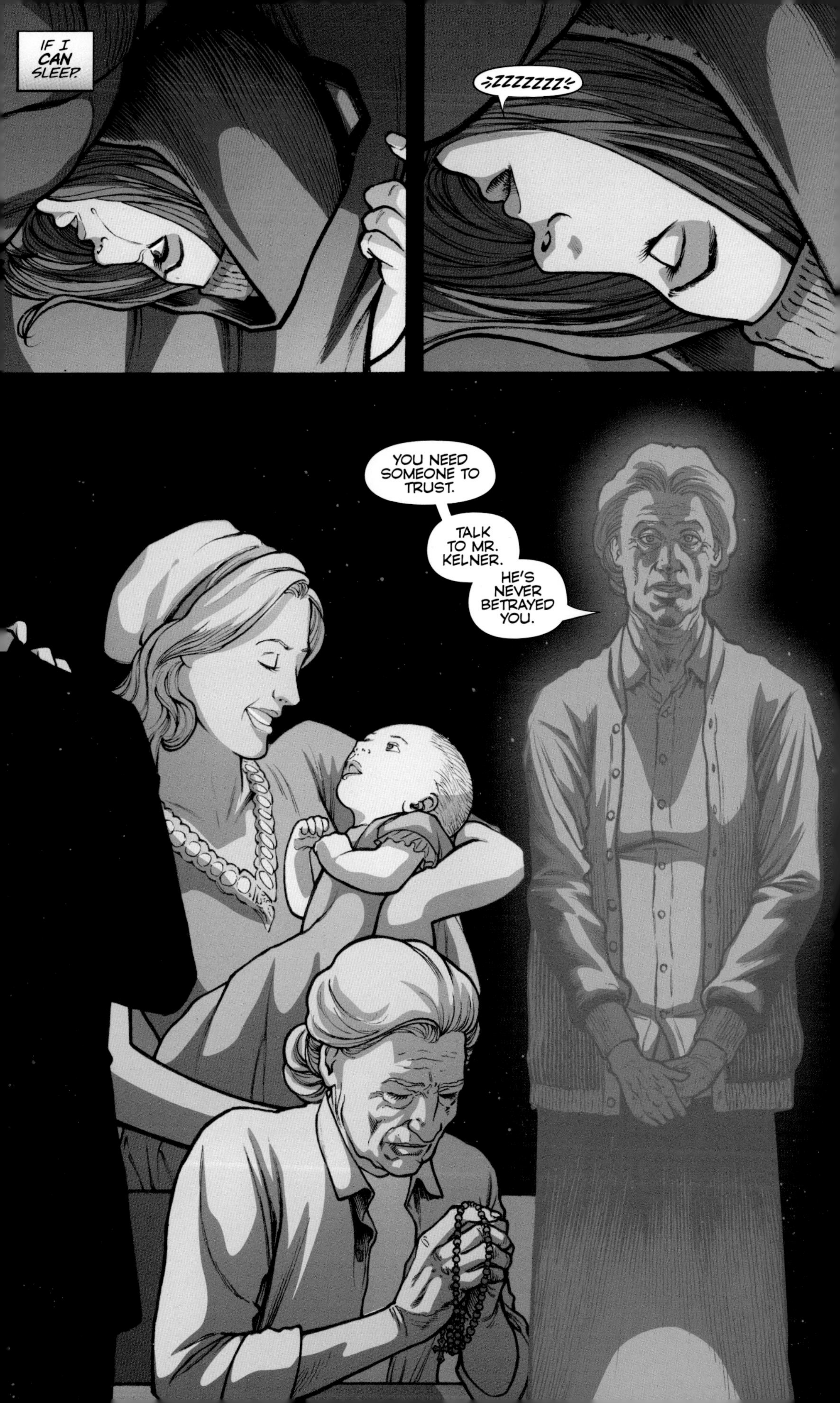
IF I CAN SLEEP.
ZZZZZZZ
YOU NEED SOMEONE TO TRUST.
TALK TO MR. KELNER.
HE'S NEVER BETRAYED YOU.

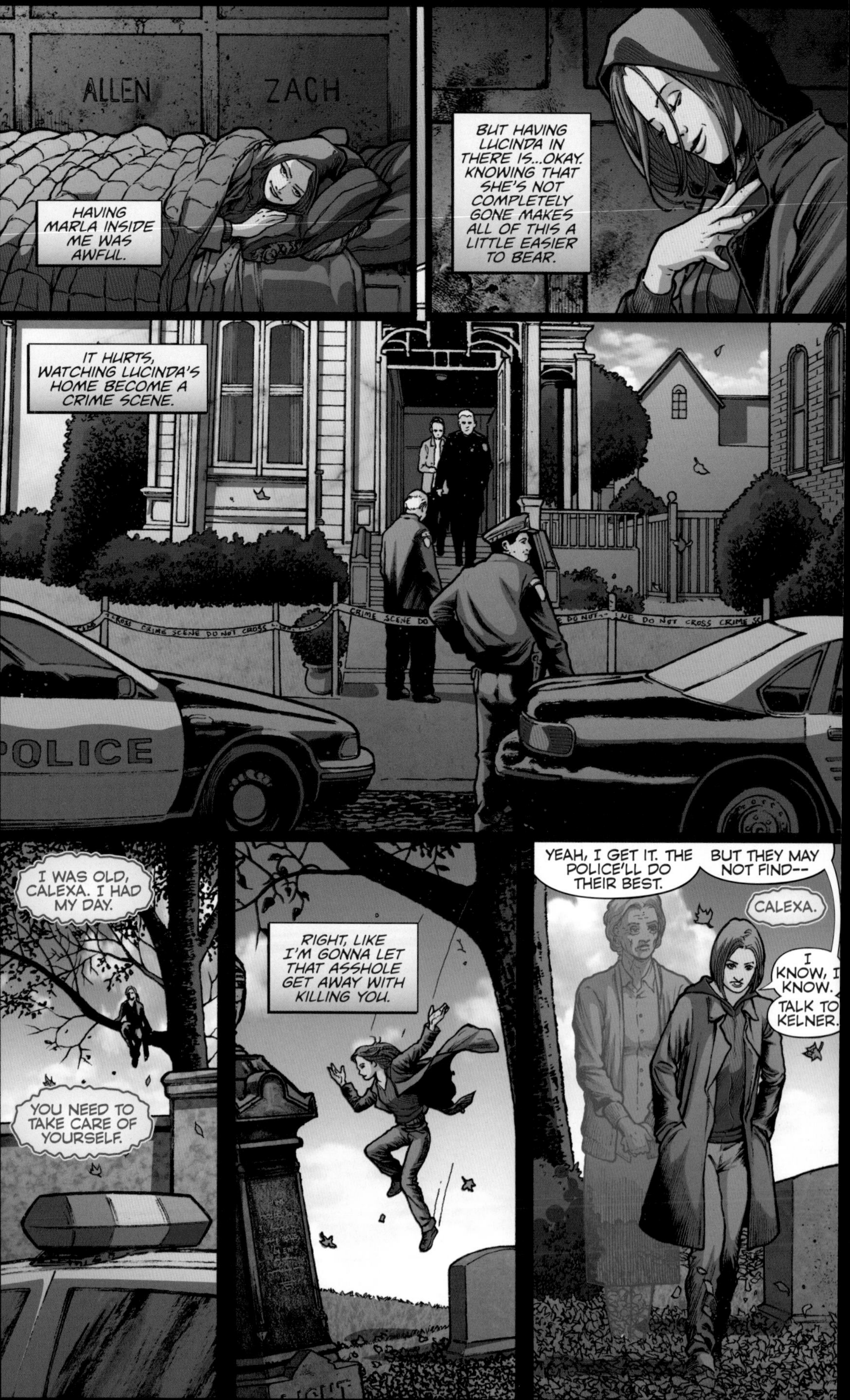
ALLEN
ZACH
HAVING MARLA INSIDE ME WAS AWFUL.
BUT HAVING LUCINDA IN THERE IS...OKAY. KNOWING THAT SHE'S NOT COMPLETELY GONE MAKES ALL OF THIS A LITTLE EASIER TO BEAR.
IT HURTS, WATCHING LUCINDA'S HOME BECOME A CRIME SCENE.
CRIME SCENE DO NOT CROSS
POLICE
I WAS OLD, CALEXA. I HAD MY DAY.
YOU NEED TO TAKE CARE OF YOURSELF.
RIGHT, LIKE I'M GONNA LET THAT ASSHOLE GET AWAY WITH KILLING YOU.
YEAH, I GET IT. THE POLICE'LL DO THEIR BEST.
BUT THEY MAY NOT FIND--
CALEXA.
I KNOW, I KNOW.
TALK TO KELNER.

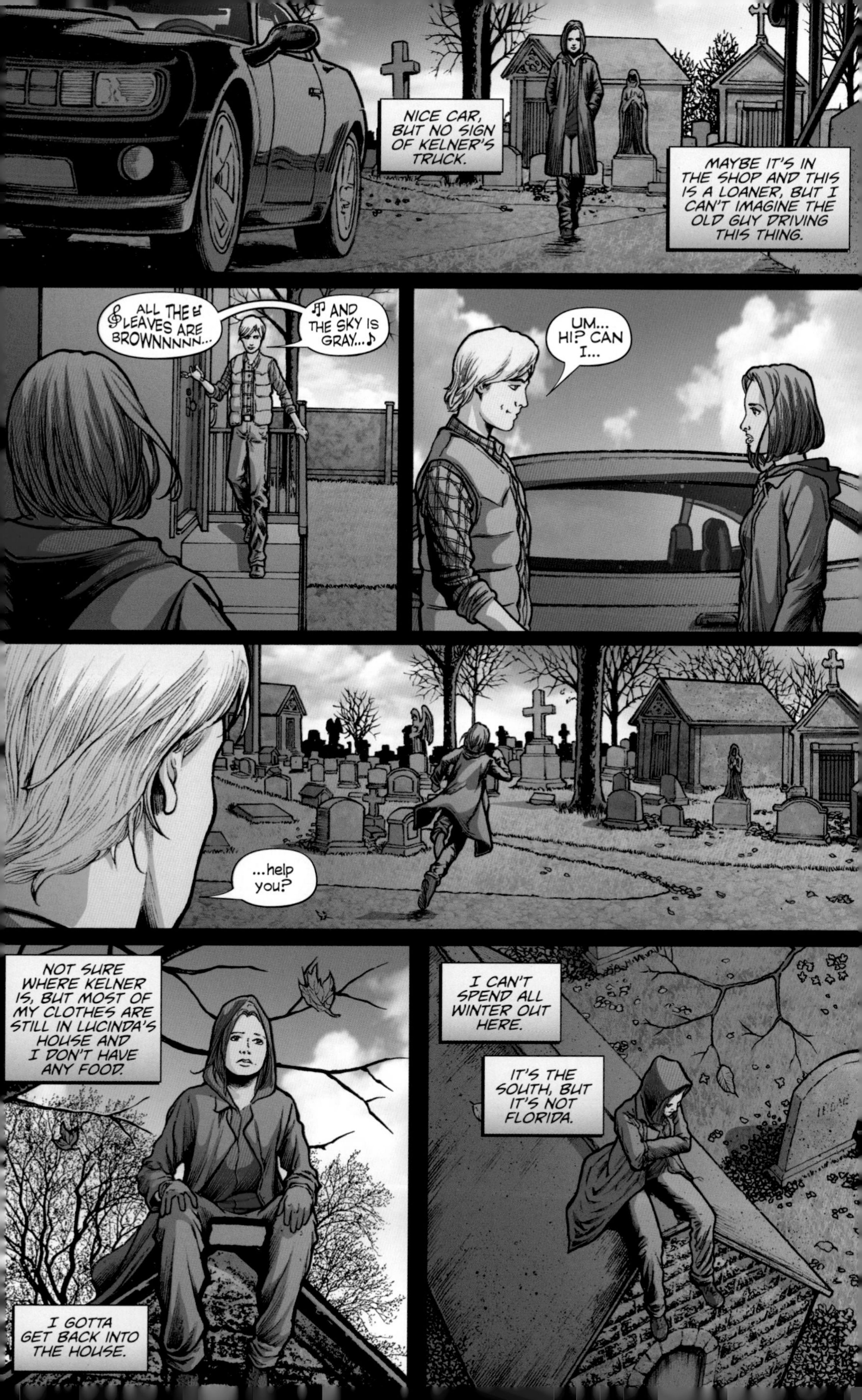
NICE CAR, BUT NO SIGN OF KELNER'S TRUCK.
MAYBE IT'S IN THE SHOP AND THIS IS A LOANER, BUT I CAN'T IMAGINE THE OLD GUY DRIVING THIS THING.
ALL THE LEAVES ARE BROWNNNNNN...
AND THE SKY IS GRAY...
UM... HI? CAN I...
...help you?
NOT SURE WHERE KELNER IS, BUT MOST OF MY CLOTHES ARE STILL IN LUCINDA'S HOUSE AND I DON'T HAVE ANY FOOD.
I GOTTA GET BACK INTO THE HOUSE.
I CAN'T SPEND ALL WINTER OUT HERE.
IT'S THE SOUTH, BUT IT'S NOT FLORIDA.

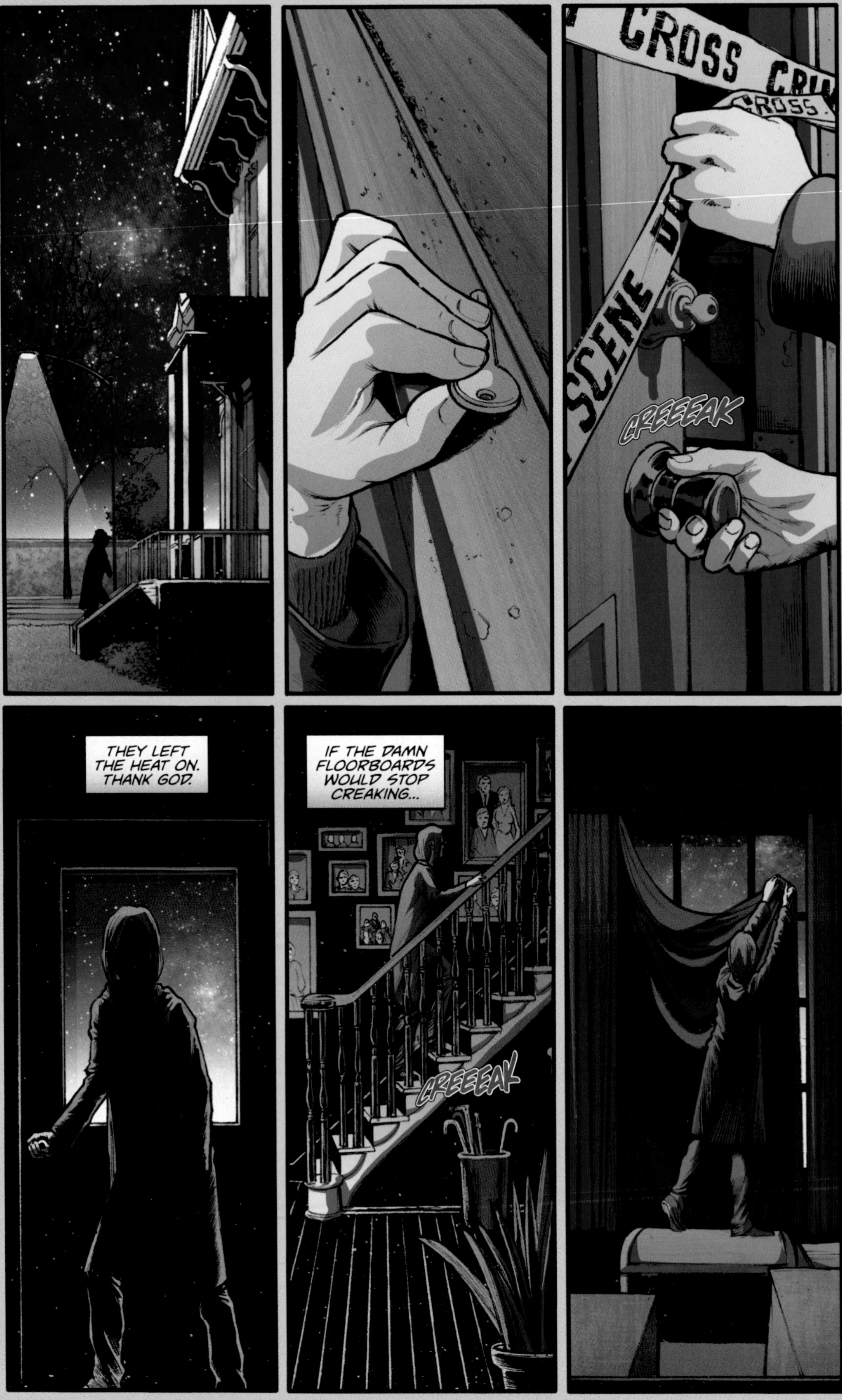
CROSS
CROSS
SCENE
CREEEAK
THEY LEFT THE HEAT ON. THANK GOD.
IF THE DAMN FLOORBOARDS WOULD STOP CREAKING...
CREEEAK

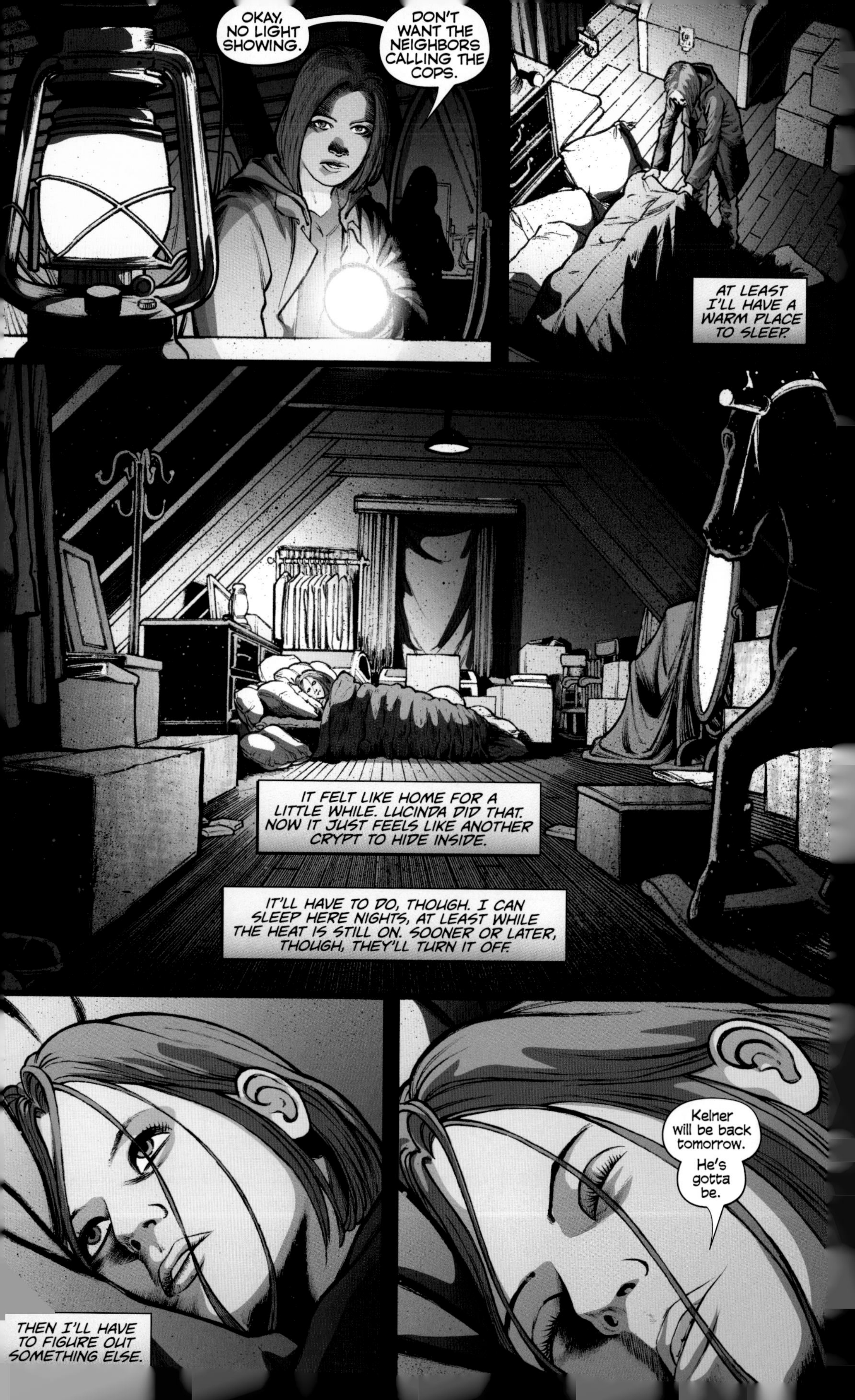
OKAY, NO LIGHT SHOWING.
DON'T WANT THE NEIGHBORS CALLING THE COPS.
AT LEAST I'LL HAVE A WARM PLACE TO SLEEP.
IT FELT LIKE HOME FOR A LITTLE WHILE. LUCINDA DID THAT. NOW IT JUST FEELS LIKE ANOTHER CRYPT TO HIDE INSIDE.
IT'LL HAVE TO DO, THOUGH. I CAN SLEEP HERE NIGHTS, AT LEAST WHILE THE HEAT IS STILL ON. SOONER OR LATER, THOUGH, THEY'LL TURN IT OFF.
THEN I'LL HAVE TO FIGURE OUT SOMETHING ELSE.
Kelner will be back tomorrow.
He's gotta be.

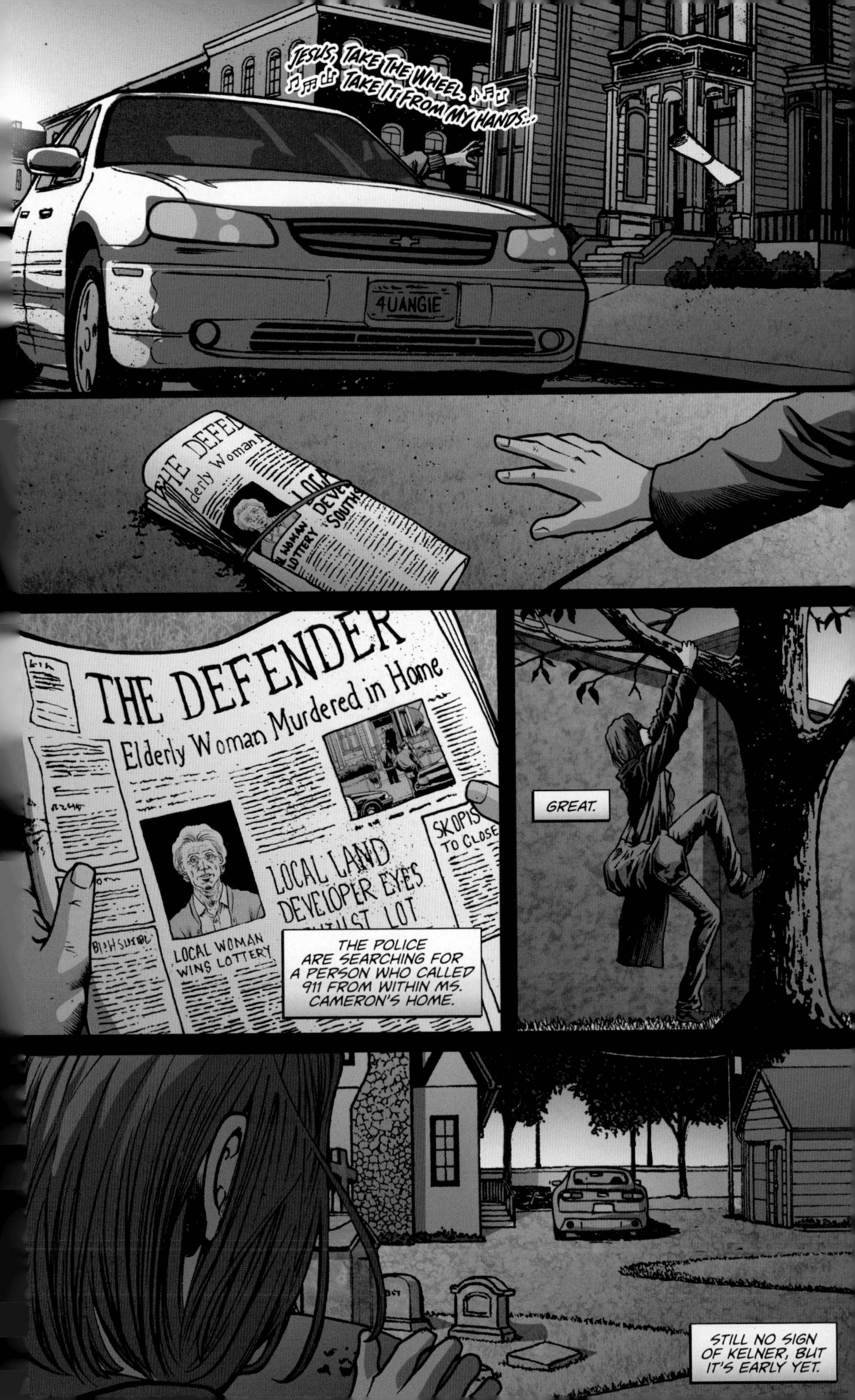
JESUS, TAKE THE WHEEL. ♪♬♪ TAKE IT FROM MY HANDS...
4UANGIE
THE DEFENDER
Elderly Woman Murdered in Home
LOCAL LAND DEVELOPER EYES
SKOPIS TO CLOSE
LOCAL WOMAN WINS LOTTERY
THE POLICE ARE SEARCHING FOR A PERSON WHO CALLED 911 FROM WITHIN MS. CAMERON'S HOME.
GREAT.
STILL NO SIGN OF KELNER, BUT IT'S EARLY YET.

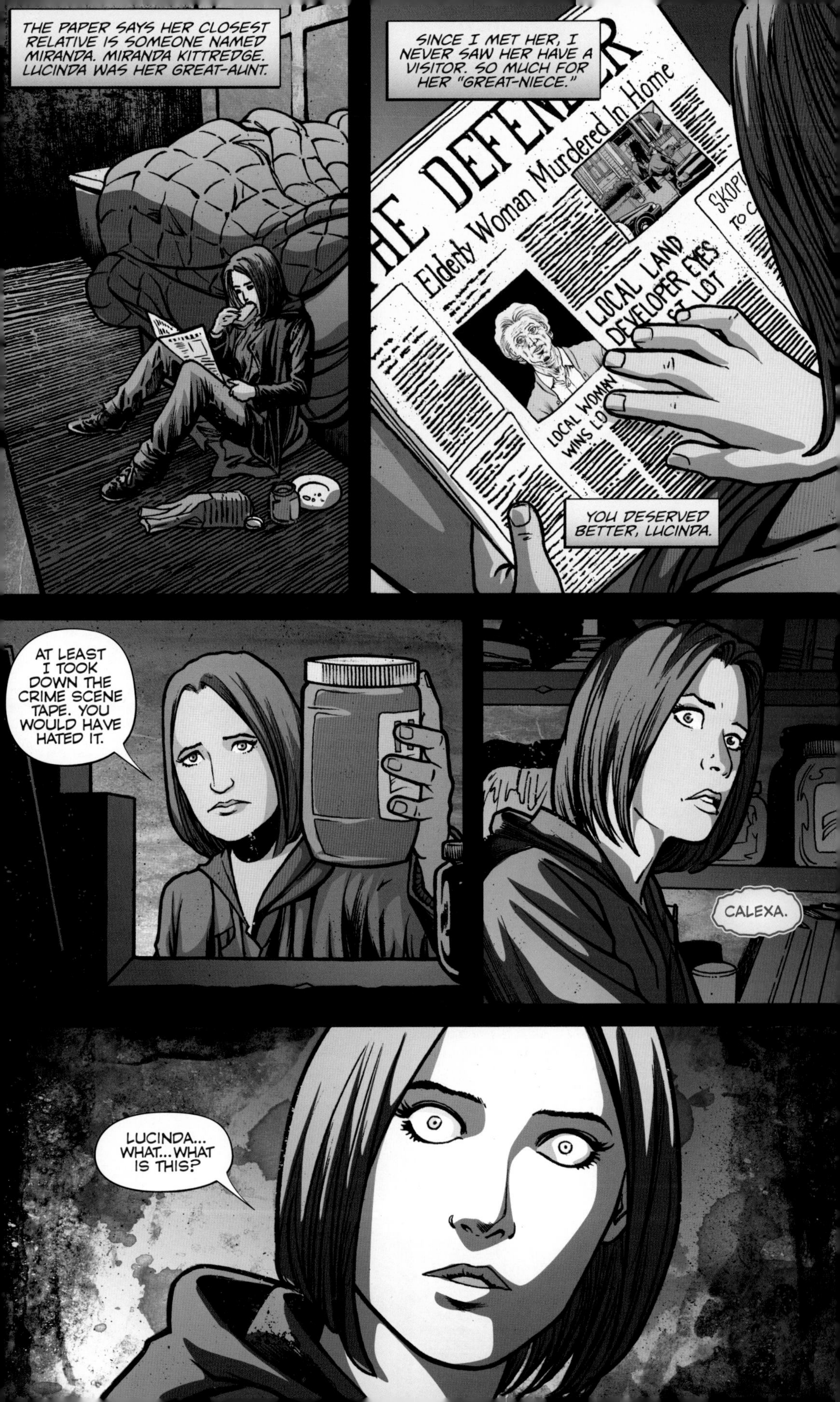
THE PAPER SAYS HER CLOSEST RELATIVE IS SOMEONE NAMED MIRANDA. MIRANDA KITTREDGE. LUCINDA WAS HER GREAT-AUNT.
SINCE I MET HER, I NEVER SAW HER HAVE A VISITOR. SO MUCH FOR HER "GREAT-NIECE."
HE DEFENDER
Elderly Woman Murdered In Home
LOCAL LAND DEVELOPER EYES
LOCAL WOMAN WINS LO
YOU DESERVED BETTER, LUCINDA.
AT LEAST I TOOK DOWN THE CRIME SCENE TAPE. YOU WOULD HAVE HATED IT.
CALEXA.
LUCINDA... WHAT...WHAT IS THIS?

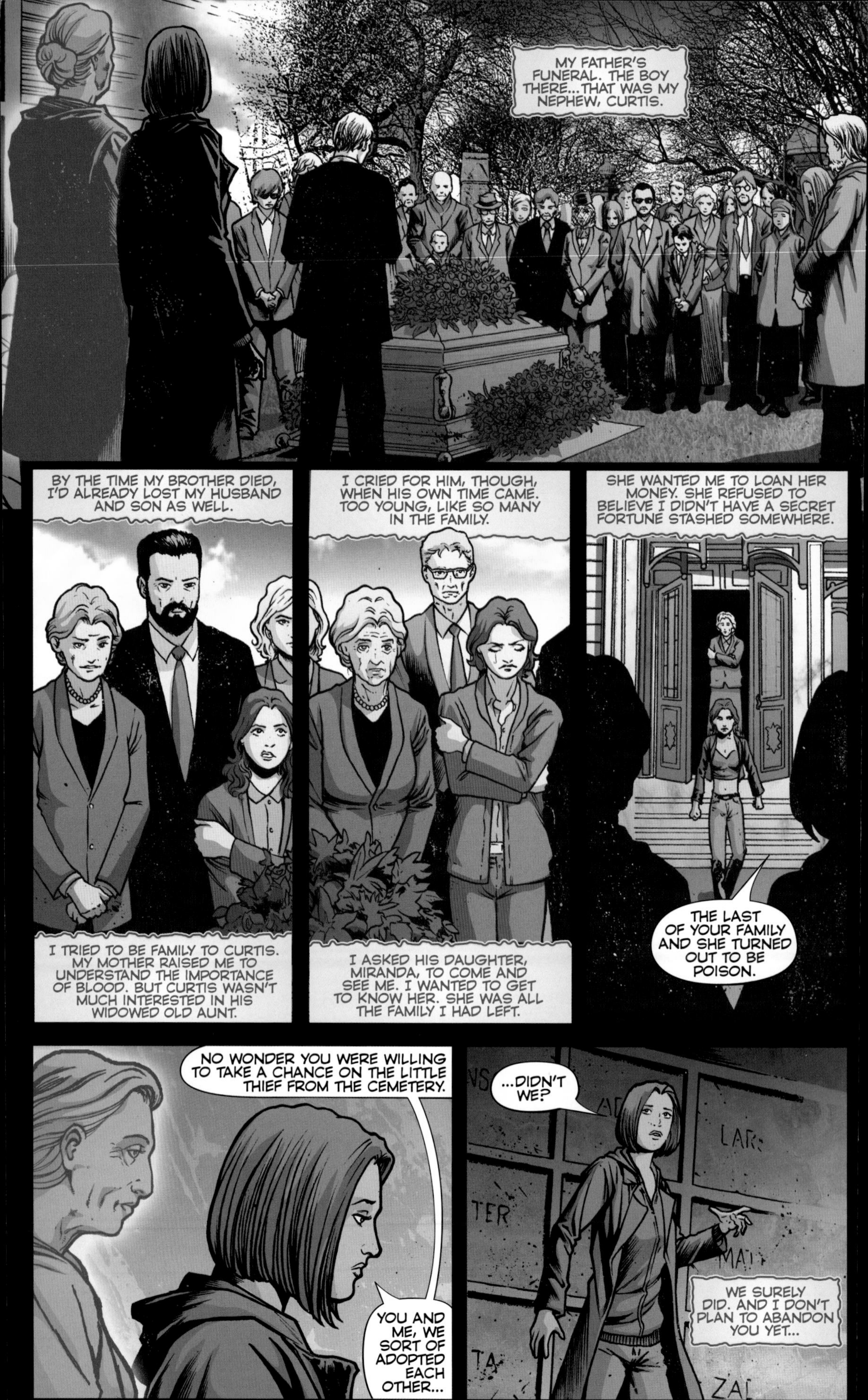
MY FATHER'S FUNERAL. THE BOY THERE...THAT WAS MY NEPHEW, CURTIS.
BY THE TIME MY BROTHER DIED, I'D ALREADY LOST MY HUSBAND AND SON AS WELL.
I TRIED TO BE FAMILY TO CURTIS. MY MOTHER RAISED ME TO UNDERSTAND THE IMPORTANCE OF BLOOD. BUT CURTIS WASN'T MUCH INTERESTED IN HIS WIDOWED OLD AUNT.
I CRIED FOR HIM, THOUGH, WHEN HIS OWN TIME CAME. TOO YOUNG, LIKE SO MANY IN THE FAMILY.
I ASKED HIS DAUGHTER, MIRANDA, TO COME AND SEE ME. I WANTED TO GET TO KNOW HER. SHE WAS ALL THE FAMILY I HAD LEFT.
SHE WANTED ME TO LOAN HER MONEY. SHE REFUSED TO BELIEVE I DIDN'T HAVE A SECRET FORTUNE STASHED SOMEWHERE.
THE LAST OF YOUR FAMILY AND SHE TURNED OUT TO BE POISON.
NO WONDER YOU WERE WILLING TO TAKE A CHANCE ON THE LITTLE THIEF FROM THE CEMETERY.
YOU AND ME, WE SORT OF ADOPTED EACH OTHER...
...DIDN'T WE?
WE SURELY DID. AND I DON'T PLAN TO ABANDON YOU YET...

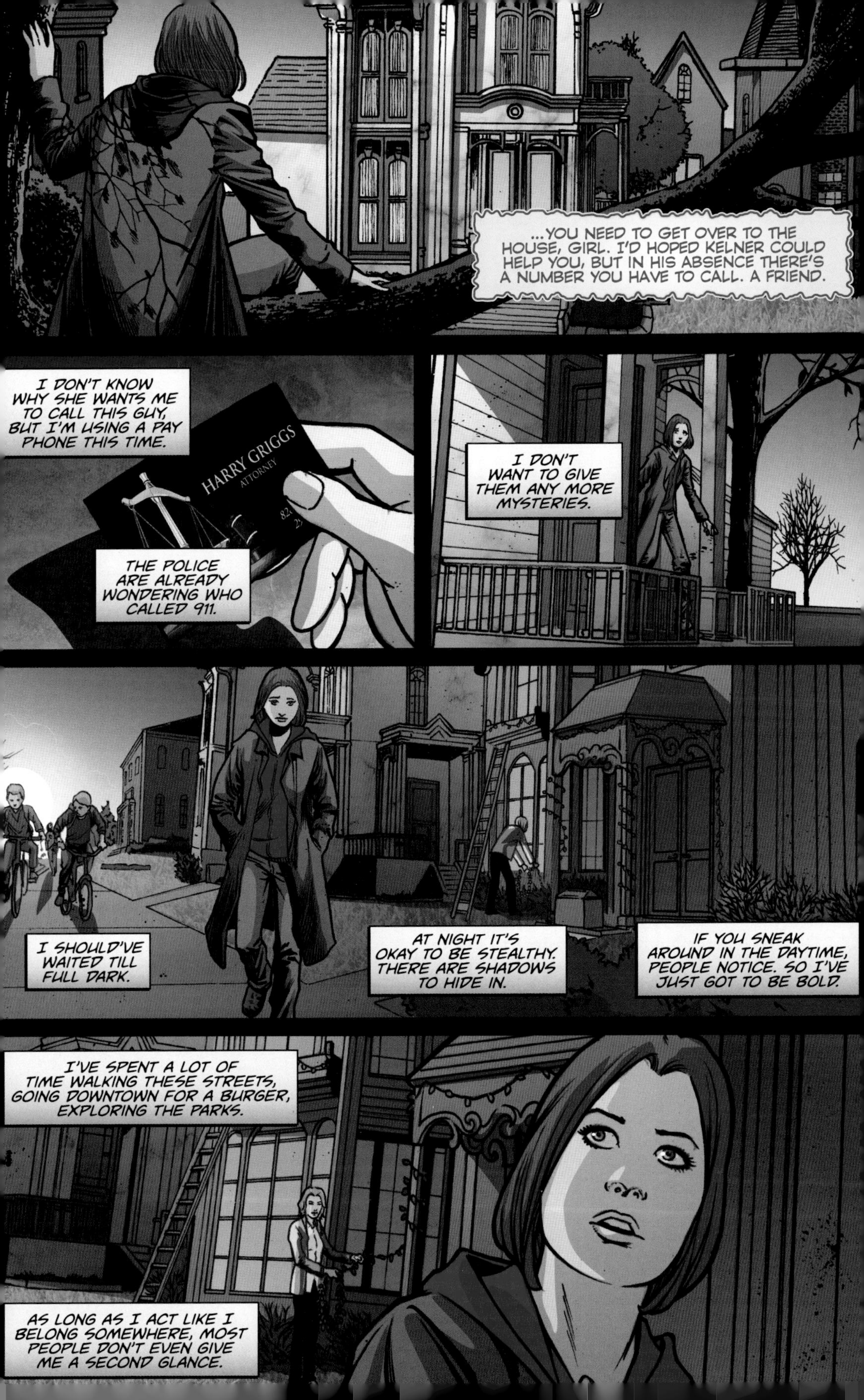
...YOU NEED TO GET OVER TO THE HOUSE, GIRL. I'D HOPED KELNER COULD HELP YOU, BUT IN HIS ABSENCE THERE'S A NUMBER YOU HAVE TO CALL. A FRIEND.
I DON'T KNOW WHY SHE WANTS ME TO CALL THIS GUY, BUT I'M USING A PAY PHONE THIS TIME.
HARRY GRIGGS
ATTORNEY
THE POLICE ARE ALREADY WONDERING WHO CALLED 911.
I DON'T WANT TO GIVE THEM ANY MORE MYSTERIES.
I SHOULD'VE WAITED TILL FULL DARK.
AT NIGHT IT'S OKAY TO BE STEALTHY. THERE ARE SHADOWS TO HIDE IN.
IF YOU SNEAK AROUND IN THE DAYTIME, PEOPLE NOTICE. SO I'VE JUST GOT TO BE BOLD.
I'VE SPENT A LOT OF TIME WALKING THESE STREETS, GOING DOWNTOWN FOR A BURGER, EXPLORING THE PARKS.
AS LONG AS I ACT LIKE I BELONG SOMEWHERE, MOST PEOPLE DON'T EVEN GIVE ME A SECOND GLANCE.

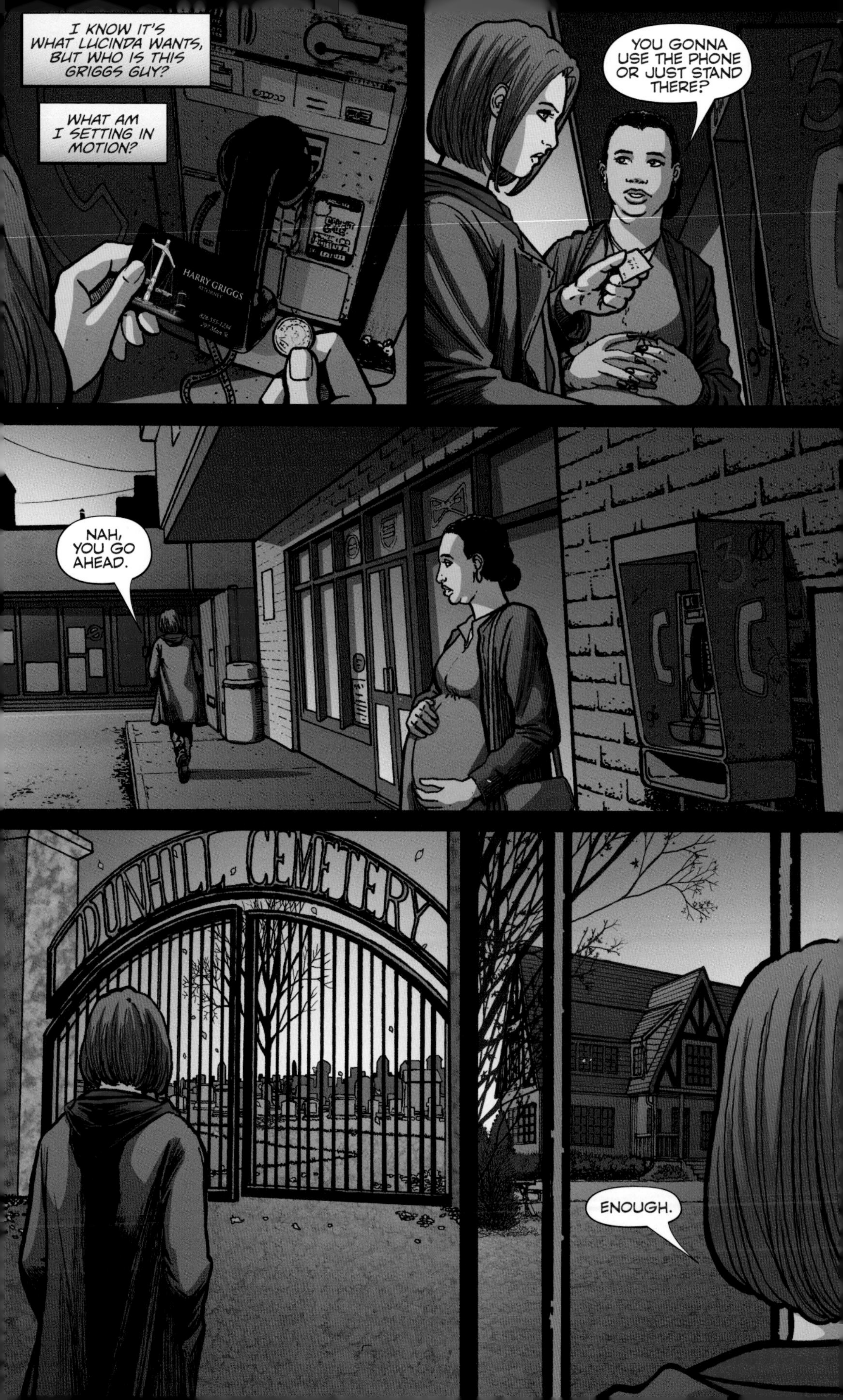
I KNOW IT'S WHAT LUCINDA WANTS, BUT WHO IS THIS GRIGGS GUY?
WHAT AM I SETTING IN MOTION?
HARRY GRIGGS
ATTORNEY
YOU GONNA USE THE PHONE OR JUST STAND THERE?
NAH, YOU GO AHEAD.
DUNHILL CEMETERY
ENOUGH.

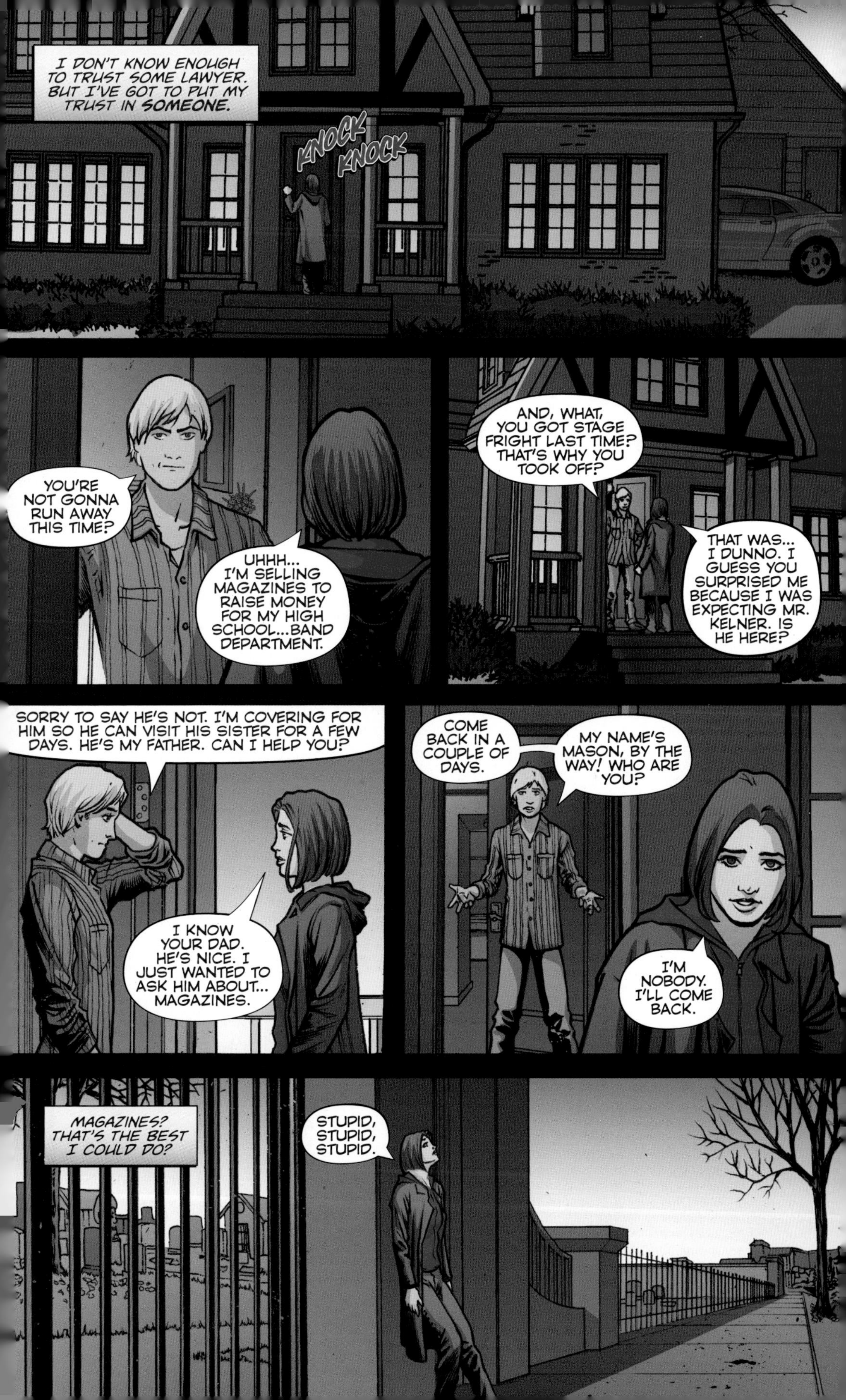
I DON'T KNOW ENOUGH TO TRUST SOME LAWYER. BUT I'VE GOT TO PUT MY TRUST IN SOMEONE.
KNOCK KNOCK
YOU'RE NOT GONNA RUN AWAY THIS TIME?
UHHH... I'M SELLING MAGAZINES TO RAISE MONEY FOR MY HIGH SCHOOL...BAND DEPARTMENT.
AND, WHAT, YOU GOT STAGE FRIGHT LAST TIME? THAT'S WHY YOU TOOK OFF?
THAT WAS... I DUNNO. I GUESS YOU SURPRISED ME BECAUSE I WAS EXPECTING MR. KELNER. IS HE HERE?
SORRY TO SAY HE'S NOT. I'M COVERING FOR HIM SO HE CAN VISIT HIS SISTER FOR A FEW DAYS. HE'S MY FATHER. CAN I HELP YOU?
I KNOW YOUR DAD. HE'S NICE. I JUST WANTED TO ASK HIM ABOUT... MAGAZINES.
COME BACK IN A COUPLE OF DAYS.
MY NAME'S MASON, BY THE WAY! WHO ARE YOU?
I'M NOBODY. I'LL COME BACK.
MAGAZINES? THAT'S THE BEST I COULD DO?
STUPID, STUPID, STUPID.

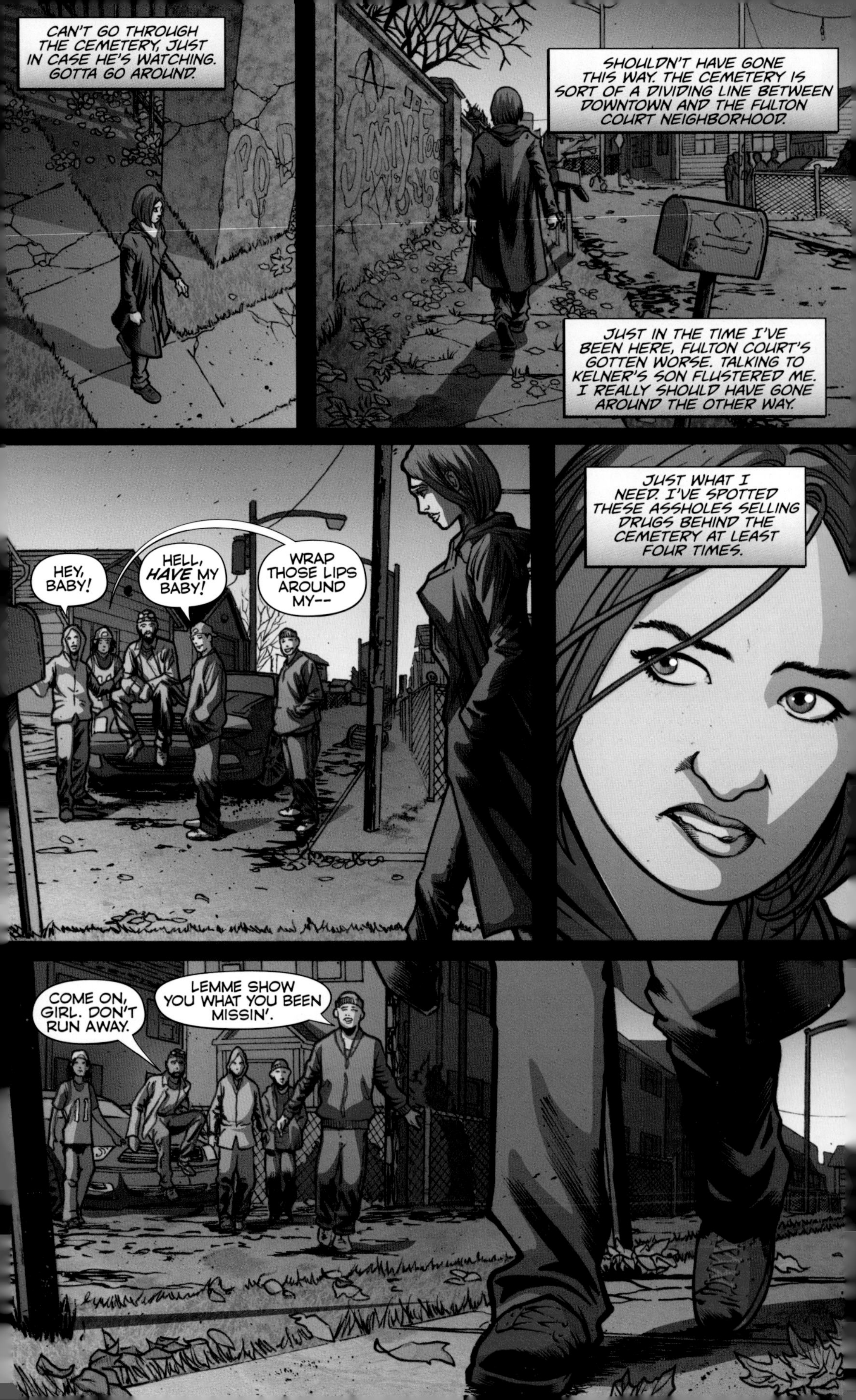
CAN'T GO THROUGH THE CEMETERY, JUST IN CASE HE'S WATCHING. GOTTA GO AROUND.
SHOULDN'T HAVE GONE THIS WAY. THE CEMETERY IS SORT OF A DIVIDING LINE BETWEEN DOWNTOWN AND THE FULTON COURT NEIGHBORHOOD.
JUST IN THE TIME I'VE BEEN HERE, FULTON COURT'S GOTTEN WORSE. TALKING TO KELNER'S SON FLUSTERED ME. I REALLY SHOULD HAVE GONE AROUND THE OTHER WAY.
HEY, BABY!
HELL, HAVE MY BABY!
WRAP THOSE LIPS AROUND MY--
JUST WHAT I NEED. I'VE SPOTTED THESE ASSHOLES SELLING DRUGS BEHIND THE CEMETERY AT LEAST FOUR TIMES.
COME ON, GIRL. DON'T RUN AWAY.
LEMME SHOW YOU WHAT YOU BEEN MISSIN'.

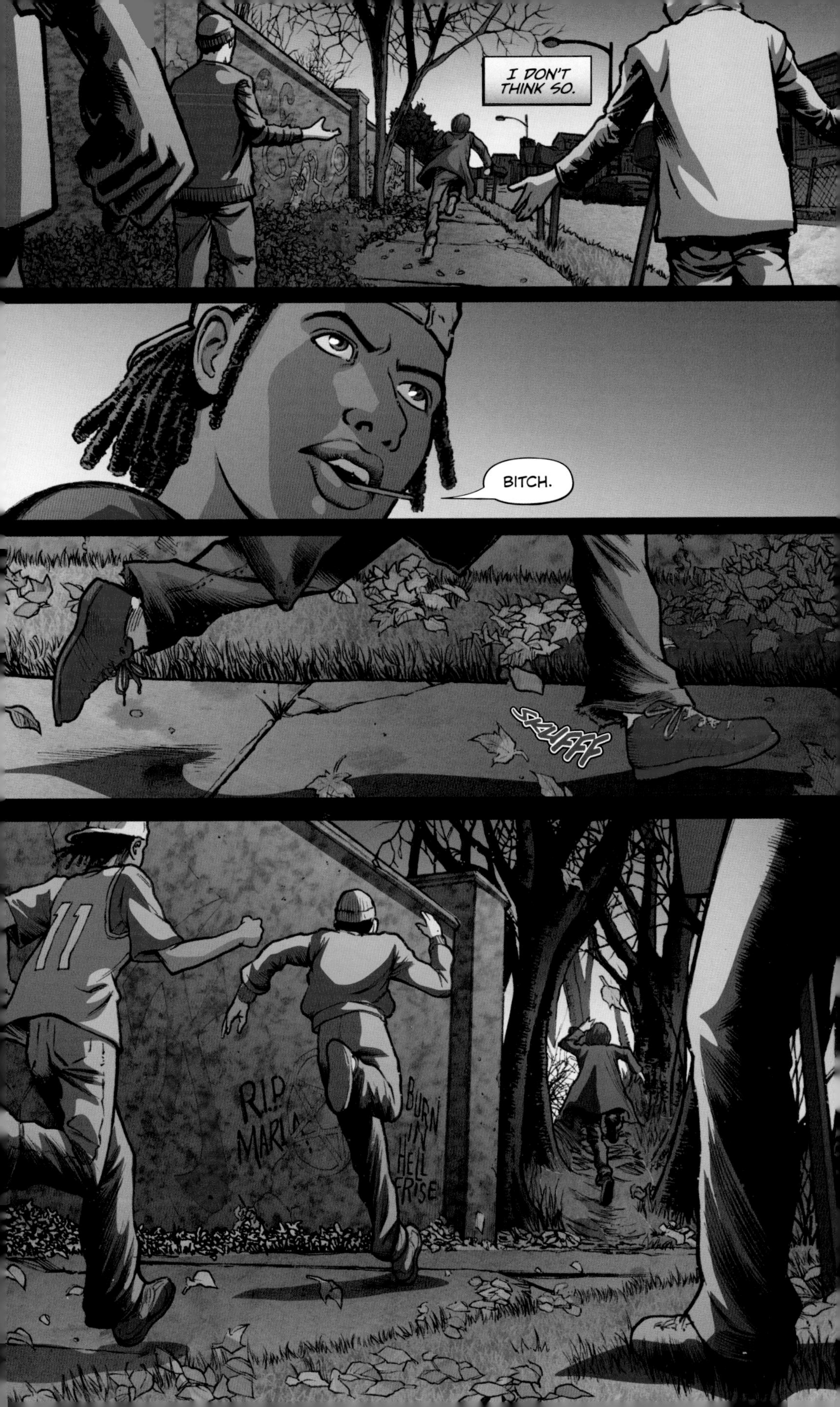
I DON'T THINK SO.
BITCH.
SKUFFF
R.I.P. MARLA
BURN IN HELL FRISE

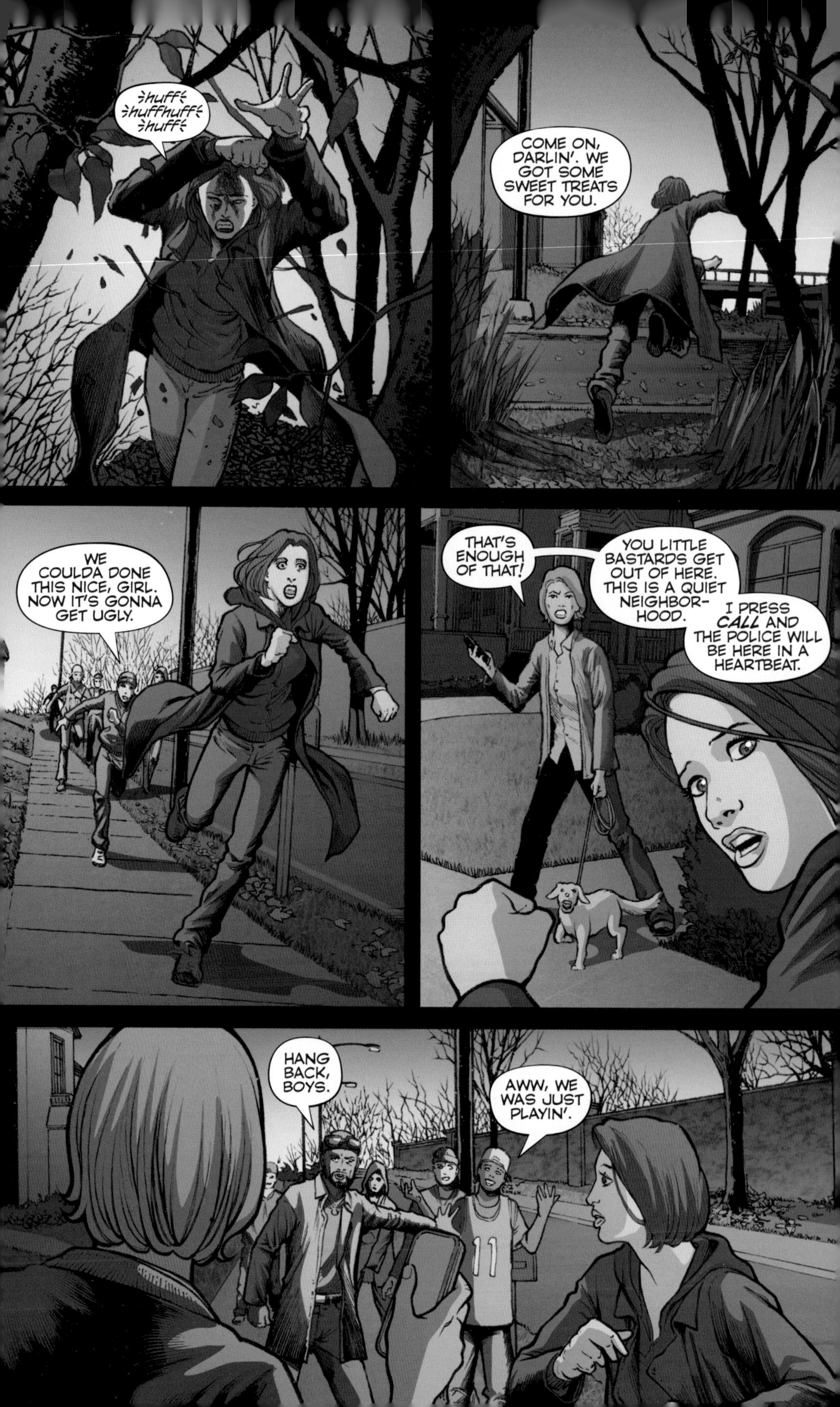

huff *huffhuff* *huff*
COME ON, DARLIN'. WE GOT SOME SWEET TREATS FOR YOU.
WE COULDA DONE THIS NICE, GIRL. NOW IT'S GONNA GET UGLY.
THAT'S ENOUGH OF THAT!
YOU LITTLE BASTARDS GET OUT OF HERE. THIS IS A QUIET NEIGHBOR-HOOD.
I PRESS *CALL* AND THE POLICE WILL BE HERE IN A HEARTBEAT.
HANG BACK, BOYS.
AWW, WE WAS JUST PLAYIN'.

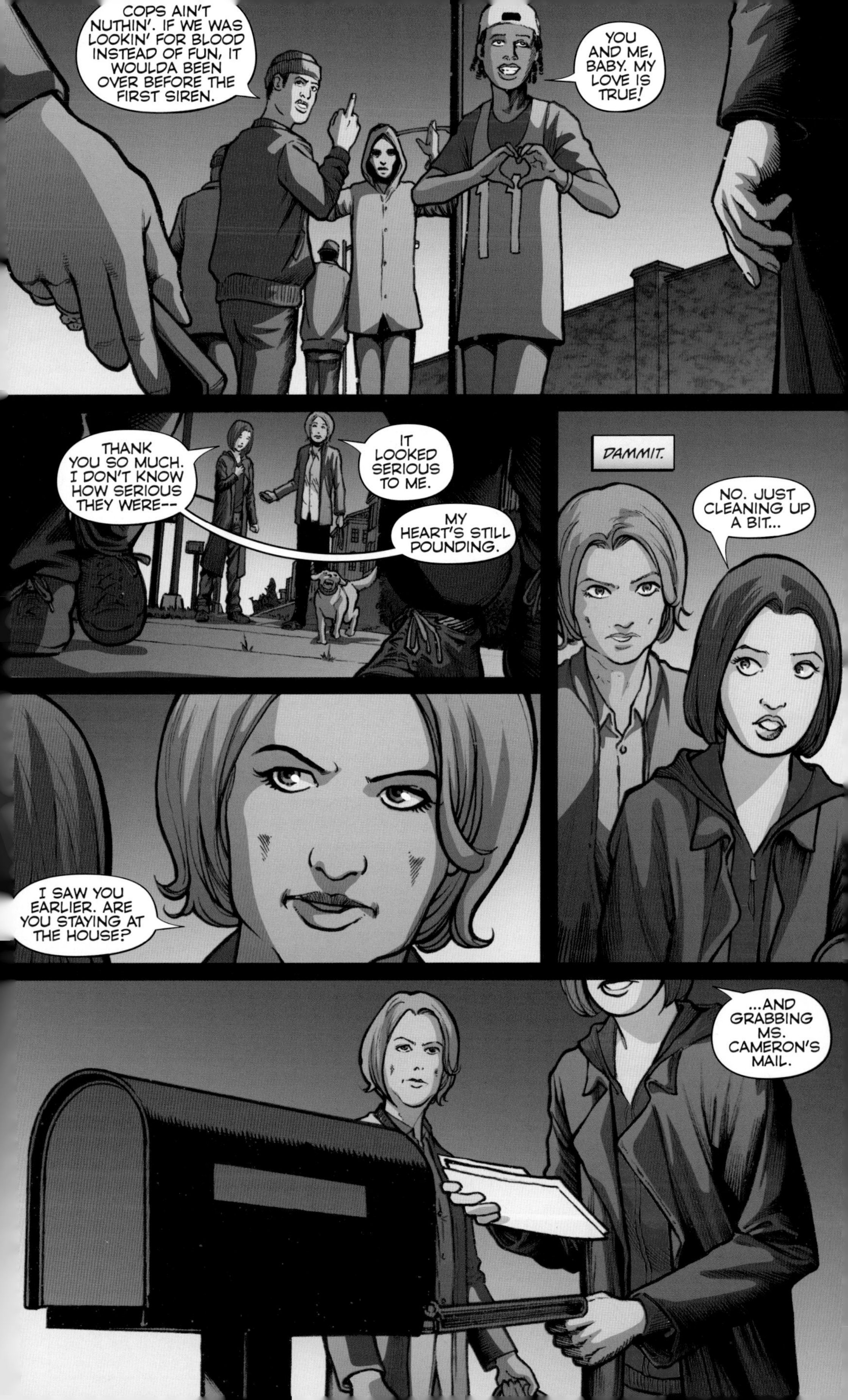
COPS AIN'T NUTHIN'. IF WE WAS LOOKIN' FOR BLOOD INSTEAD OF FUN, IT WOULDA BEEN OVER BEFORE THE FIRST SIREN.
YOU AND ME, BABY. MY LOVE IS TRUE!
THANK YOU SO MUCH. I DON'T KNOW HOW SERIOUS THEY WERE--
IT LOOKED SERIOUS TO ME.
MY HEART'S STILL POUNDING.
DAMMIT.
I SAW YOU EARLIER. ARE YOU STAYING AT THE HOUSE?
NO. JUST CLEANING UP A BIT...
...AND GRABBING MS. CAMERON'S MAIL.

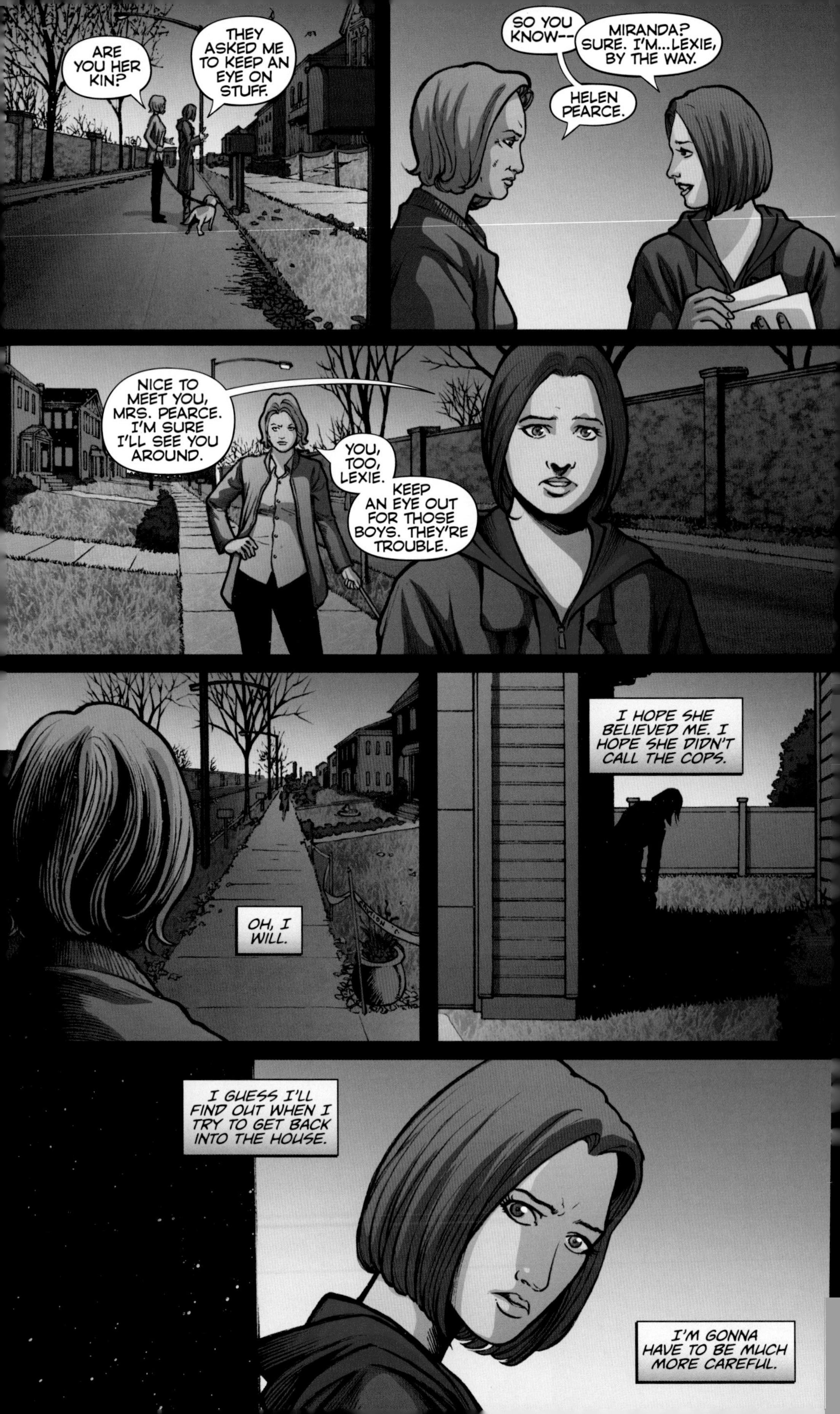
ARE YOU HER KIN?
THEY ASKED ME TO KEEP AN EYE ON STUFF.
SO YOU KNOW--
MIRANDA? SURE. I'M...LEXIE, BY THE WAY.
HELEN PEARCE.
NICE TO MEET YOU, MRS. PEARCE. I'M SURE I'LL SEE YOU AROUND.
YOU, TOO, LEXIE.
KEEP AN EYE OUT FOR THOSE BOYS. THEY'RE TROUBLE.
OH, I WILL.
I HOPE SHE BELIEVED ME. I HOPE SHE DIDN'T CALL THE COPS.
I GUESS I'LL FIND OUT WHEN I TRY TO GET BACK INTO THE HOUSE.
I'M GONNA HAVE TO BE MUCH MORE CAREFUL.

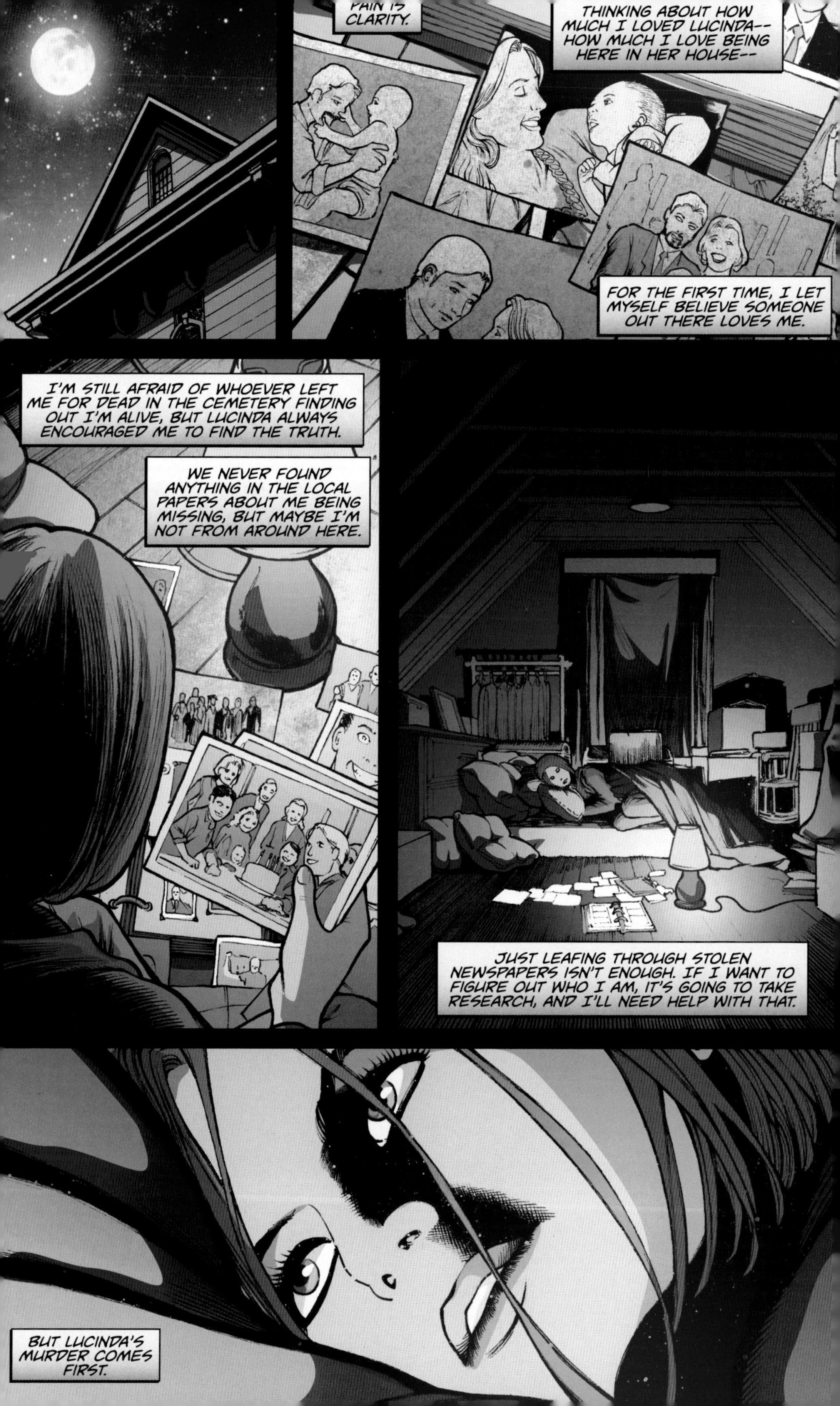
PAIN IS CLARITY.
THINKING ABOUT HOW MUCH I LOVED LUCINDA-- HOW MUCH I LOVE BEING HERE IN HER HOUSE--
FOR THE FIRST TIME, I LET MYSELF BELIEVE SOMEONE OUT THERE LOVES ME.
I'M STILL AFRAID OF WHOEVER LEFT ME FOR DEAD IN THE CEMETERY FINDING OUT I'M ALIVE, BUT LUCINDA ALWAYS ENCOURAGED ME TO FIND THE TRUTH.
WE NEVER FOUND ANYTHING IN THE LOCAL PAPERS ABOUT ME BEING MISSING, BUT MAYBE I'M NOT FROM AROUND HERE.
JUST LEAFING THROUGH STOLEN NEWSPAPERS ISN'T ENOUGH. IF I WANT TO FIGURE OUT WHO I AM, IT'S GOING TO TAKE RESEARCH, AND I'LL NEED HELP WITH THAT.
BUT LUCINDA'S MURDER COMES FIRST.

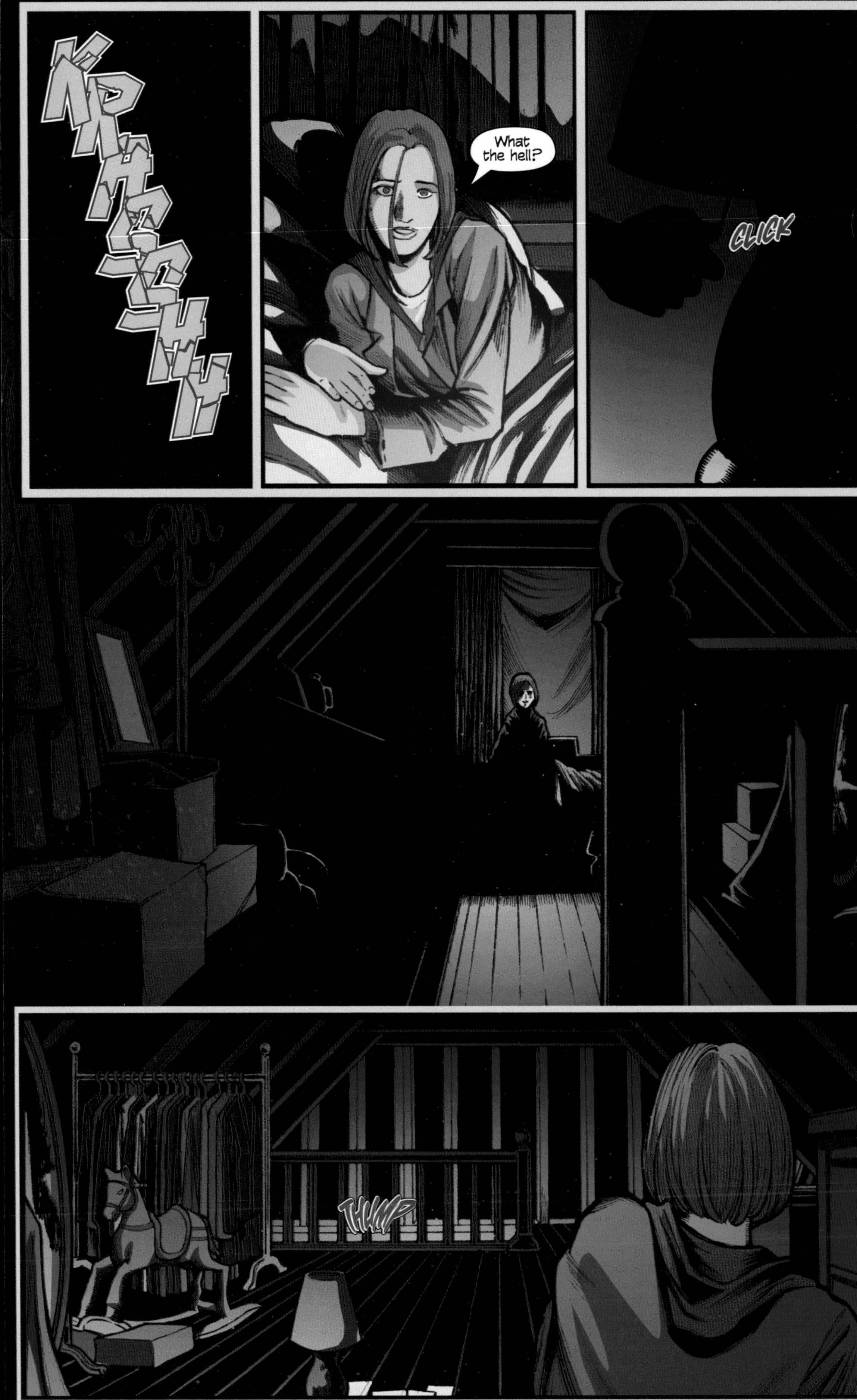
What the hell?
CLICK
THUMP

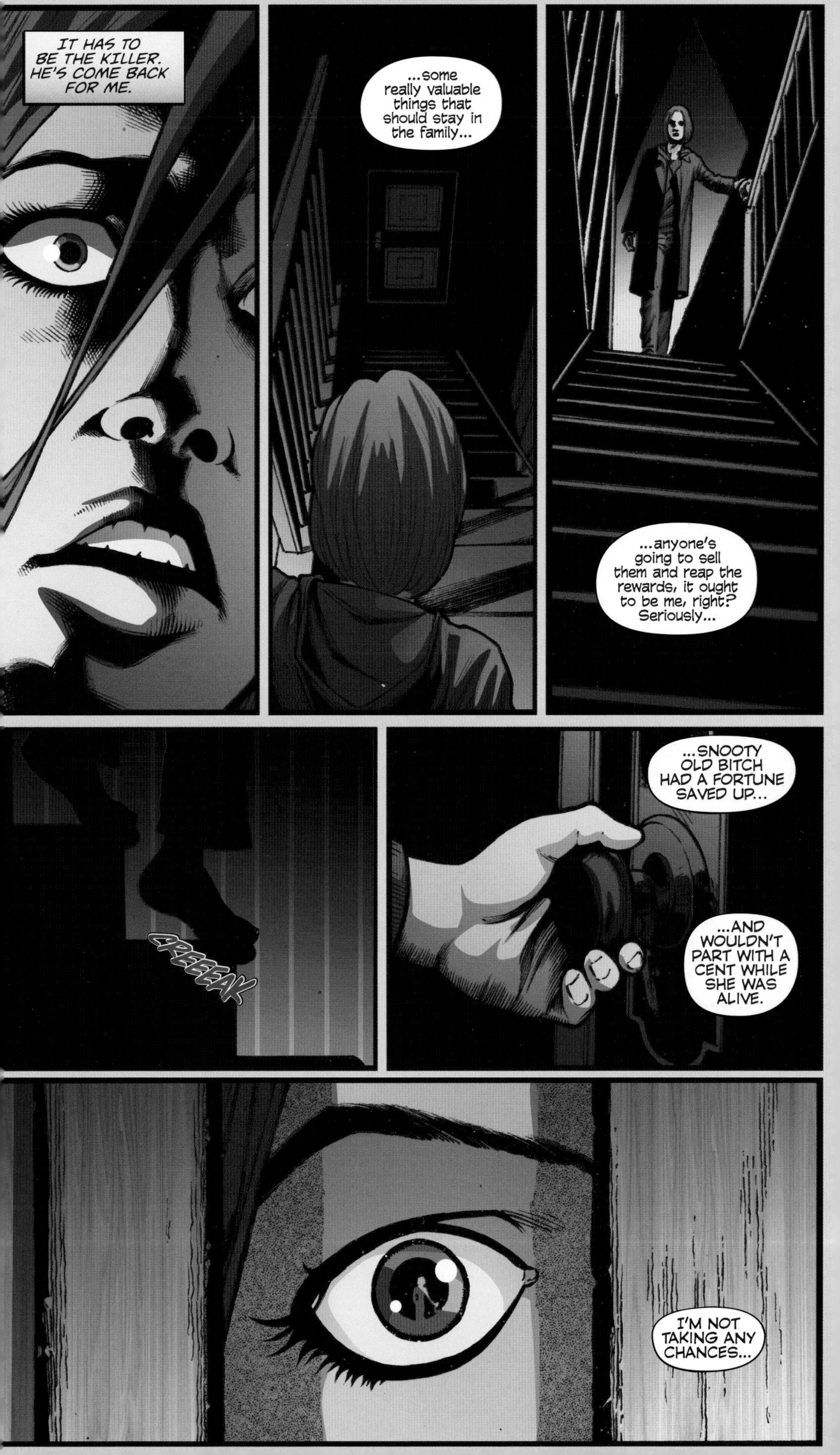
IT HAS TO BE THE KILLER. HE'S COME BACK FOR ME.
...some really valuable things that should stay in the family...
...anyone's going to sell them and reap the rewards, it ought to be me, right? Seriously...
CREEEAK
...SNOOTY OLD BITCH HAD A FORTUNE SAVED UP...
...AND WOULDN'T PART WITH A CENT WHILE SHE WAS ALIVE.
I'M NOT TAKING ANY CHANCES...

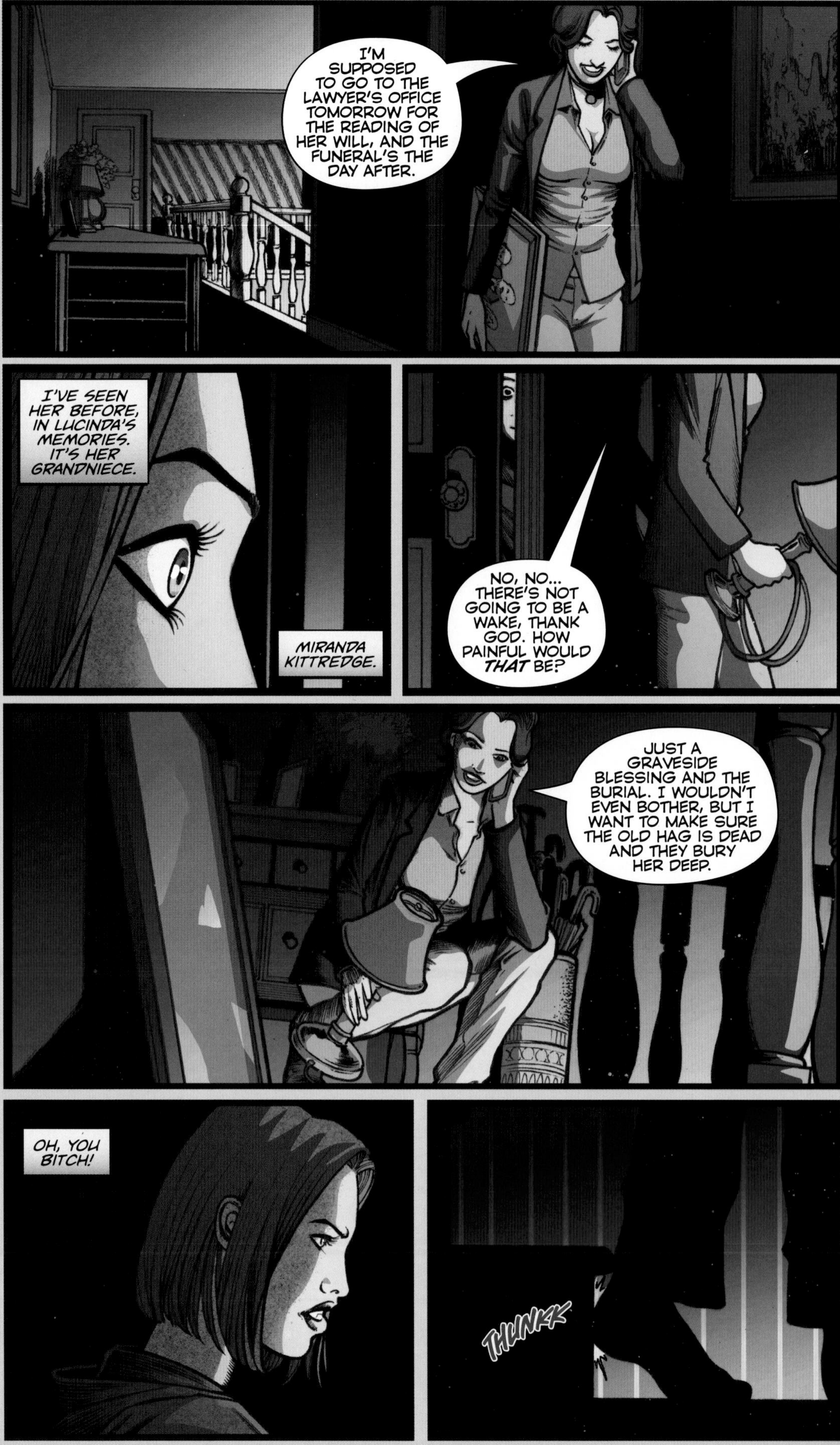
I'M SUPPOSED TO GO TO THE LAWYER'S OFFICE TOMORROW FOR THE READING OF HER WILL, AND THE FUNERAL'S THE DAY AFTER.
I'VE SEEN HER BEFORE, IN LUCINDA'S MEMORIES. IT'S HER GRANDNIECE.
MIRANDA KITTREDGE.
NO, NO... THERE'S NOT GOING TO BE A WAKE, THANK GOD. HOW PAINFUL WOULD *THAT* BE?
JUST A GRAVESIDE BLESSING AND THE BURIAL. I WOULDN'T EVEN BOTHER, BUT I WANT TO MAKE SURE THE OLD HAG IS DEAD AND THEY BURY HER DEEP.
OH, YOU BITCH!
THUNKK

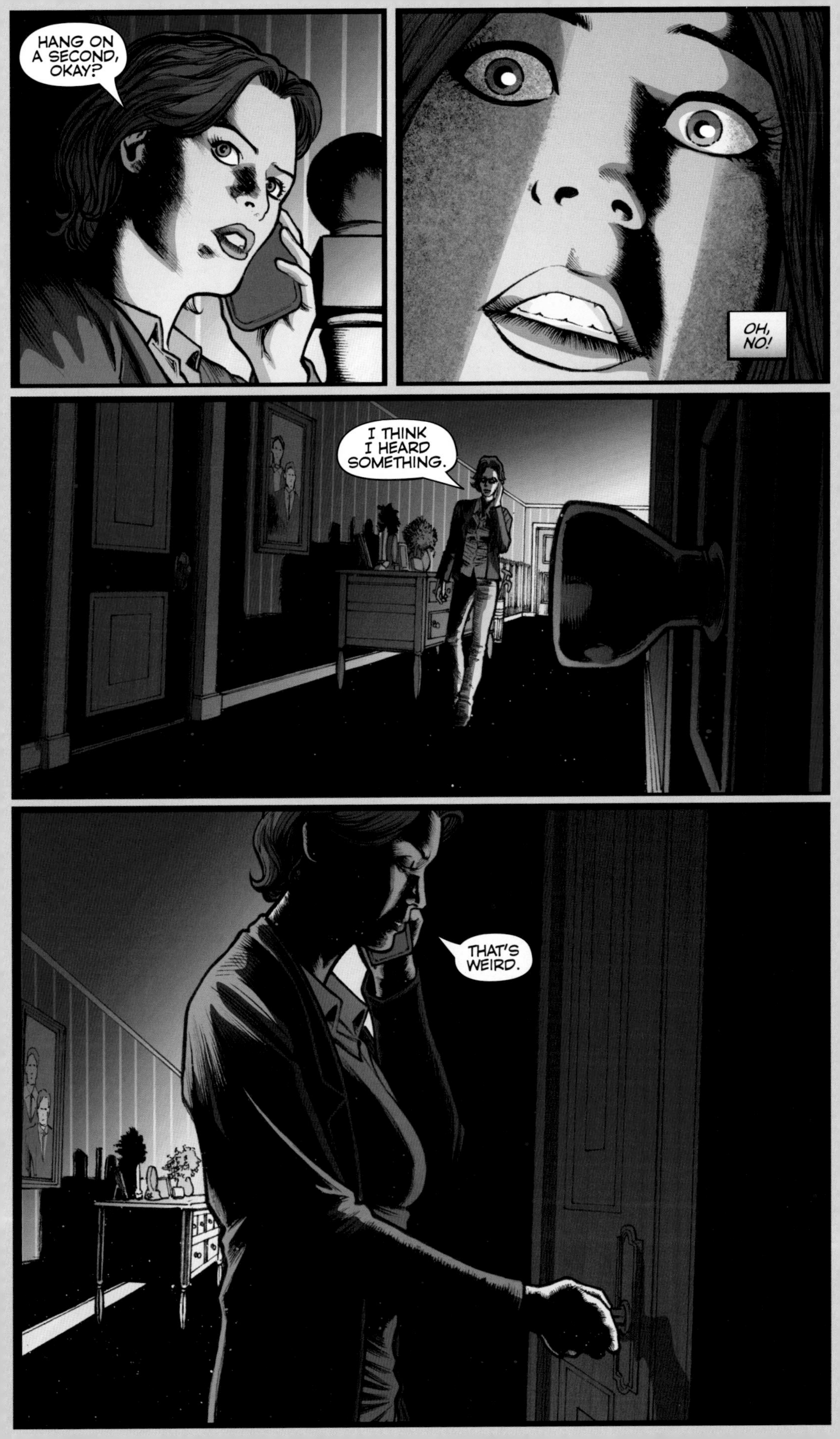
HANG ON A SECOND, OKAY?
OH, NO!
I THINK I HEARD SOMETHING.
THAT'S WEIRD.

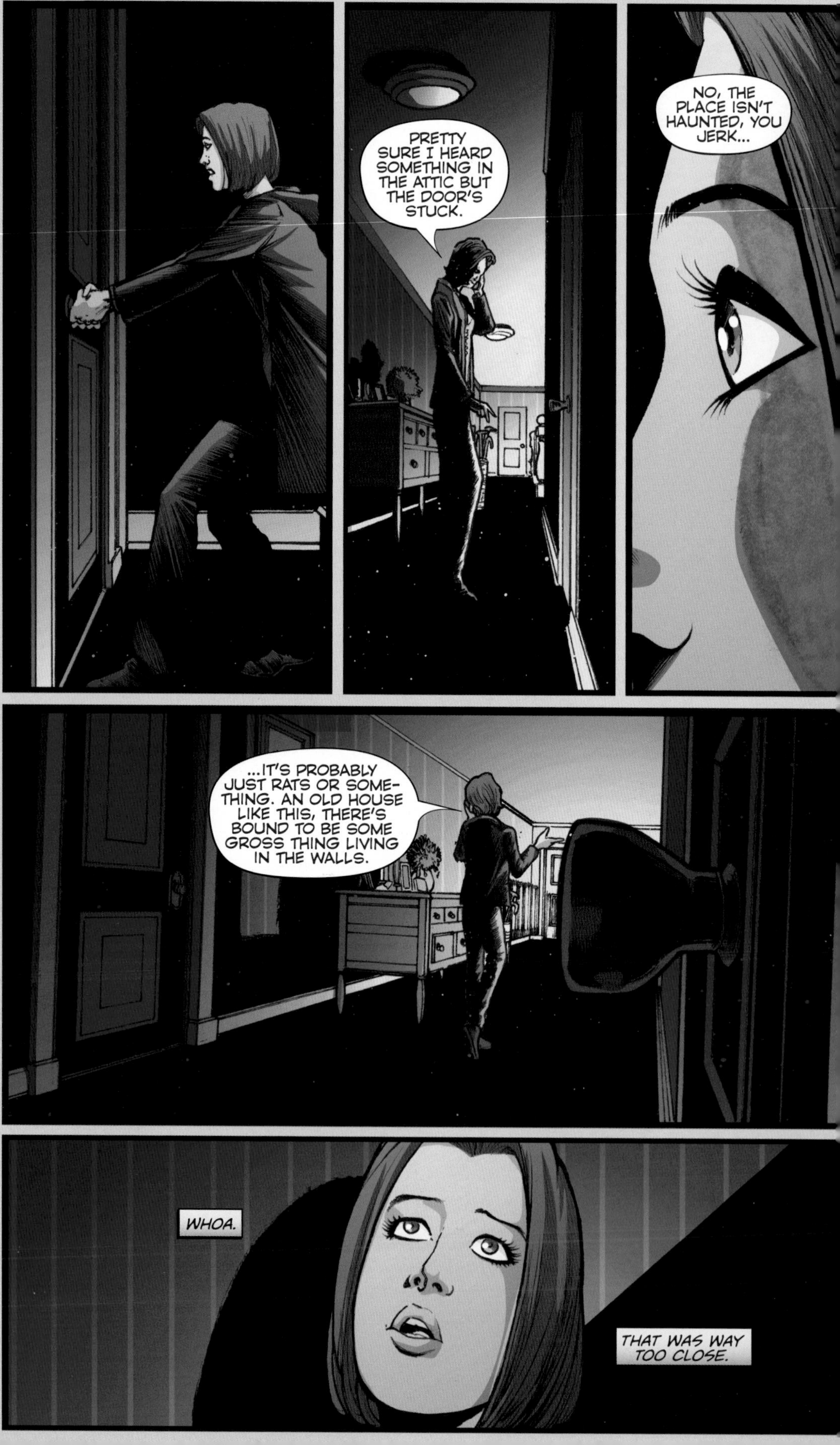
PRETTY SURE I HEARD SOMETHING IN THE ATTIC BUT THE DOOR'S STUCK.
NO, THE PLACE ISN'T HAUNTED, YOU JERK...
...IT'S PROBABLY JUST RATS OR SOME-THING. AN OLD HOUSE LIKE THIS, THERE'S BOUND TO BE SOME GROSS THING LIVING IN THE WALLS.
WHOA.
THAT WAS WAY TOO CLOSE.

THE WOMAN'S A MONSTER. THE THINGS SHE WAS SAYING...DISGUSTING.

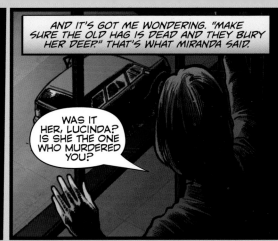

AND IT'S GOT ME WONDERING. "MAKE SURE THE OLD HAG IS DEAD AND THEY BURY HER DEEP." THAT'S WHAT MIRANDA SAID.

WAS IT HER, LUCINDA? IS SHE THE ONE WHO MURDERED YOU?

I CAN'T EVEN BELIEVE YOU, AUNTIE.

ALL I WANTED WAS A LITTLE LOAN. IT'S NOT AS IF YOU DON'T HAVE THE MONEY!

WE ALL KNOW YOU'VE GOT IT SOCKED AWAY SOME-WHERE!

I ONLY WISH THAT WERE TRUE. I'D LIKE TO HELP YOU, MIRANDA. NO MATTER HOW RUDE YOU ARE TO ME, YOU'RE STILL FAMILY, AND I'VE LOST TOO MANY OF MY KIN.

IT WASN'T ALWAYS LIKE THAT, YOU KNOW.

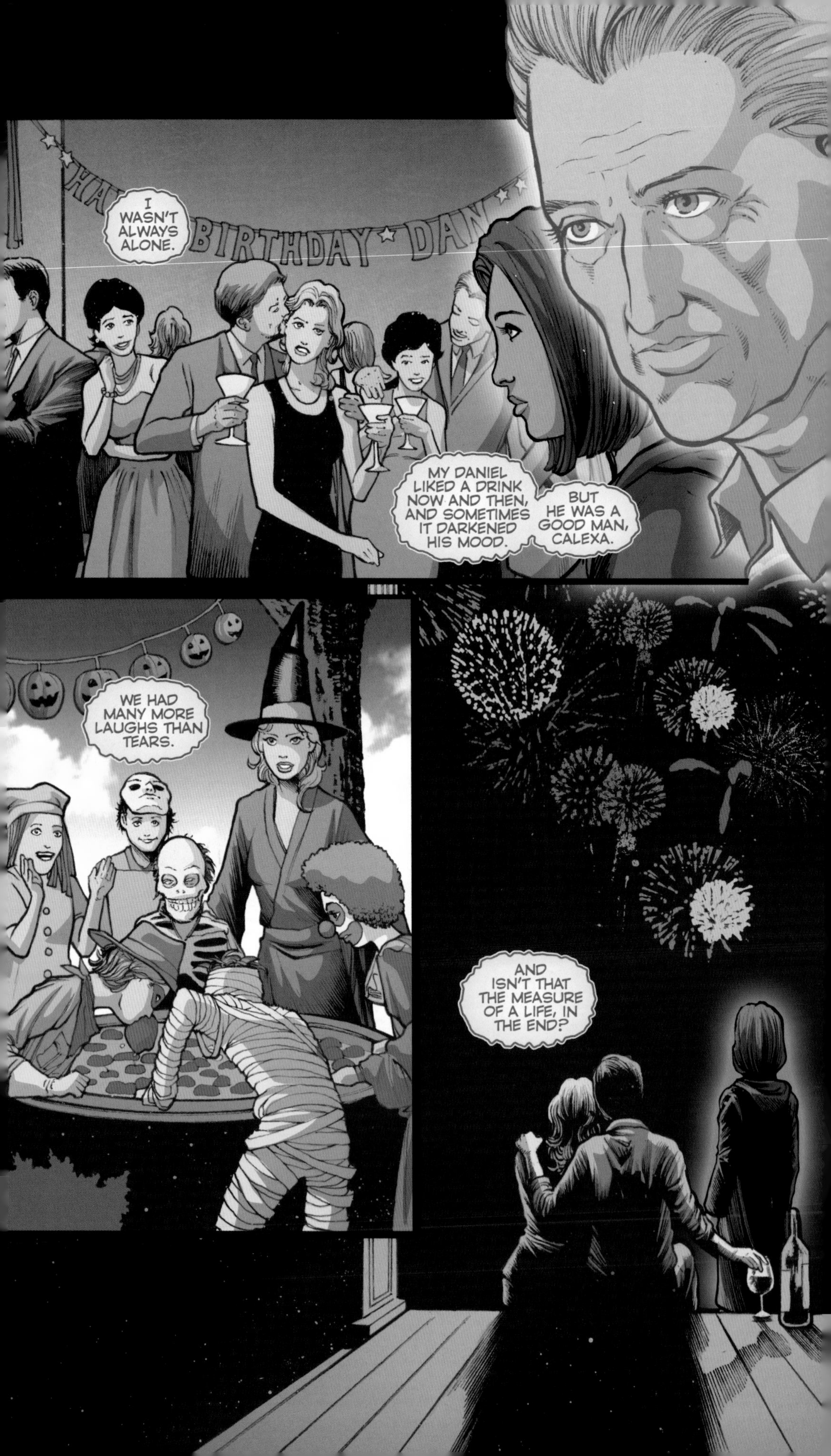
HA BIRTHDAY DAN
I WASN'T ALWAYS ALONE.
MY DANIEL LIKED A DRINK NOW AND THEN, AND SOMETIMES IT DARKENED HIS MOOD.
BUT HE WAS A GOOD MAN, CALEXA.
WE HAD MANY MORE LAUGHS THAN TEARS.
AND ISN'T THAT THE MEASURE OF A LIFE, IN THE END?

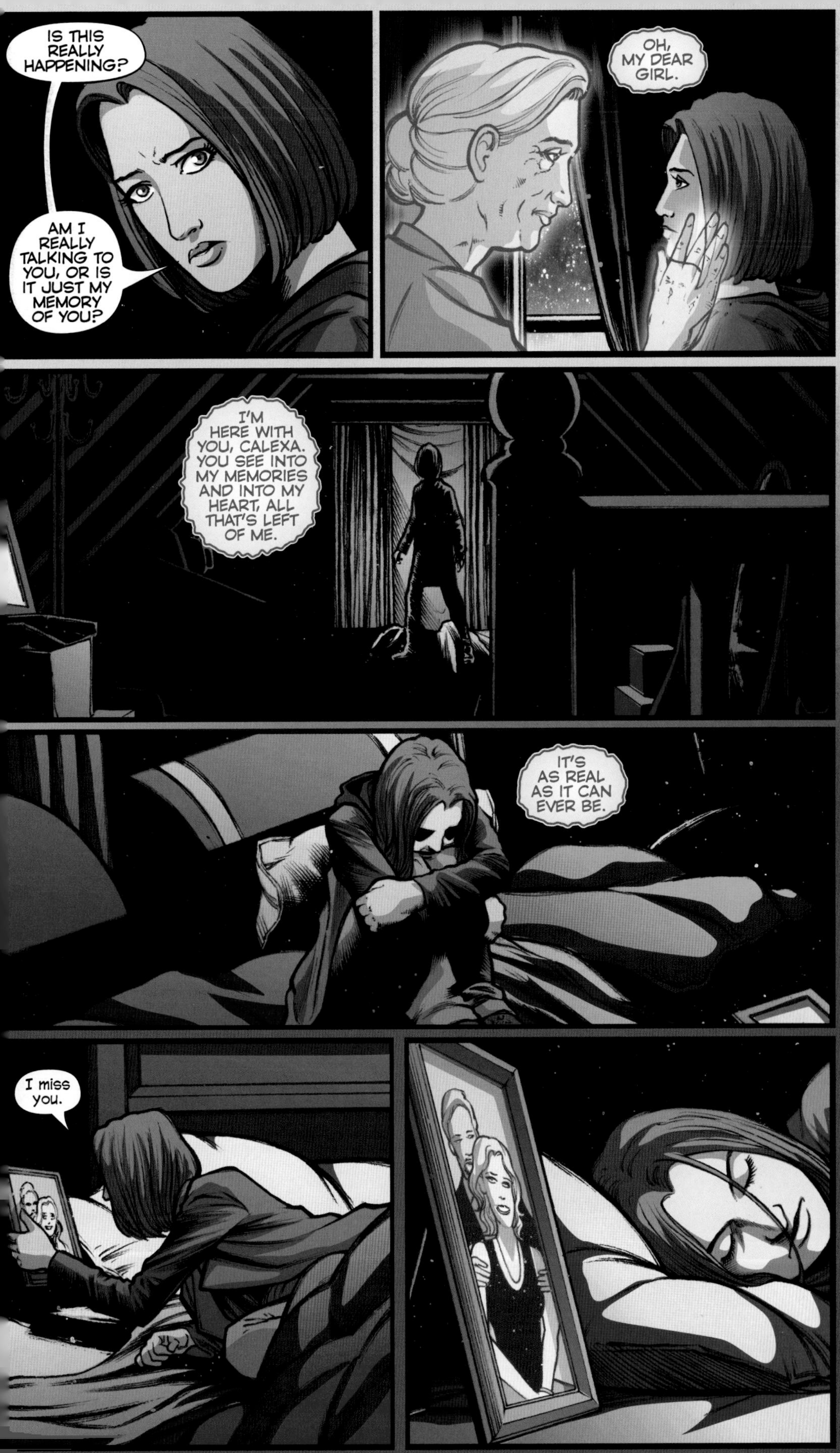
IS THIS REALLY HAPPENING?
AM I REALLY TALKING TO YOU, OR IS IT JUST MY MEMORY OF YOU?
OH, MY DEAR GIRL.
I'M HERE WITH YOU, CALEXA. YOU SEE INTO MY MEMORIES AND INTO MY HEART, ALL THAT'S LEFT OF ME.
IT'S AS REAL AS IT CAN EVER BE.
I miss you.

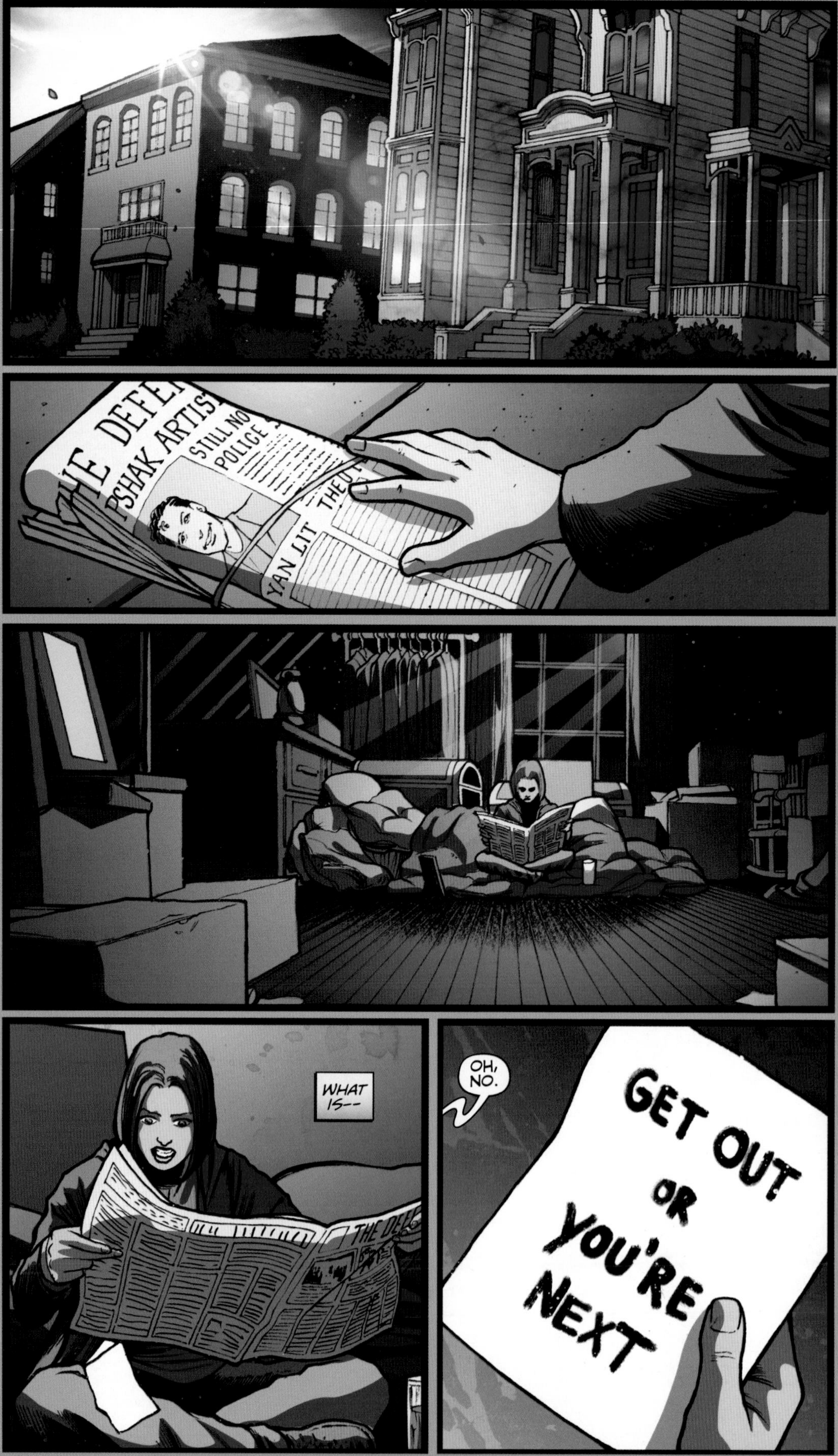
STILL NO POLICE
WHAT IS--
OH, NO.
GET OUT OR YOU'RE NEXT

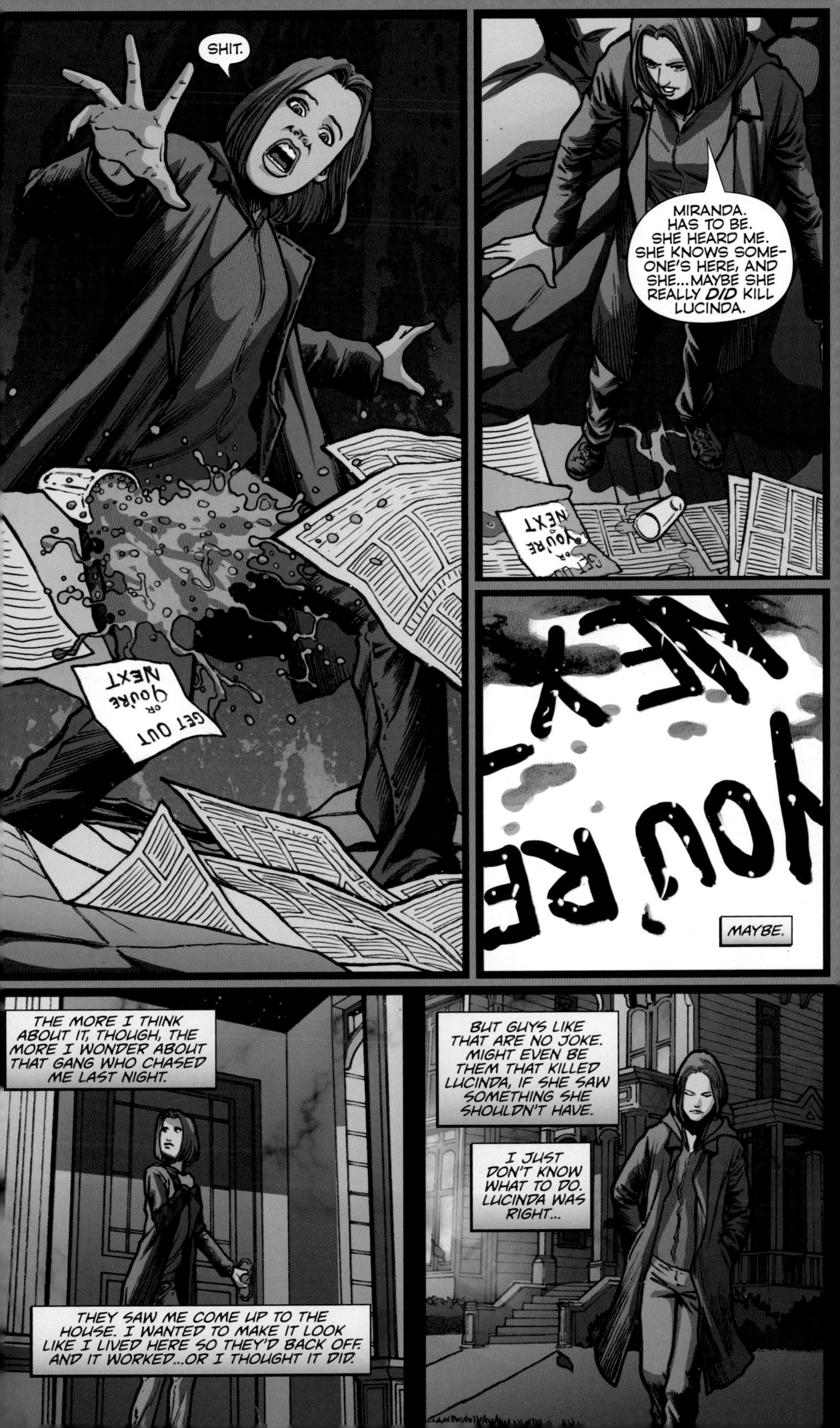
SHIT.
GET OUT OR YOU'RE NEXT
MIRANDA. HAS TO BE. SHE HEARD ME. SHE KNOWS SOME-ONE'S HERE, AND SHE...MAYBE SHE REALLY *DID* KILL LUCINDA.
YOU'RE NEX
MAYBE.
THE MORE I THINK ABOUT IT, THOUGH, THE MORE I WONDER ABOUT THAT GANG WHO CHASED ME LAST NIGHT.
THEY SAW ME COME UP TO THE HOUSE. I WANTED TO MAKE IT LOOK LIKE I LIVED HERE SO THEY'D BACK OFF. AND IT WORKED...OR I THOUGHT IT DID.
BUT GUYS LIKE THAT ARE NO JOKE. MIGHT EVEN BE THEM THAT KILLED LUCINDA, IF SHE SAW SOMETHING SHE SHOULDN'T HAVE.
I JUST DON'T KNOW WHAT TO DO. LUCINDA WAS RIGHT...

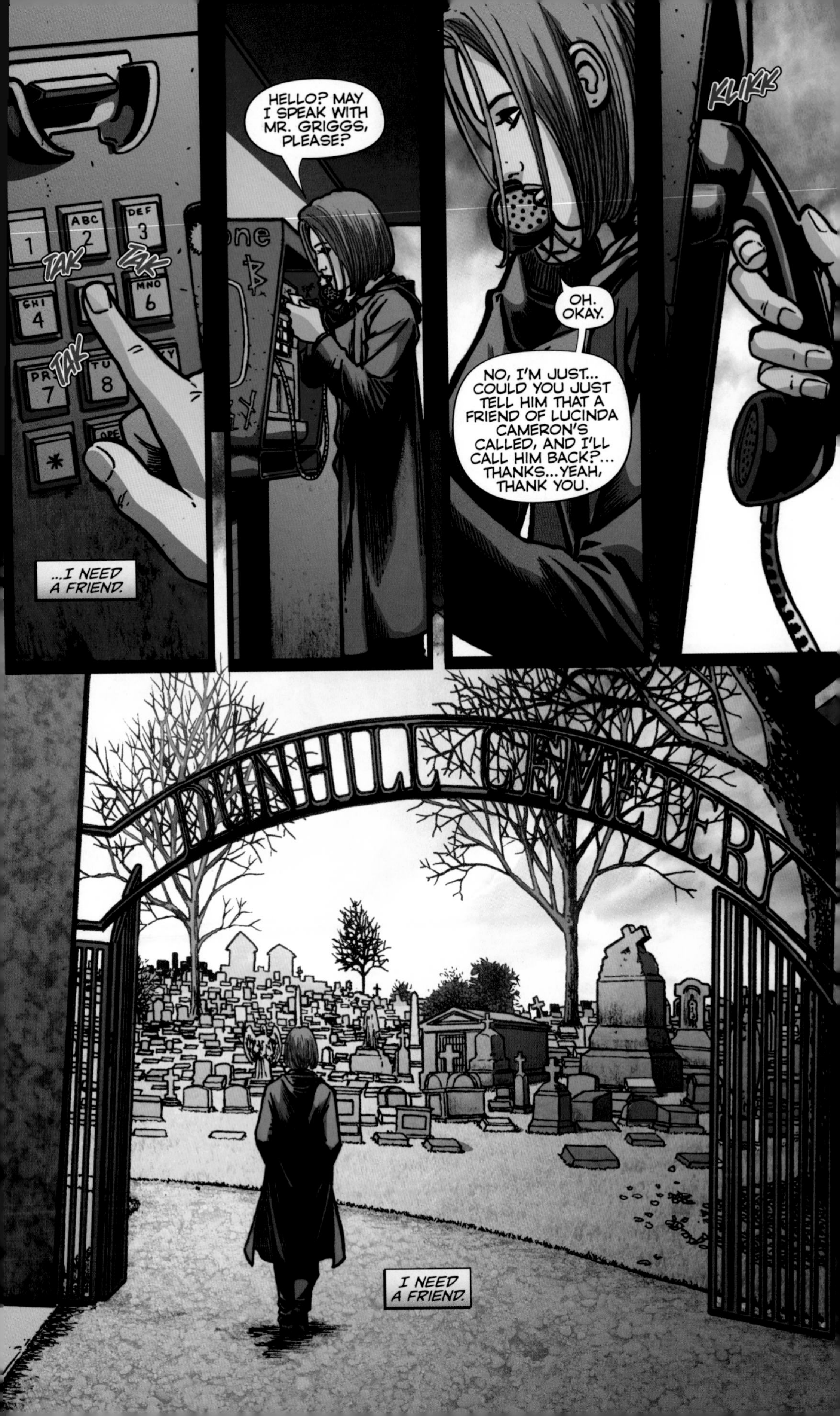
TAK
TAK
TAK
...I NEED A FRIEND.
HELLO? MAY I SPEAK WITH MR. GRIGGS, PLEASE?
OH. OKAY.
NO, I'M JUST... COULD YOU JUST TELL HIM THAT A FRIEND OF LUCINDA CAMERON'S CALLED, AND I'LL CALL HIM BACK?... THANKS...YEAH, THANK YOU.
KLIKK
DUNHILL CEMETERY
I NEED A FRIEND.

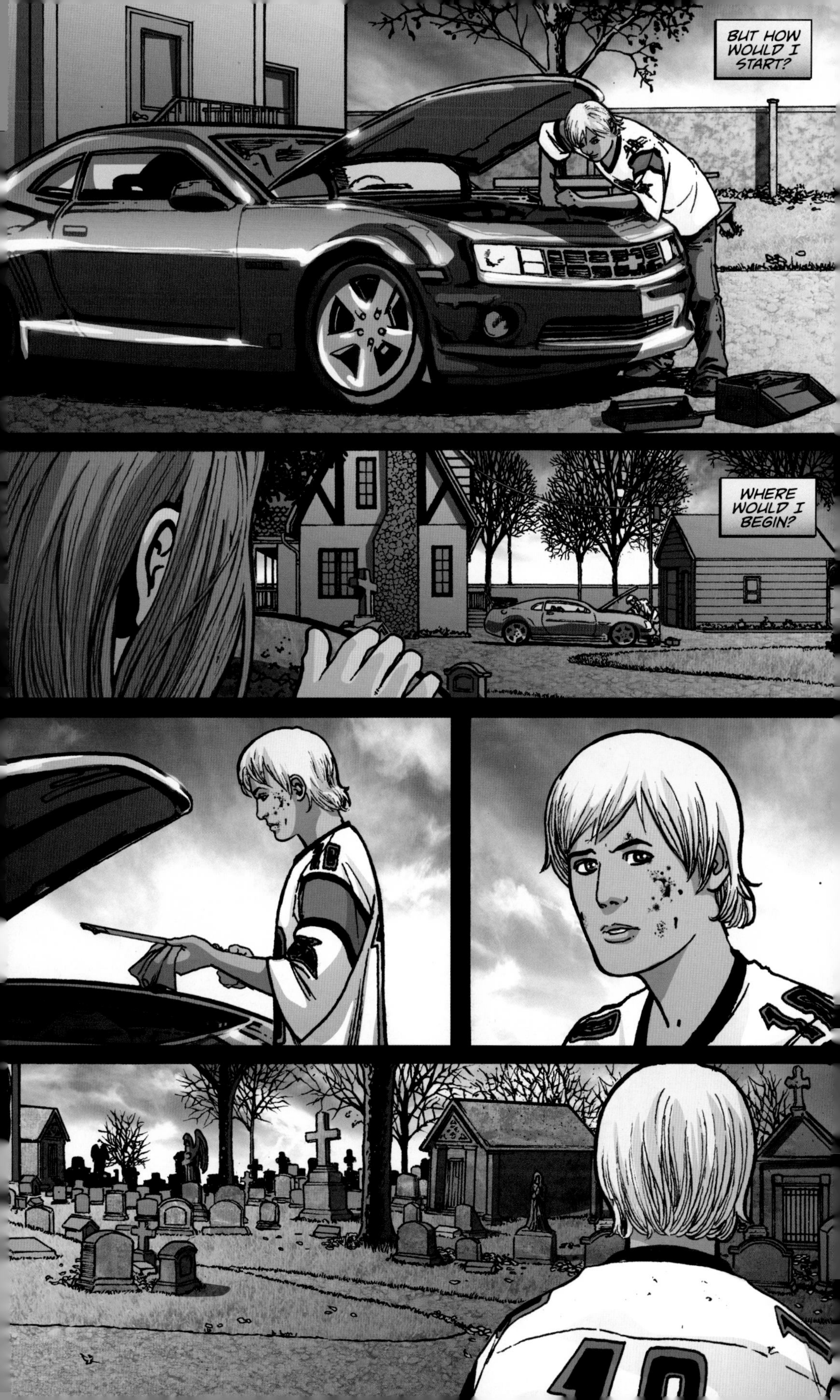
BUT HOW WOULD I START?
WHERE WOULD I BEGIN?

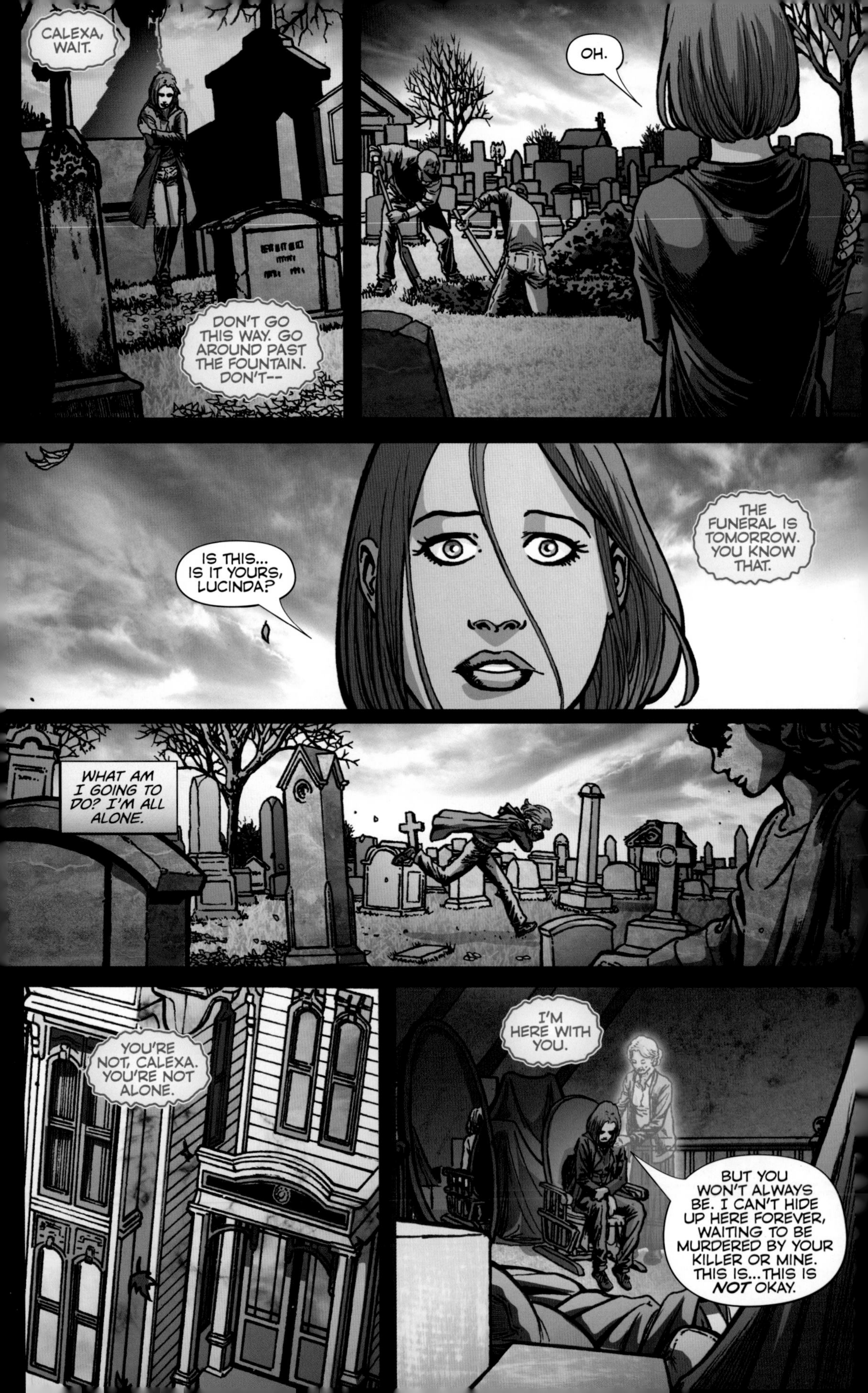
CALEXA, WAIT.
DON'T GO THIS WAY. GO AROUND PAST THE FOUNTAIN. DON'T--
OH.
IS THIS... IS IT YOURS, LUCINDA?
THE FUNERAL IS TOMORROW. YOU KNOW THAT.
WHAT AM I GOING TO DO? I'M ALL ALONE.
YOU'RE NOT, CALEXA. YOU'RE NOT ALONE.
I'M HERE WITH YOU.
BUT YOU WON'T ALWAYS BE. I CAN'T HIDE UP HERE FOREVER, WAITING TO BE MURDERED BY YOUR KILLER OR MINE. THIS IS...THIS IS NOT OKAY.

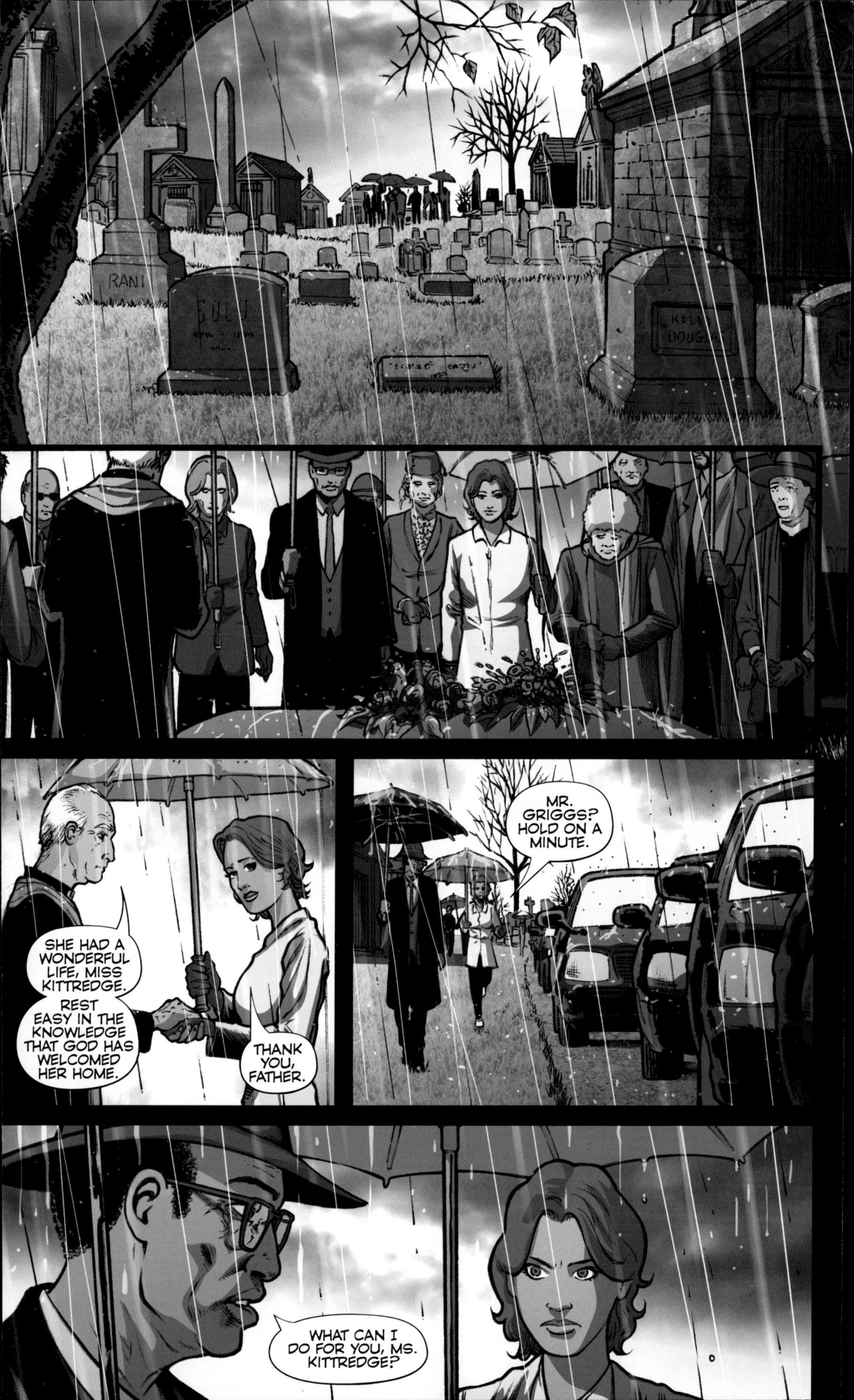
RANI
SHE HAD A WONDERFUL LIFE, MISS KITTREDGE.
REST EASY IN THE KNOWLEDGE THAT GOD HAS WELCOMED HER HOME.
THANK YOU, FATHER.
MR. GRIGGS? HOLD ON A MINUTE.
WHAT CAN I DO FOR YOU, MS. KITTREDGE?

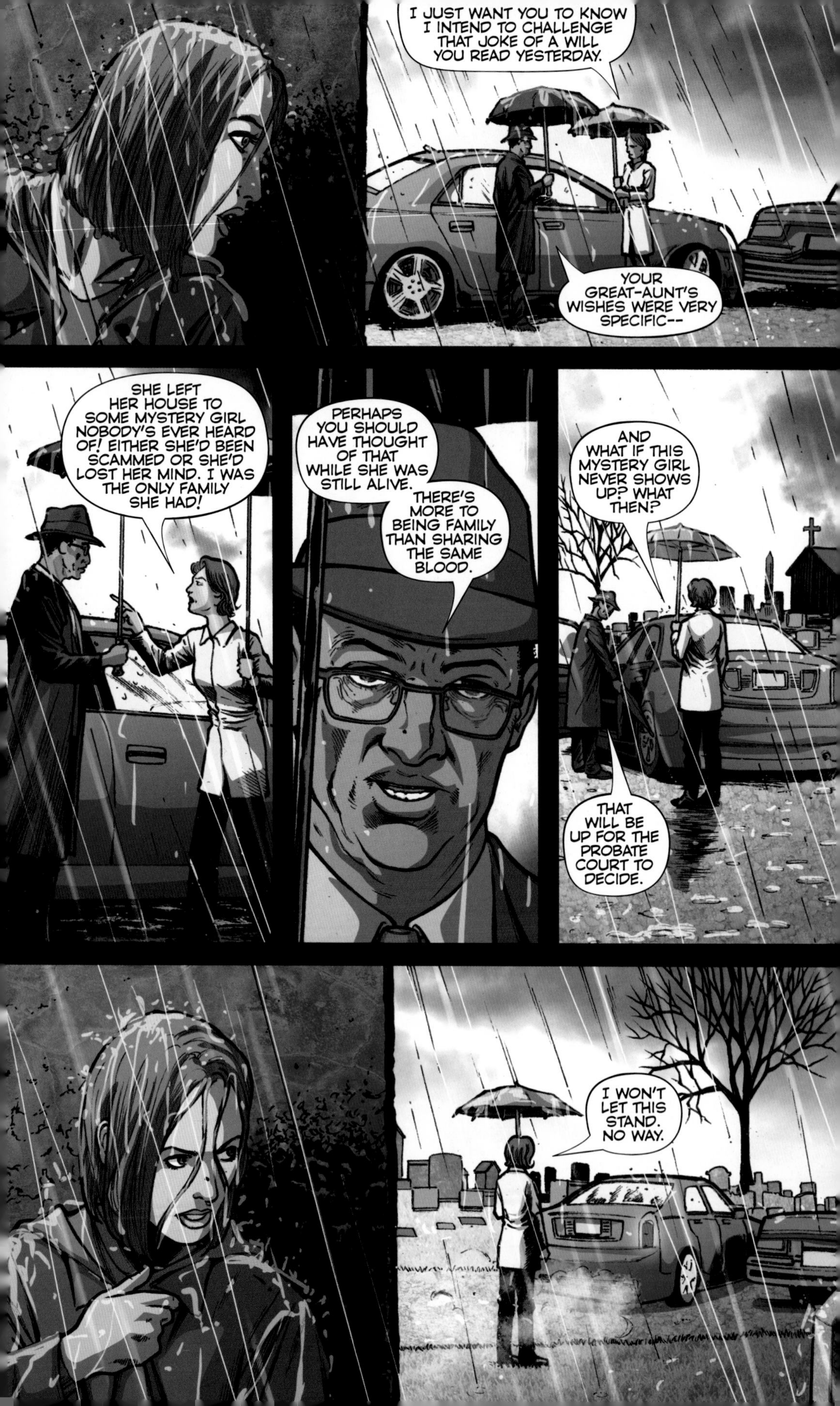
I JUST WANT YOU TO KNOW I INTEND TO CHALLENGE THAT JOKE OF A WILL YOU READ YESTERDAY.
YOUR GREAT-AUNT'S WISHES WERE VERY SPECIFIC--
SHE LEFT HER HOUSE TO SOME MYSTERY GIRL NOBODY'S EVER HEARD OF! EITHER SHE'D BEEN SCAMMED OR SHE'D LOST HER MIND. I WAS THE ONLY FAMILY SHE HAD!
PERHAPS YOU SHOULD HAVE THOUGHT OF THAT WHILE SHE WAS STILL ALIVE.
THERE'S MORE TO BEING FAMILY THAN SHARING THE SAME BLOOD.
AND WHAT IF THIS MYSTERY GIRL NEVER SHOWS UP? WHAT THEN?
THAT WILL BE UP FOR THE PROBATE COURT TO DECIDE.
I WON'T LET THIS STAND. NO WAY.

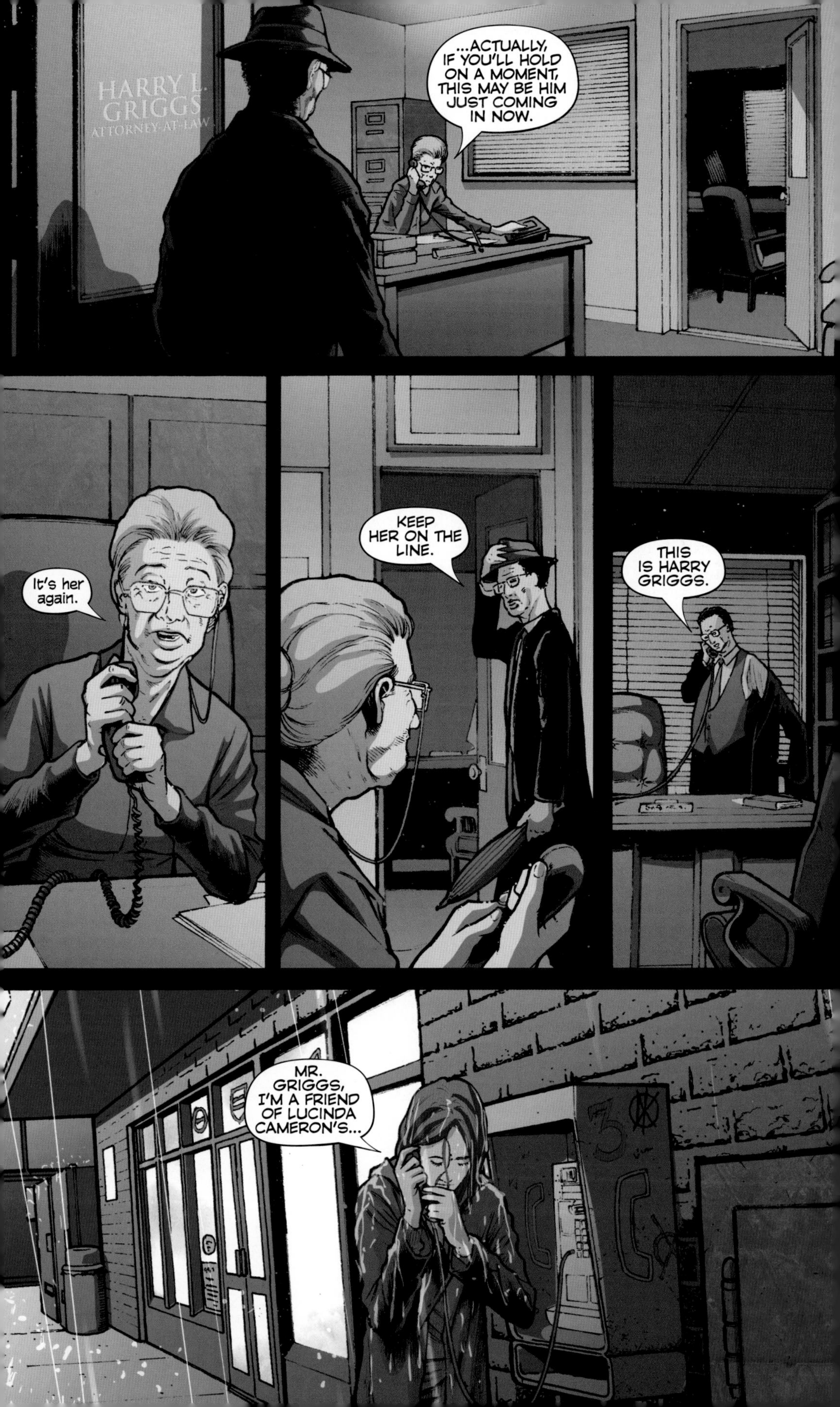
HARRY L. GRIGGS ATTORNEY-AT-LAW
...ACTUALLY, IF YOU'LL HOLD ON A MOMENT, THIS MAY BE HIM JUST COMING IN NOW.
It's her again.
KEEP HER ON THE LINE.
THIS IS HARRY GRIGGS.
MR. GRIGGS, I'M A FRIEND OF LUCINDA CAMERON'S...

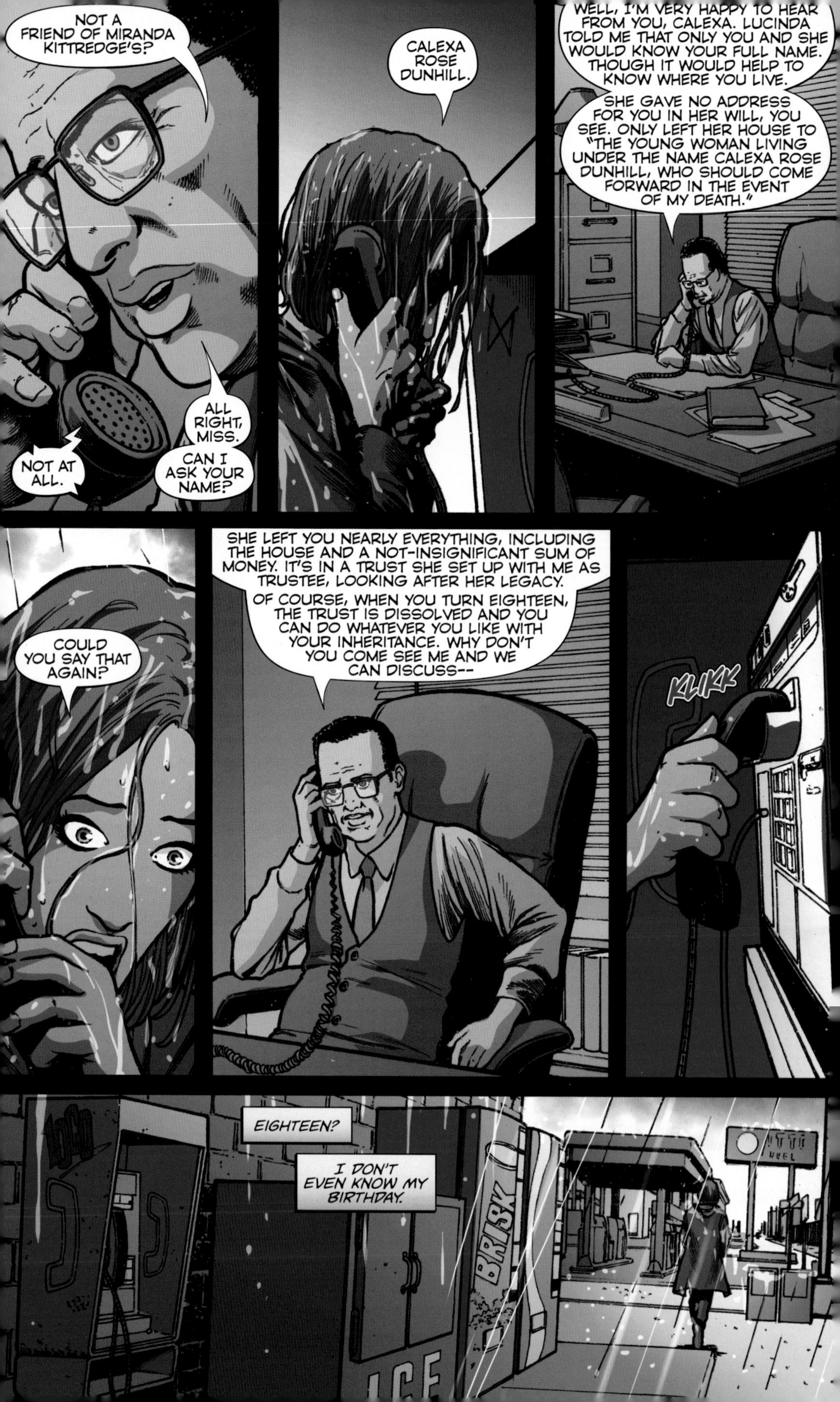
NOT A FRIEND OF MIRANDA KITTREDGE'S?
NOT AT ALL.
ALL RIGHT, MISS.
CAN I ASK YOUR NAME?
CALEXA ROSE DUNHILL.
WELL, I'M VERY HAPPY TO HEAR FROM YOU, CALEXA. LUCINDA TOLD ME THAT ONLY YOU AND SHE WOULD KNOW YOUR FULL NAME. THOUGH IT WOULD HELP TO KNOW WHERE YOU LIVE.
SHE GAVE NO ADDRESS FOR YOU IN HER WILL, YOU SEE. ONLY LEFT HER HOUSE TO "THE YOUNG WOMAN LIVING UNDER THE NAME CALEXA ROSE DUNHILL, WHO SHOULD COME FORWARD IN THE EVENT OF MY DEATH."
COULD YOU SAY THAT AGAIN?
SHE LEFT YOU NEARLY EVERYTHING, INCLUDING THE HOUSE AND A NOT-INSIGNIFICANT SUM OF MONEY. IT'S IN A TRUST SHE SET UP WITH ME AS TRUSTEE, LOOKING AFTER HER LEGACY.
OF COURSE, WHEN YOU TURN EIGHTEEN, THE TRUST IS DISSOLVED AND YOU CAN DO WHATEVER YOU LIKE WITH YOUR INHERITANCE. WHY DON'T YOU COME SEE ME AND WE CAN DISCUSS--
KLIKK
EIGHTEEN?
I DON'T EVEN KNOW MY BIRTHDAY.
BRISK
ICE

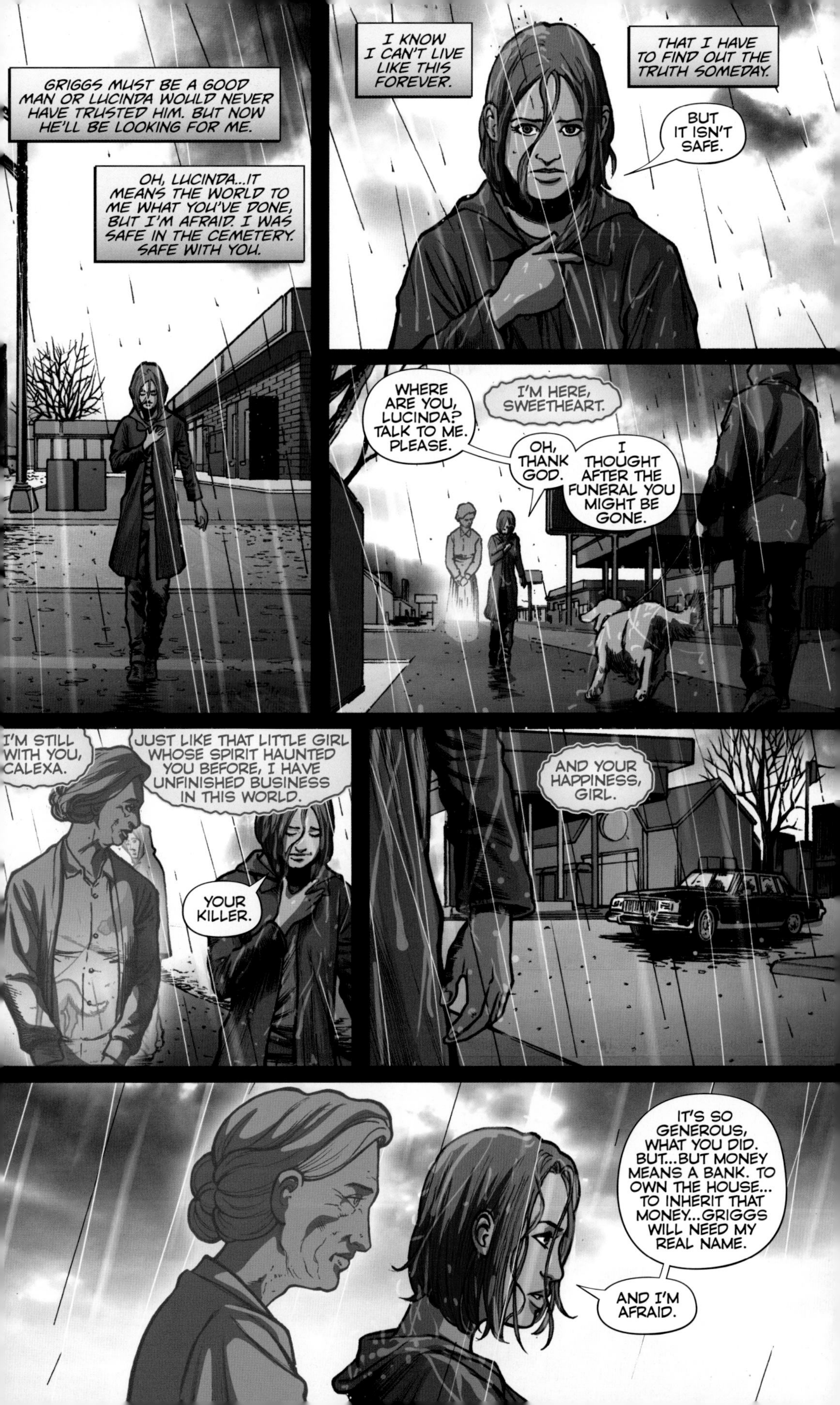
GRIGGS MUST BE A GOOD MAN OR LUCINDA WOULD NEVER HAVE TRUSTED HIM. BUT NOW HE'LL BE LOOKING FOR ME.
OH, LUCINDA...IT MEANS THE WORLD TO ME WHAT YOU'VE DONE, BUT I'M AFRAID. I WAS SAFE IN THE CEMETERY. SAFE WITH YOU.
I KNOW I CAN'T LIVE LIKE THIS FOREVER.
THAT I HAVE TO FIND OUT THE TRUTH SOMEDAY.
BUT IT ISN'T SAFE.
WHERE ARE YOU, LUCINDA? TALK TO ME. PLEASE.
I'M HERE, SWEETHEART.
OH, THANK GOD.
I THOUGHT AFTER THE FUNERAL YOU MIGHT BE GONE.
I'M STILL WITH YOU, CALEXA.
JUST LIKE THAT LITTLE GIRL WHOSE SPIRIT HAUNTED YOU BEFORE, I HAVE UNFINISHED BUSINESS IN THIS WORLD.
YOUR KILLER.
AND YOUR HAPPINESS, GIRL.
IT'S SO GENEROUS, WHAT YOU DID. BUT...BUT MONEY MEANS A BANK. TO OWN THE HOUSE... TO INHERIT THAT MONEY...GRIGGS WILL NEED MY REAL NAME.
AND I'M AFRAID.

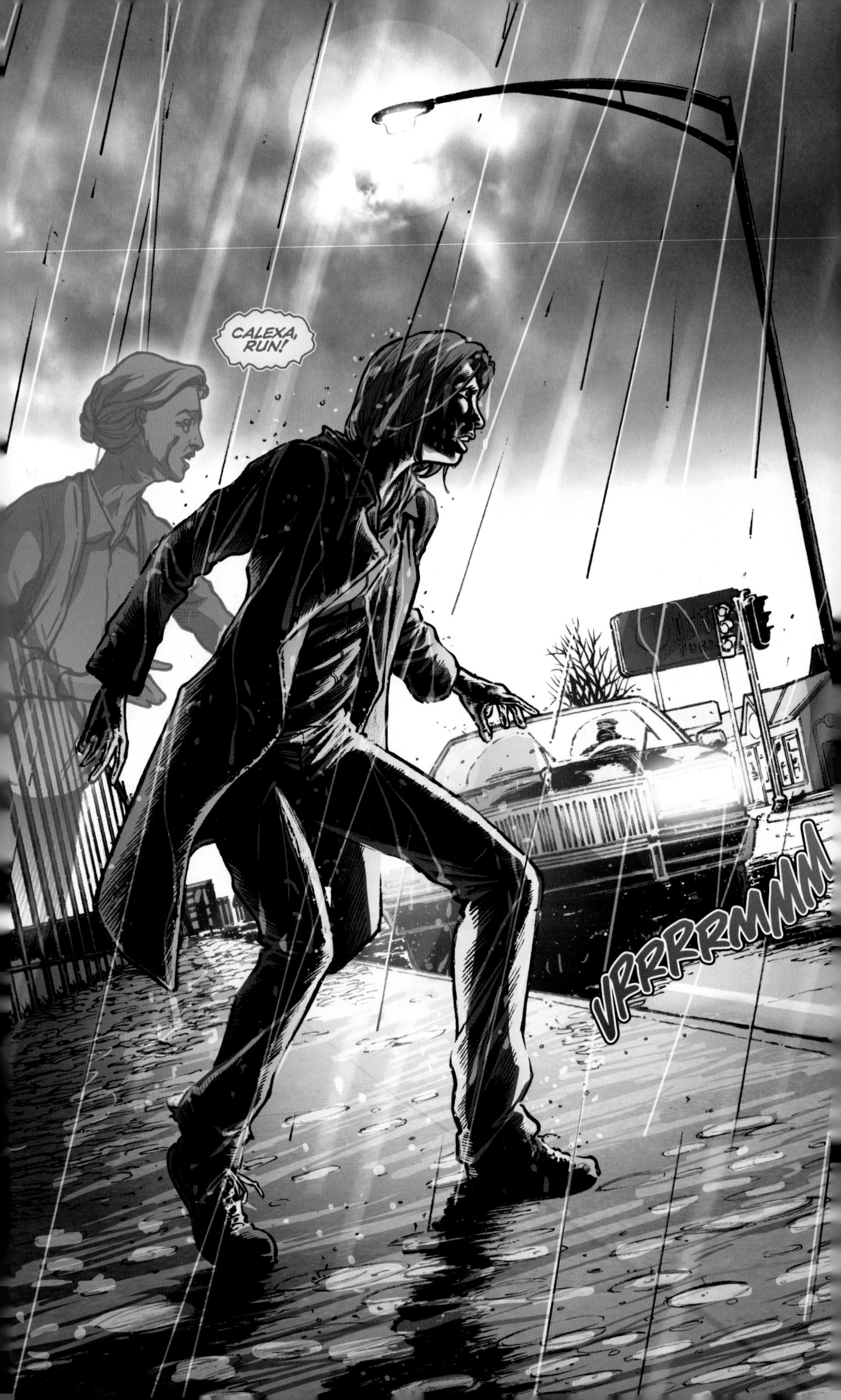
CALEXA, RUN!
VRRRRMMMM

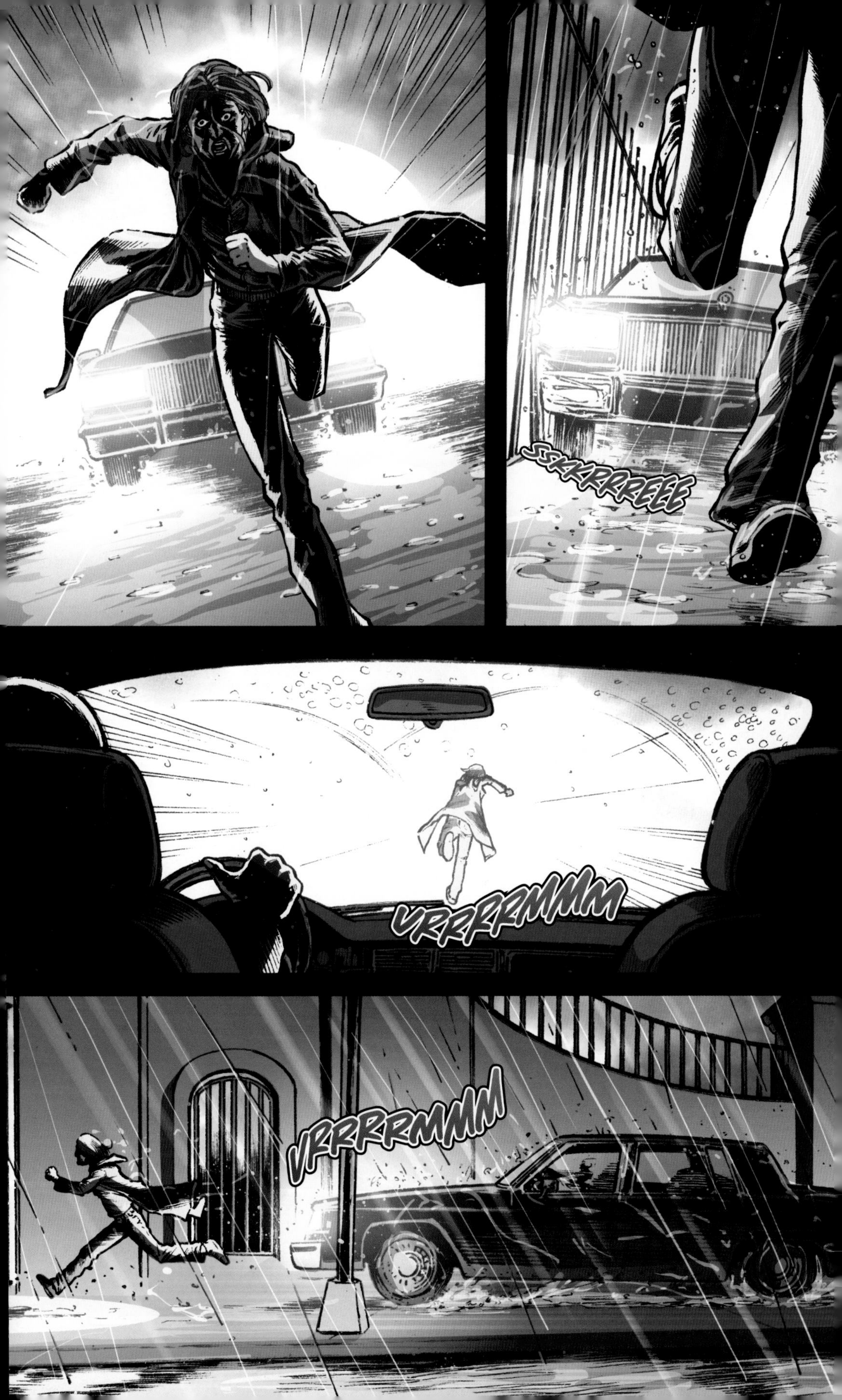
SSKKRRRREEE
VRRRRMMM
VRRRRMMM

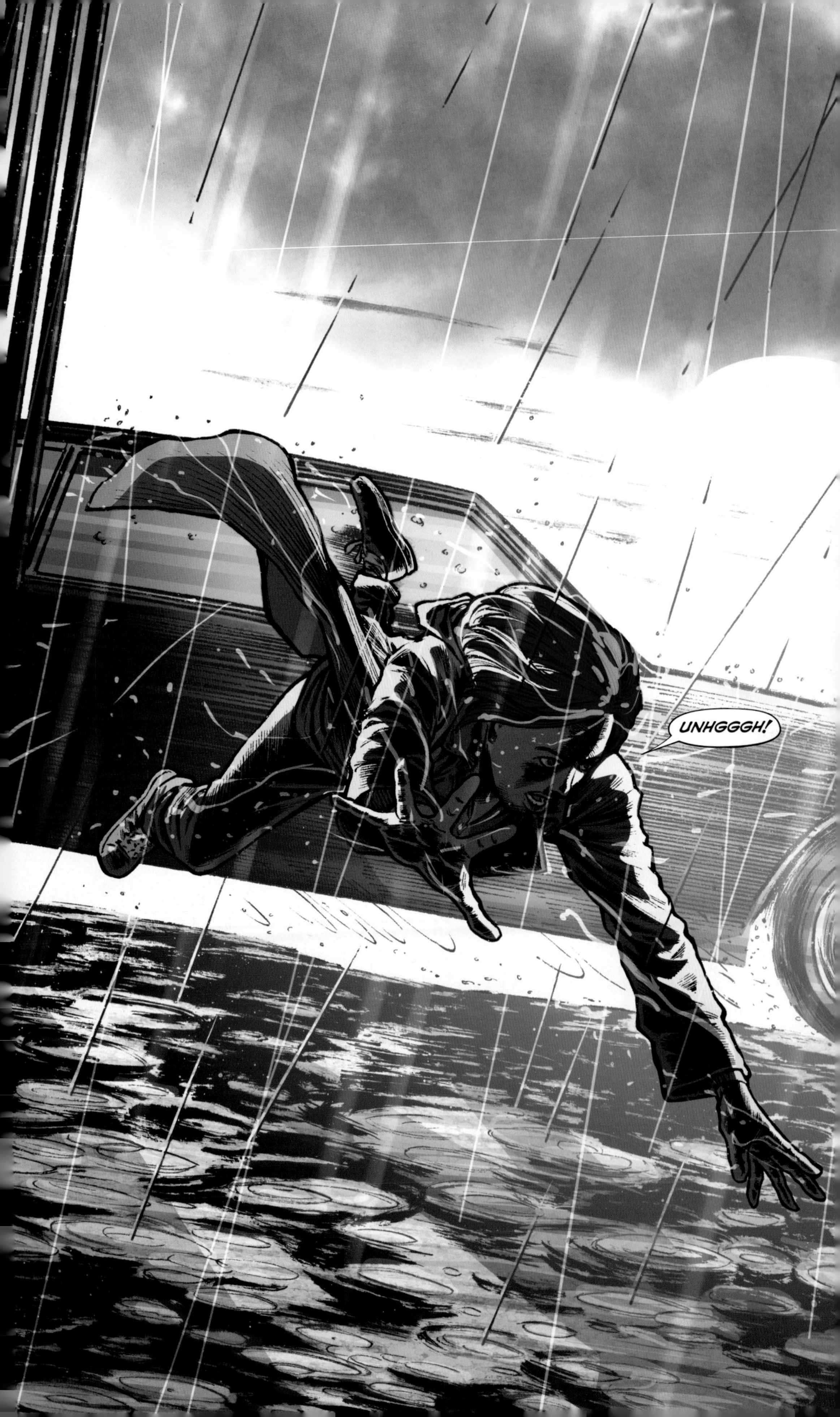
UNHGGGH!

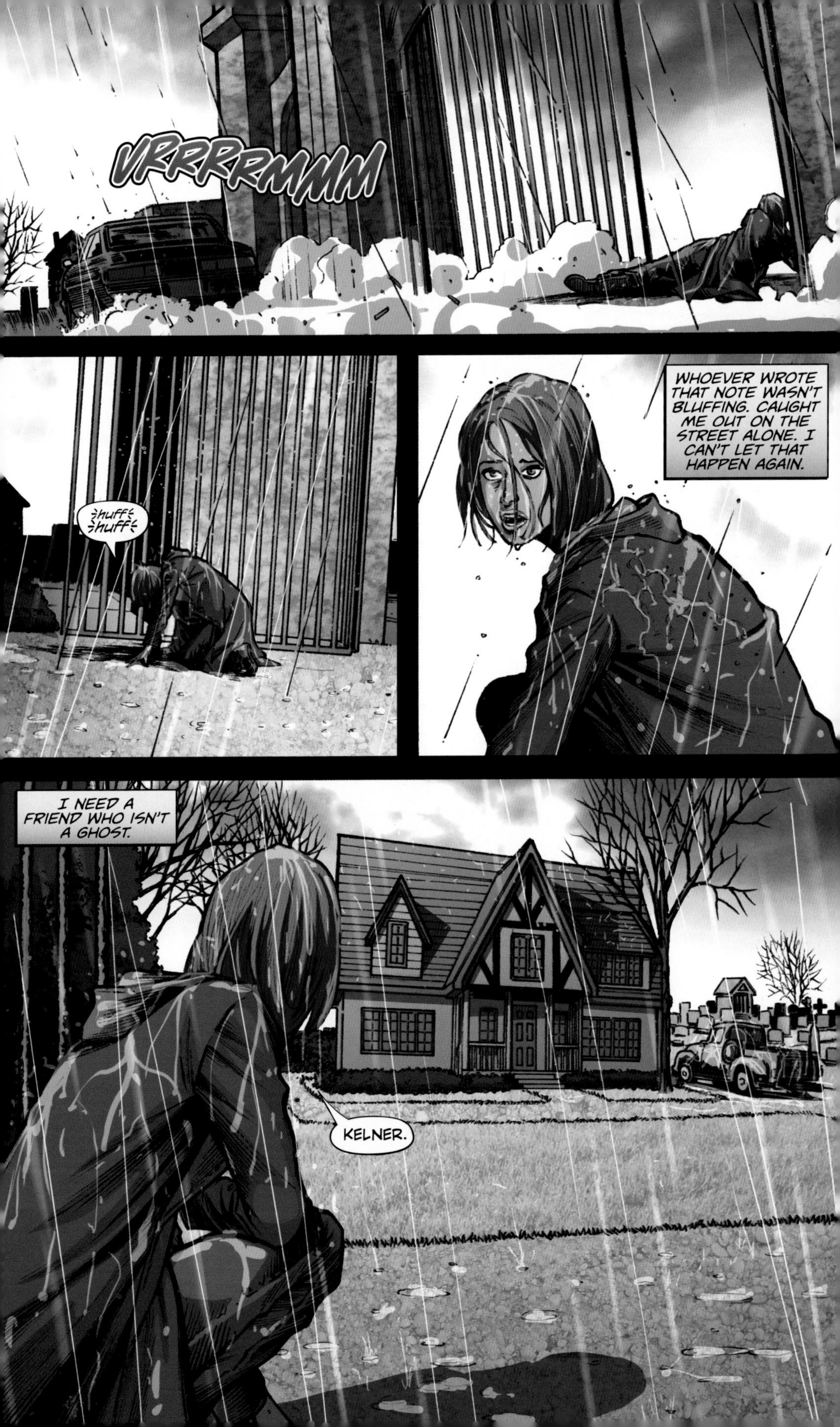
VRRRRMMMM
huff huff
WHOEVER WROTE THAT NOTE WASN'T BLUFFING. CAUGHT ME OUT ON THE STREET ALONE. I CAN'T LET THAT HAPPEN AGAIN.
I NEED A FRIEND WHO ISN'T A GHOST.
KELNER.

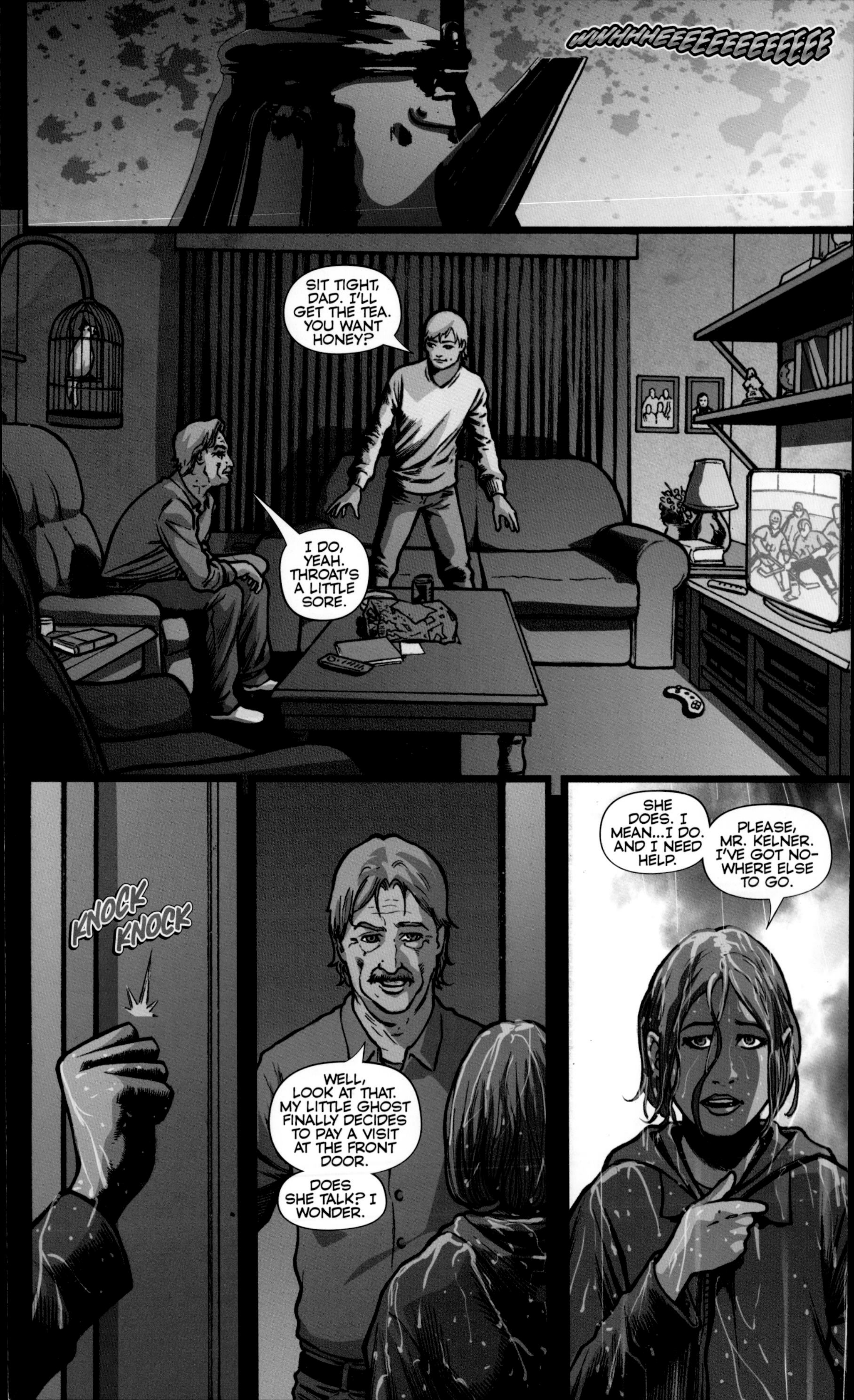
WWHHHEEEEEEEEEEEE
SIT TIGHT, DAD. I'LL GET THE TEA. YOU WANT HONEY?
I DO, YEAH. THROAT'S A LITTLE SORE.
KNOCK KNOCK
WELL, LOOK AT THAT. MY LITTLE GHOST FINALLY DECIDES TO PAY A VISIT AT THE FRONT DOOR.
DOES SHE TALK? I WONDER.
SHE DOES. I MEAN...I DO. AND I NEED HELP.
PLEASE, MR. KELNER. I'VE GOT NO-WHERE ELSE TO GO.

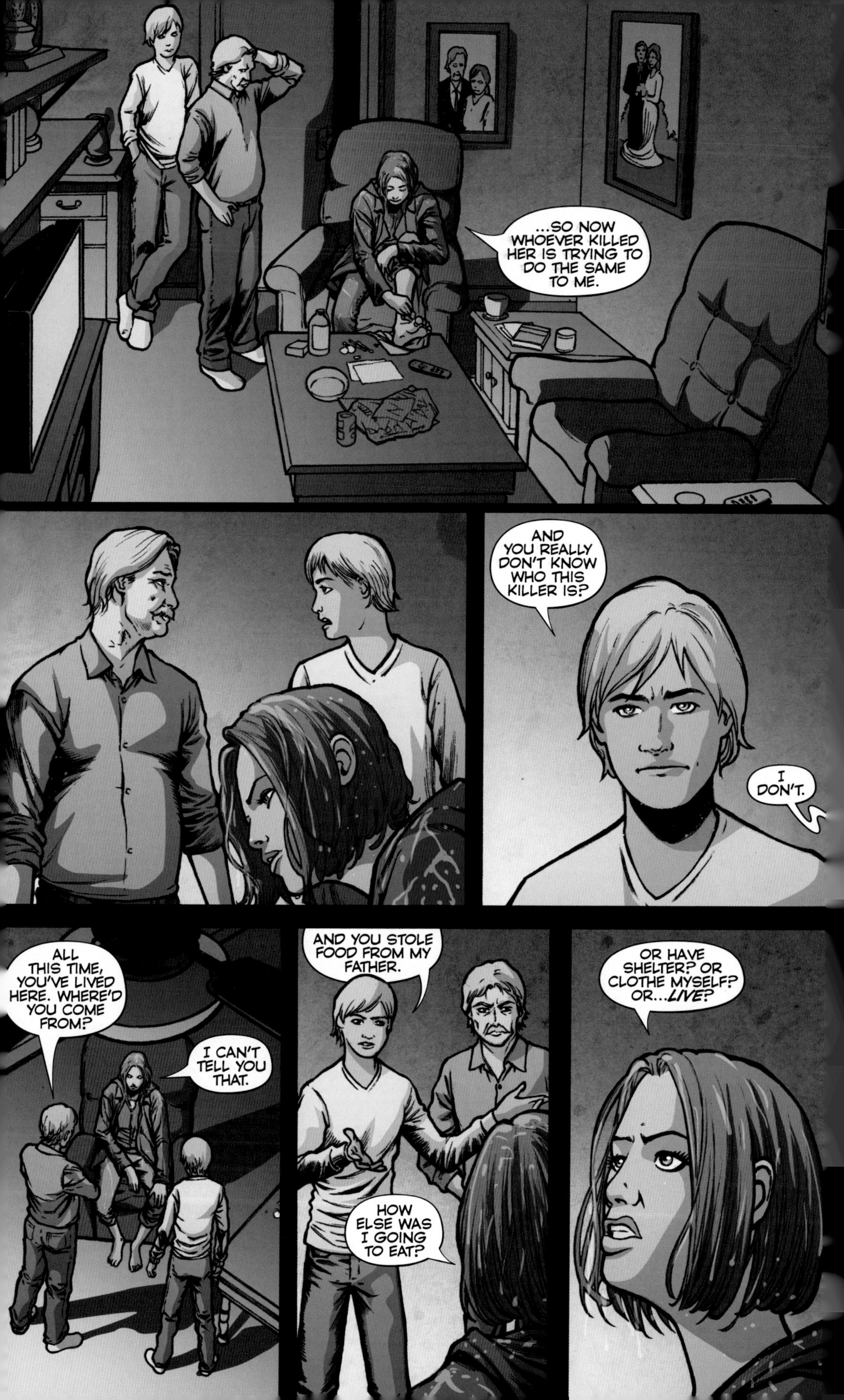
...SO NOW WHOEVER KILLED HER IS TRYING TO DO THE SAME TO ME.
AND YOU REALLY DON'T KNOW WHO THIS KILLER IS?
I DON'T.
ALL THIS TIME, YOU'VE LIVED HERE. WHERE'D YOU COME FROM?
I CAN'T TELL YOU THAT.
AND YOU STOLE FOOD FROM MY FATHER.
HOW ELSE WAS I GOING TO EAT?
OR HAVE SHELTER? OR CLOTHE MYSELF? OR...*LIVE*?

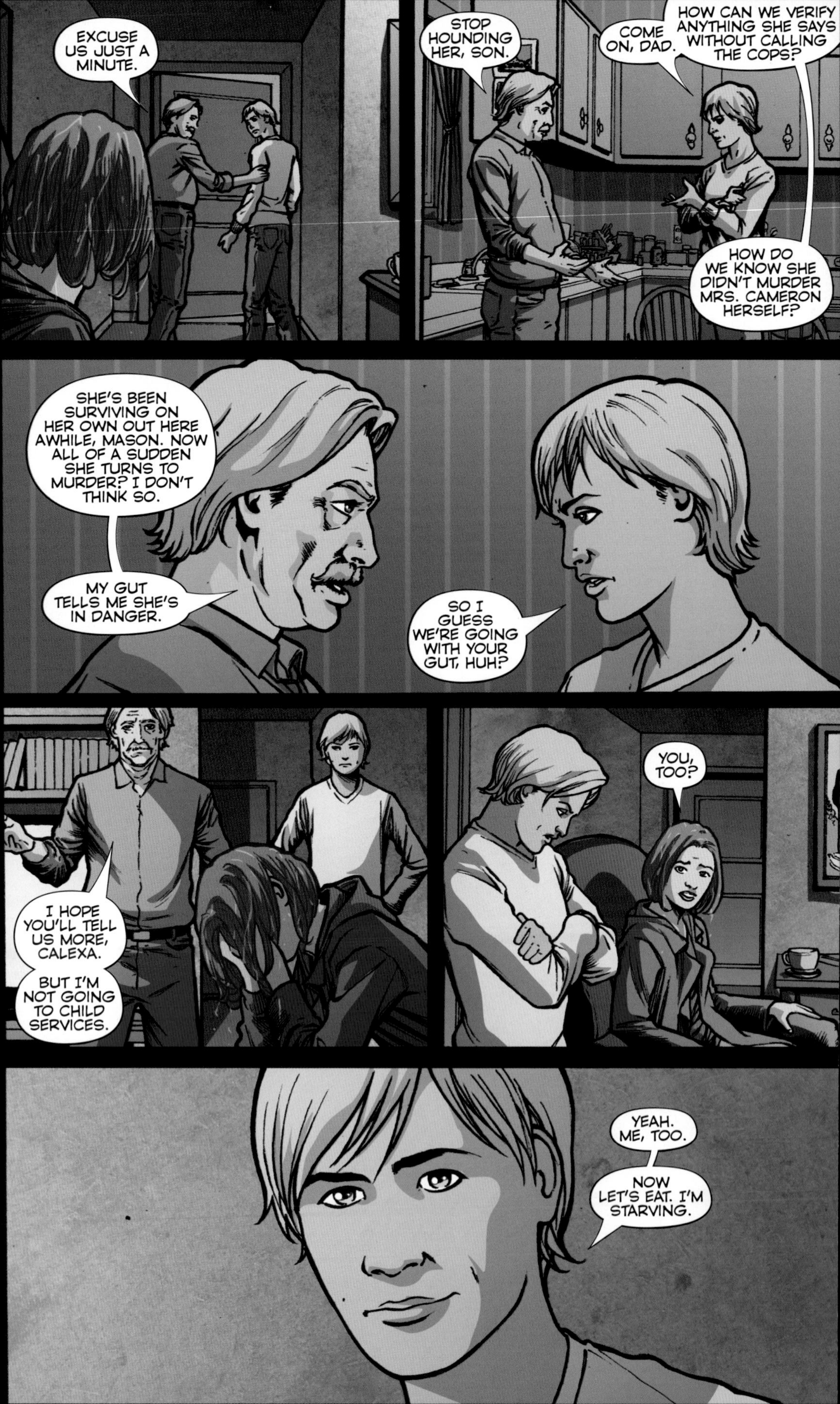

EXCUSE US JUST A MINUTE.
STOP HOUNDING HER, SON.
COME ON, DAD.
HOW CAN WE VERIFY ANYTHING SHE SAYS WITHOUT CALLING THE COPS?
HOW DO WE KNOW SHE DIDN'T MURDER MRS. CAMERON HERSELF?
SHE'S BEEN SURVIVING ON HER OWN OUT HERE AWHILE, MASON. NOW ALL OF A SUDDEN SHE TURNS TO MURDER? I DON'T THINK SO.
MY GUT TELLS ME SHE'S IN DANGER.
SO I GUESS WE'RE GOING WITH YOUR GUT, HUH?
I HOPE YOU'LL TELL US MORE, CALEXA.
BUT I'M NOT GOING TO CHILD SERVICES.
YOU, TOO?
YEAH. ME, TOO.
NOW LET'S EAT. I'M STARVING.

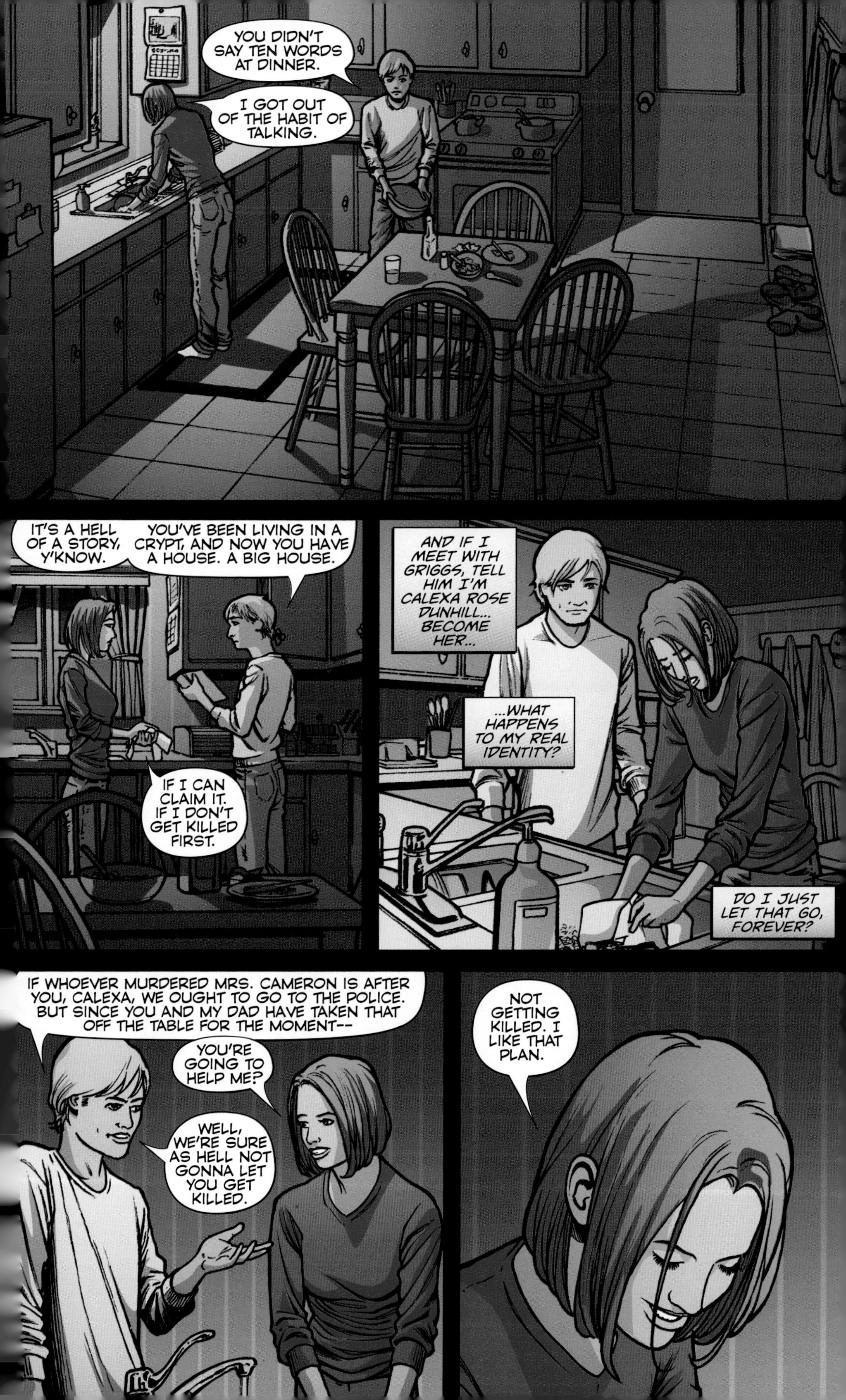
YOU DIDN'T SAY TEN WORDS AT DINNER.
I GOT OUT OF THE HABIT OF TALKING.
IT'S A HELL OF A STORY, Y'KNOW.
YOU'VE BEEN LIVING IN A CRYPT, AND NOW YOU HAVE A HOUSE. A BIG HOUSE.
IF I CAN CLAIM IT. IF I DON'T GET KILLED FIRST.
AND IF I MEET WITH GRIGGS, TELL HIM I'M CALEXA ROSE DUNHILL... BECOME HER...
...WHAT HAPPENS TO MY REAL IDENTITY?
DO I JUST LET THAT GO, FOREVER?
IF WHOEVER MURDERED MRS. CAMERON IS AFTER YOU, CALEXA, WE OUGHT TO GO TO THE POLICE. BUT SINCE YOU AND MY DAD HAVE TAKEN THAT OFF THE TABLE FOR THE MOMENT--
YOU'RE GOING TO HELP ME?
WELL, WE'RE SURE AS HELL NOT GONNA LET YOU GET KILLED.
NOT GETTING KILLED. I LIKE THAT PLAN.

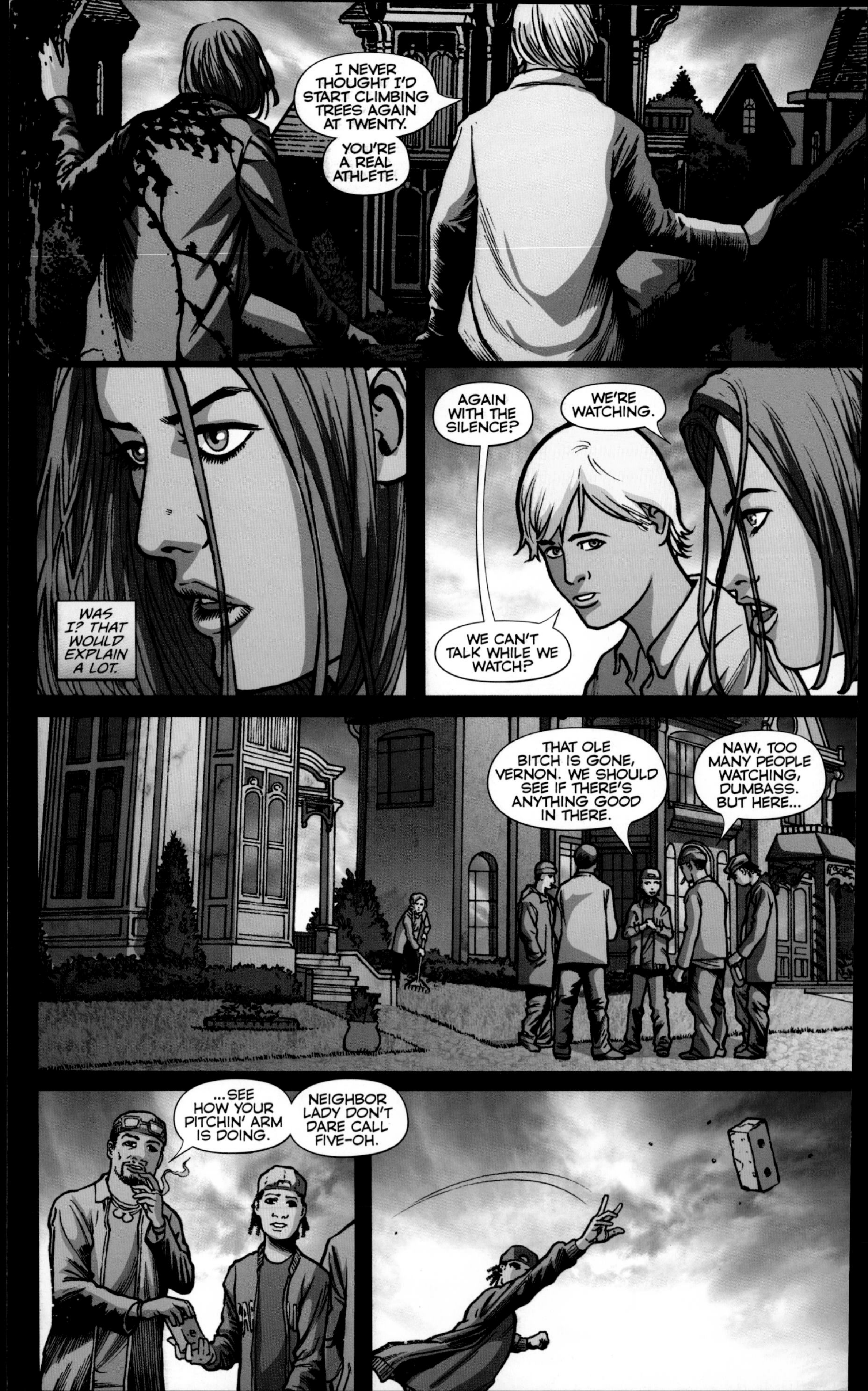
I NEVER THOUGHT I'D START CLIMBING TREES AGAIN AT TWENTY.
YOU'RE A REAL ATHLETE.
WAS I? THAT WOULD EXPLAIN A LOT.
AGAIN WITH THE SILENCE?
WE'RE WATCHING.
WE CAN'T TALK WHILE WE WATCH?
THAT OLE BITCH IS GONE, VERNON. WE SHOULD SEE IF THERE'S ANYTHING GOOD IN THERE.
NAW, TOO MANY PEOPLE WATCHING, DUMBASS. BUT HERE...
...SEE HOW YOUR PITCHIN' ARM IS DOING.
NEIGHBOR LADY DON'T DARE CALL FIVE-OH.

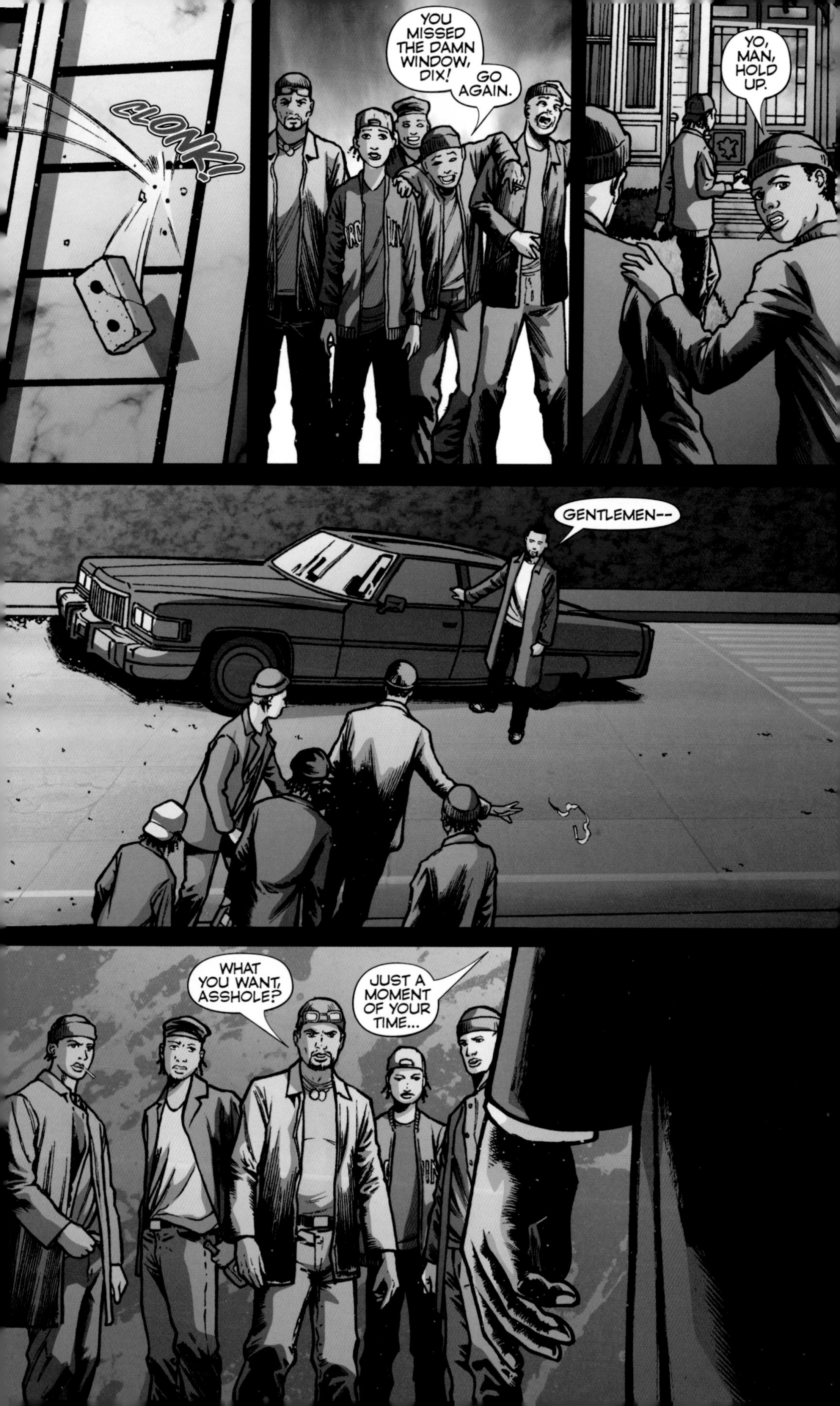
CLONK!!
YOU MISSED THE DAMN WINDOW, DIX!
GO AGAIN.
YO, MAN, HOLD UP.
GENTLEMEN--
WHAT YOU WANT, ASSHOLE?
JUST A MOMENT OF YOUR TIME...

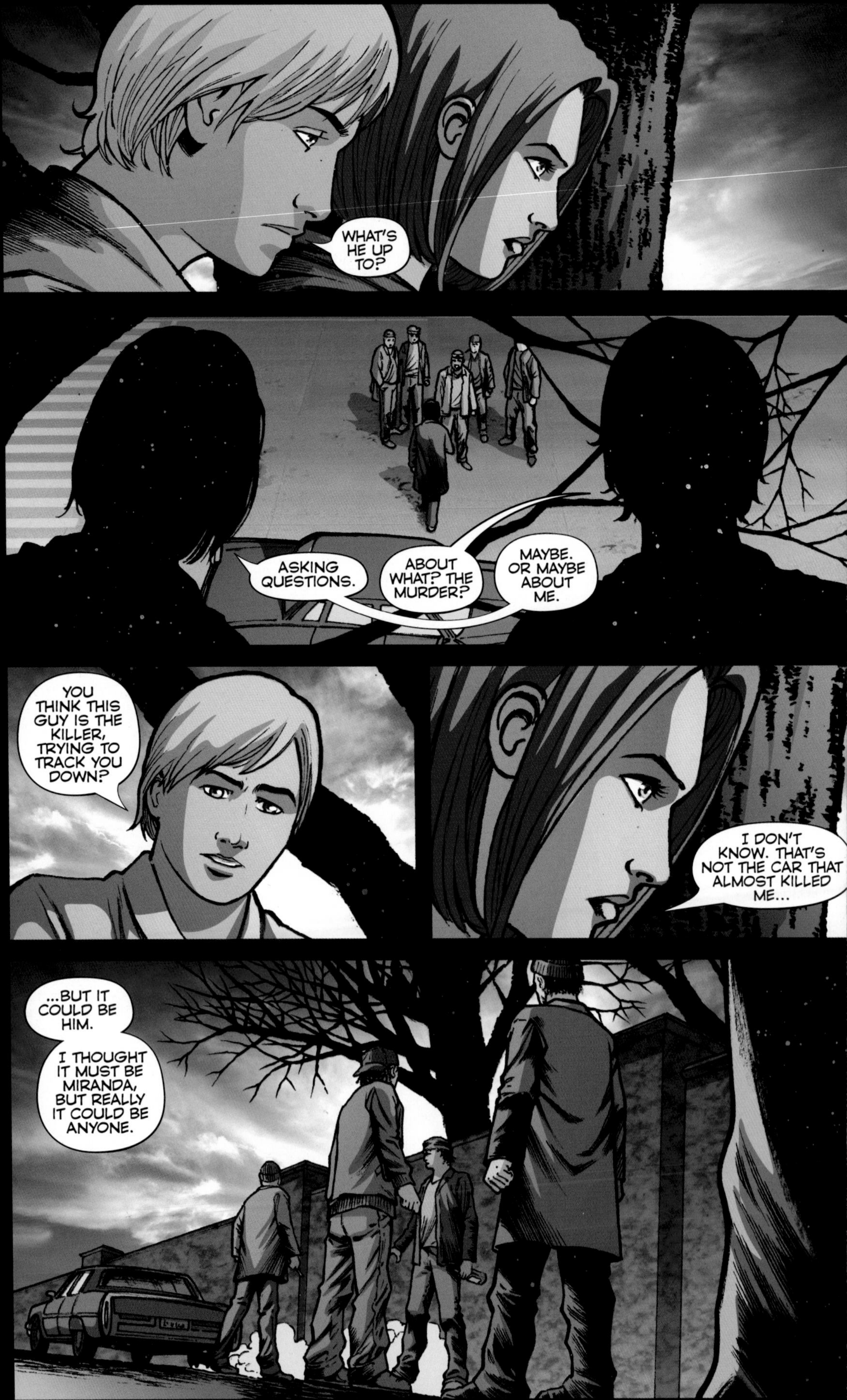
WHAT'S HE UP TO?
ASKING QUESTIONS.
ABOUT WHAT? THE MURDER?
MAYBE. OR MAYBE ABOUT ME.
YOU THINK THIS GUY IS THE KILLER, TRYING TO TRACK YOU DOWN?
I DON'T KNOW. THAT'S NOT THE CAR THAT ALMOST KILLED ME...
...BUT IT COULD BE HIM.
I THOUGHT IT MUST BE MIRANDA, BUT REALLY IT COULD BE ANYONE.

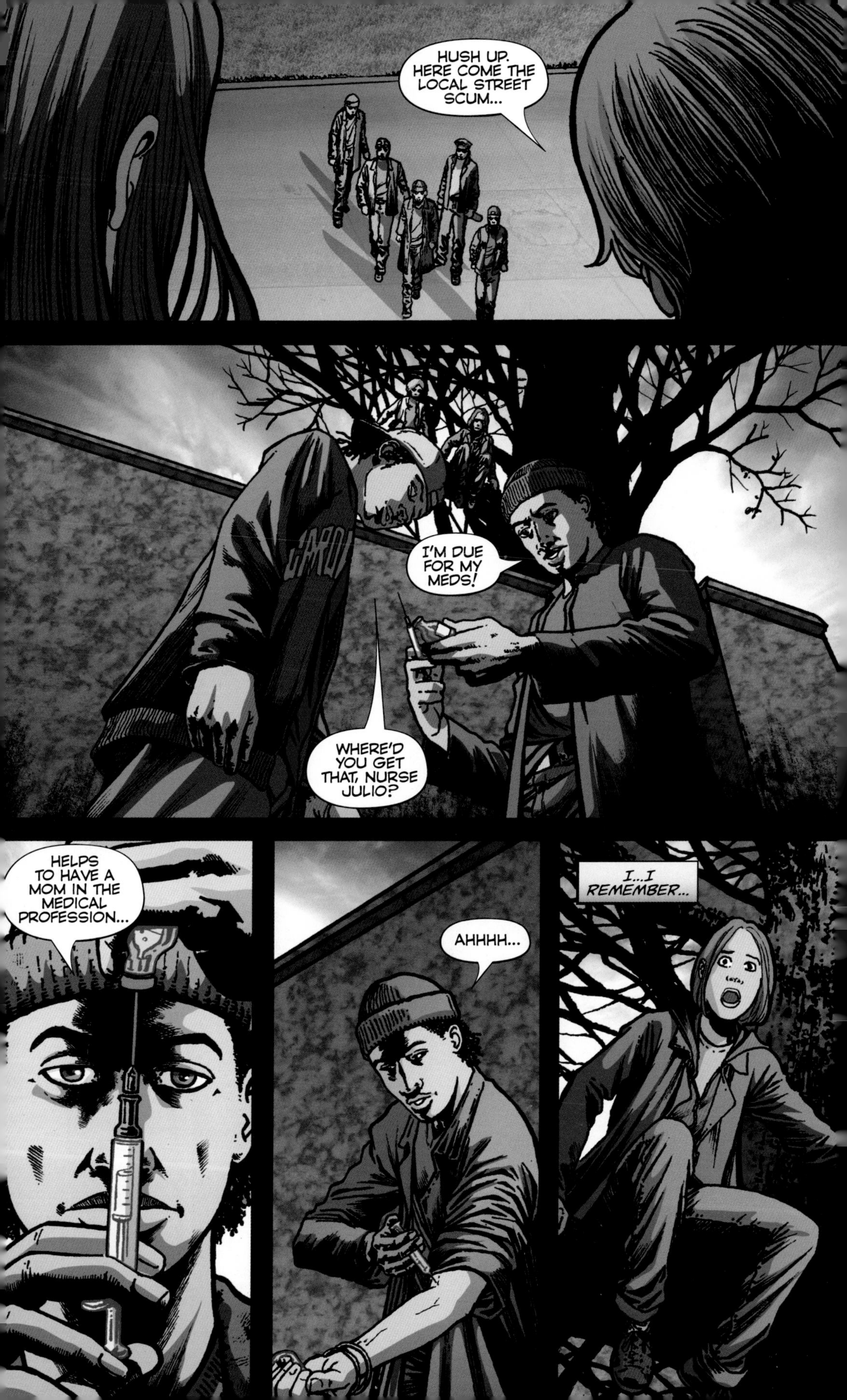
HUSH UP. HERE COME THE LOCAL STREET SCUM...
I'M DUE FOR MY MEDS!
WHERE'D YOU GET THAT, NURSE JULIO?
HELPS TO HAVE A MOM IN THE MEDICAL PROFESSION...
AHHHH...
I...I REMEMBER...

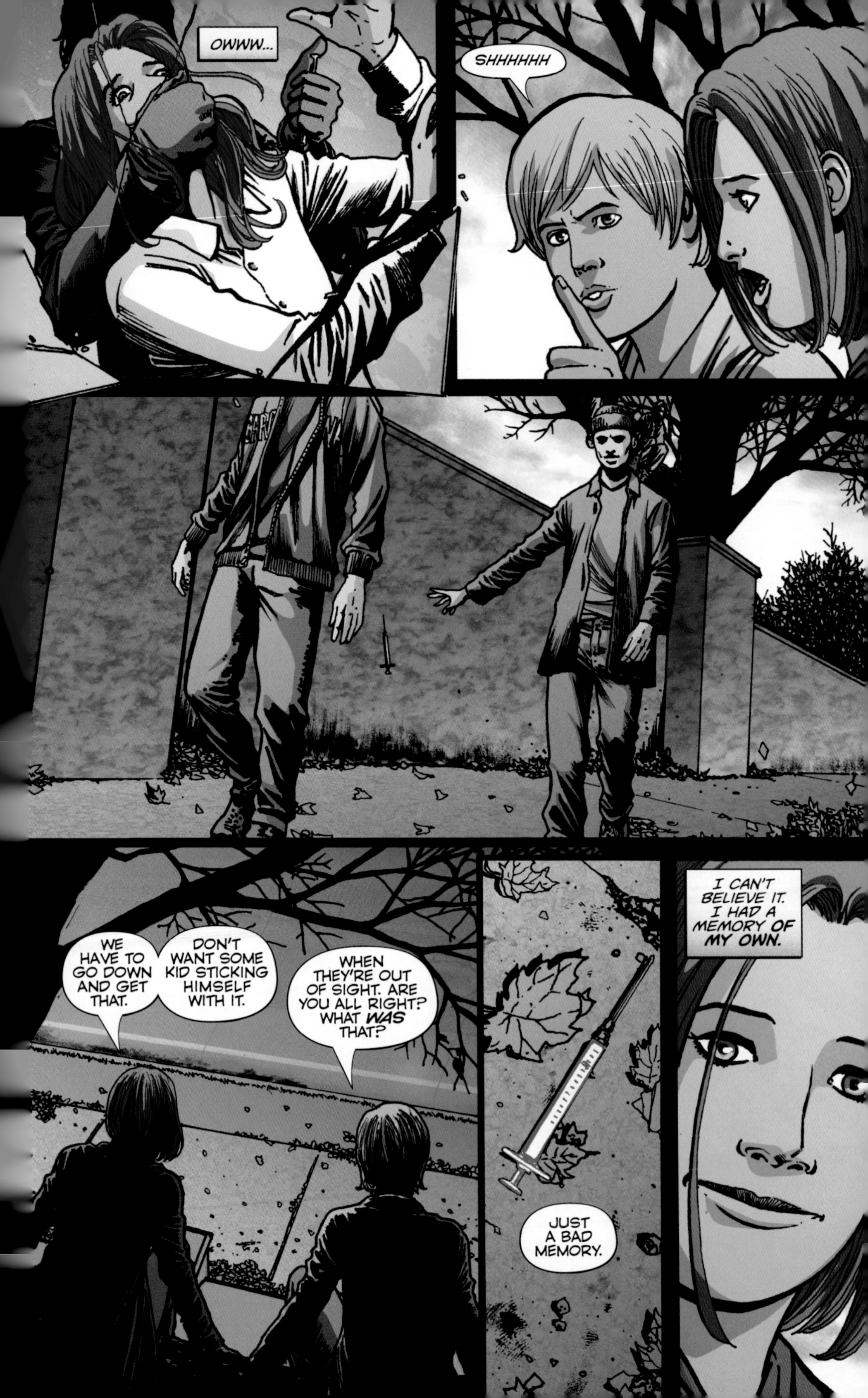
OWWW...
SHHHHHH
WE HAVE TO GO DOWN AND GET THAT.
DON'T WANT SOME KID STICKING HIMSELF WITH IT.
WHEN THEY'RE OUT OF SIGHT. ARE YOU ALL RIGHT? WHAT WAS THAT?
JUST A BAD MEMORY.
I CAN'T BELIEVE IT. I HAD A MEMORY OF MY OWN.

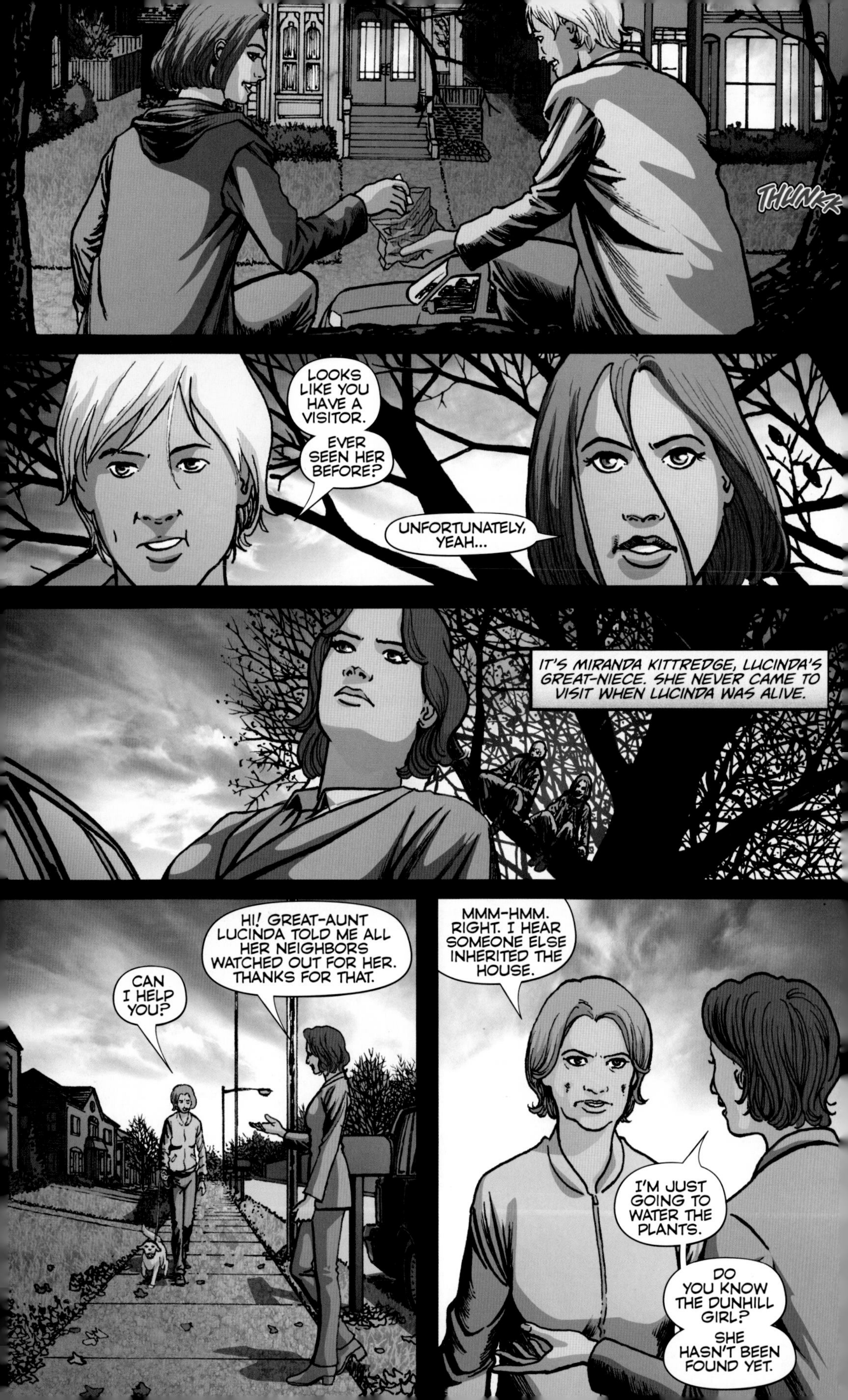
THUNK
LOOKS LIKE YOU HAVE A VISITOR.
EVER SEEN HER BEFORE?
UNFORTUNATELY, YEAH...
IT'S MIRANDA KITTREDGE, LUCINDA'S GREAT-NIECE. SHE NEVER CAME TO VISIT WHEN LUCINDA WAS ALIVE.
CAN I HELP YOU?
HI! GREAT-AUNT LUCINDA TOLD ME ALL HER NEIGHBORS WATCHED OUT FOR HER. THANKS FOR THAT.
MMM-HMM. RIGHT. I HEAR SOMEONE ELSE INHERITED THE HOUSE.
I'M JUST GOING TO WATER THE PLANTS.
DO YOU KNOW THE DUNHILL GIRL?
SHE HASN'T BEEN FOUND YET.

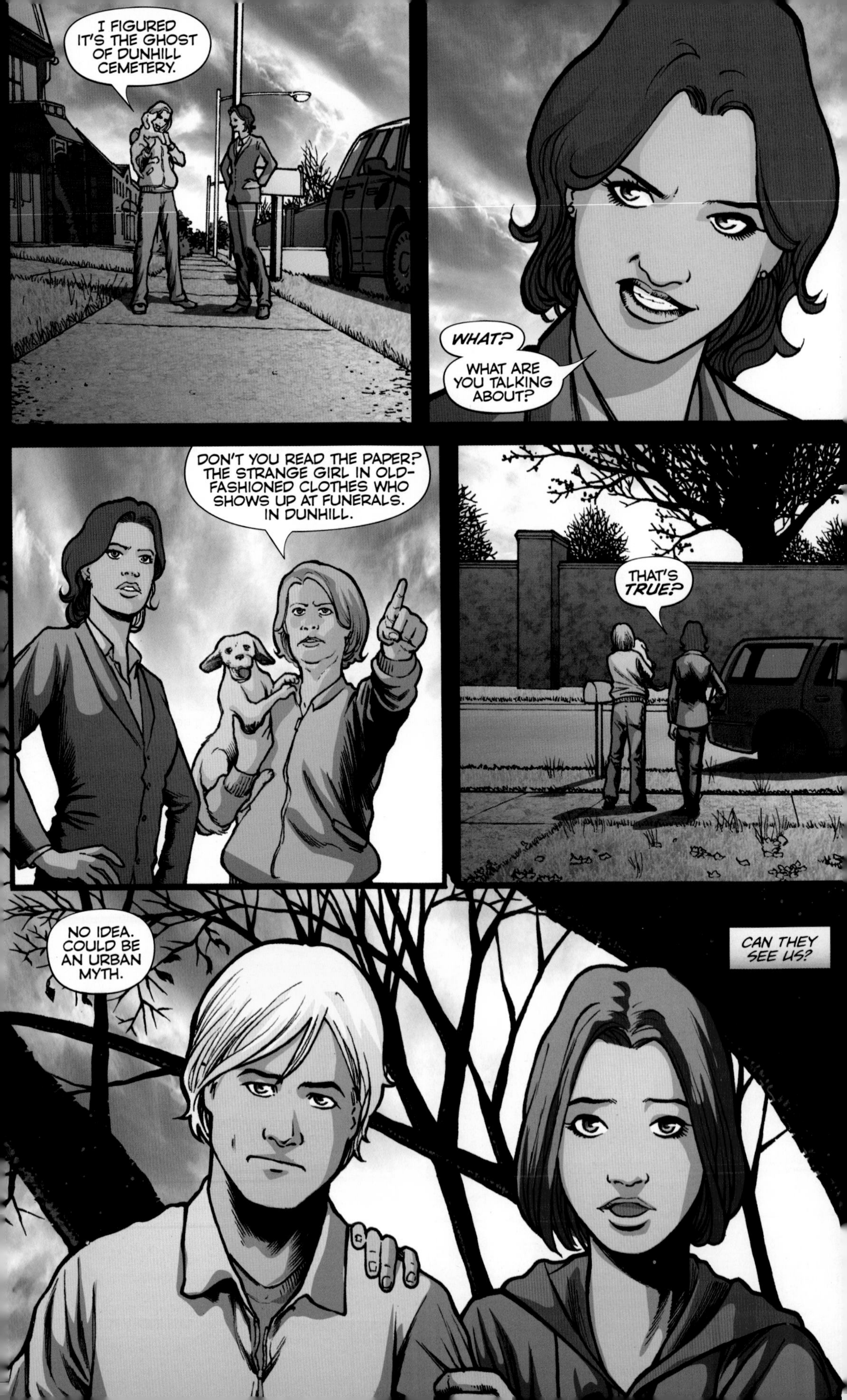
I FIGURED IT'S THE GHOST OF DUNHILL CEMETERY.
WHAT?
WHAT ARE YOU TALKING ABOUT?
DON'T YOU READ THE PAPER? THE STRANGE GIRL IN OLD-FASHIONED CLOTHES WHO SHOWS UP AT FUNERALS. IN DUNHILL.
THAT'S TRUE?
NO IDEA. COULD BE AN URBAN MYTH.
CAN THEY SEE US?

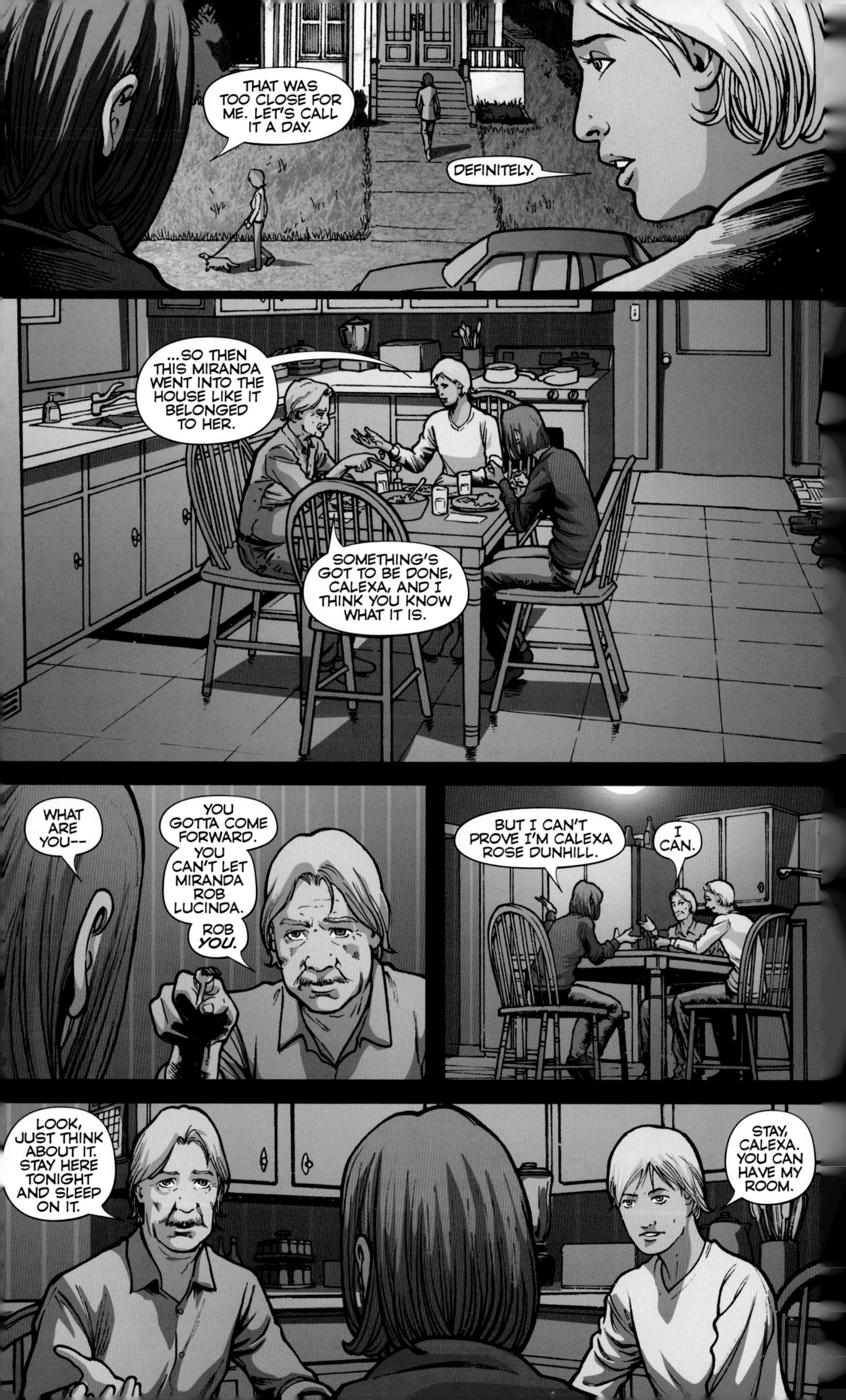
THAT WAS TOO CLOSE FOR ME. LET'S CALL IT A DAY.
DEFINITELY.
...SO THEN THIS MIRANDA WENT INTO THE HOUSE LIKE IT BELONGED TO HER.
SOMETHING'S GOT TO BE DONE, CALEXA, AND I THINK YOU KNOW WHAT IT IS.
WHAT ARE YOU--
YOU GOTTA COME FORWARD. YOU CAN'T LET MIRANDA ROB LUCINDA. ROB *YOU*.
BUT I CAN'T PROVE I'M CALEXA ROSE DUNHILL.
I CAN.
LOOK, JUST THINK ABOUT IT. STAY HERE TONIGHT AND SLEEP ON IT.
STAY, CALEXA. YOU CAN HAVE MY ROOM.

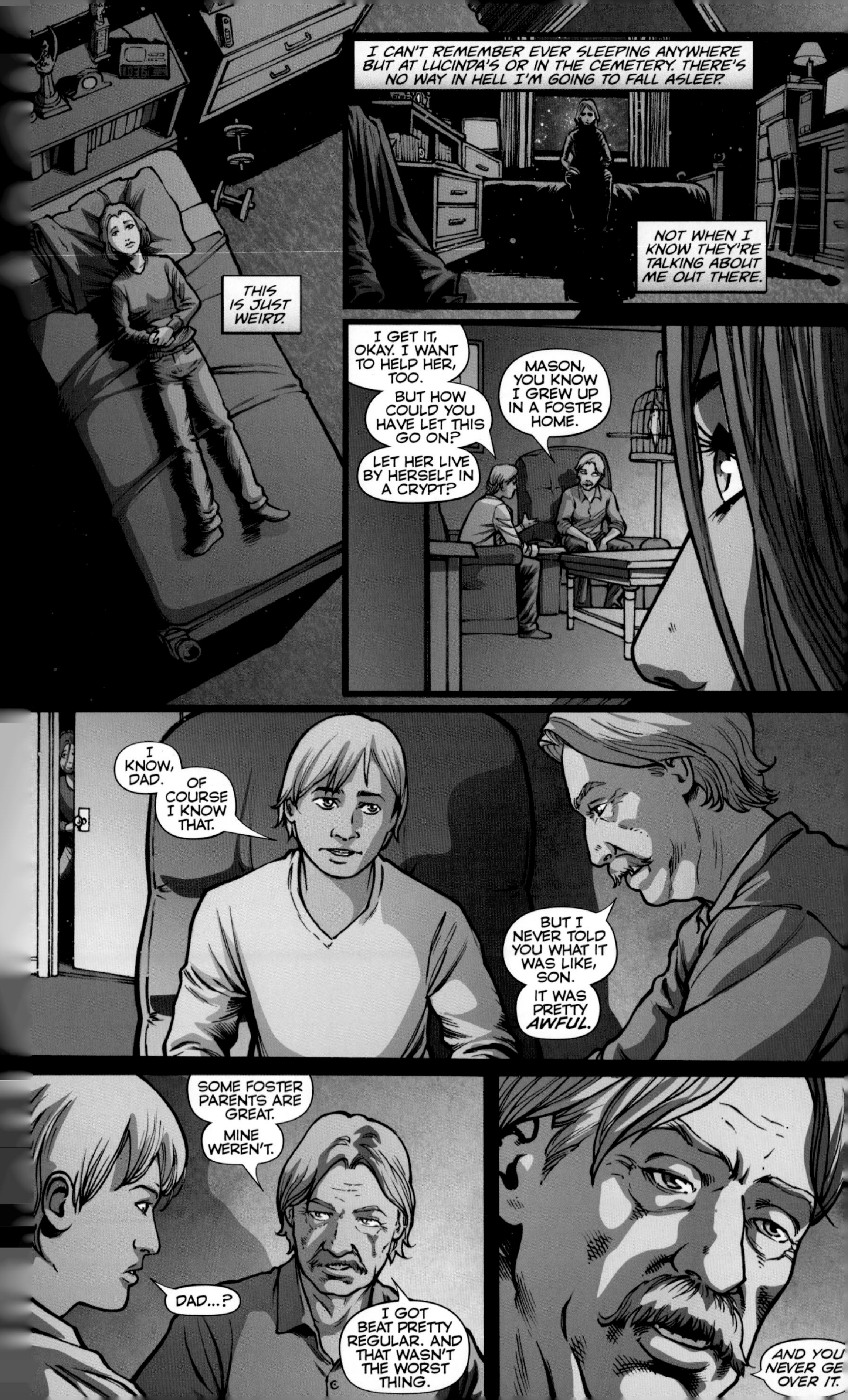
THIS IS JUST WEIRD.
I CAN'T REMEMBER EVER SLEEPING ANYWHERE BUT AT LUCINDA'S OR IN THE CEMETERY. THERE'S NO WAY IN HELL I'M GOING TO FALL ASLEEP.
NOT WHEN I KNOW THEY'RE TALKING ABOUT ME OUT THERE.
I GET IT, OKAY. I WANT TO HELP HER, TOO.
BUT HOW COULD YOU HAVE LET THIS GO ON?
LET HER LIVE BY HERSELF IN A CRYPT?
MASON, YOU KNOW I GREW UP IN A FOSTER HOME.
I KNOW, DAD.
OF COURSE I KNOW THAT.
BUT I NEVER TOLD YOU WHAT IT WAS LIKE, SON.
IT WAS PRETTY AWFUL.
SOME FOSTER PARENTS ARE GREAT.
MINE WEREN'T.
DAD...?
I GOT BEAT PRETTY REGULAR. AND THAT WASN'T THE WORST THING.
AND YOU NEVER GE OVER IT.

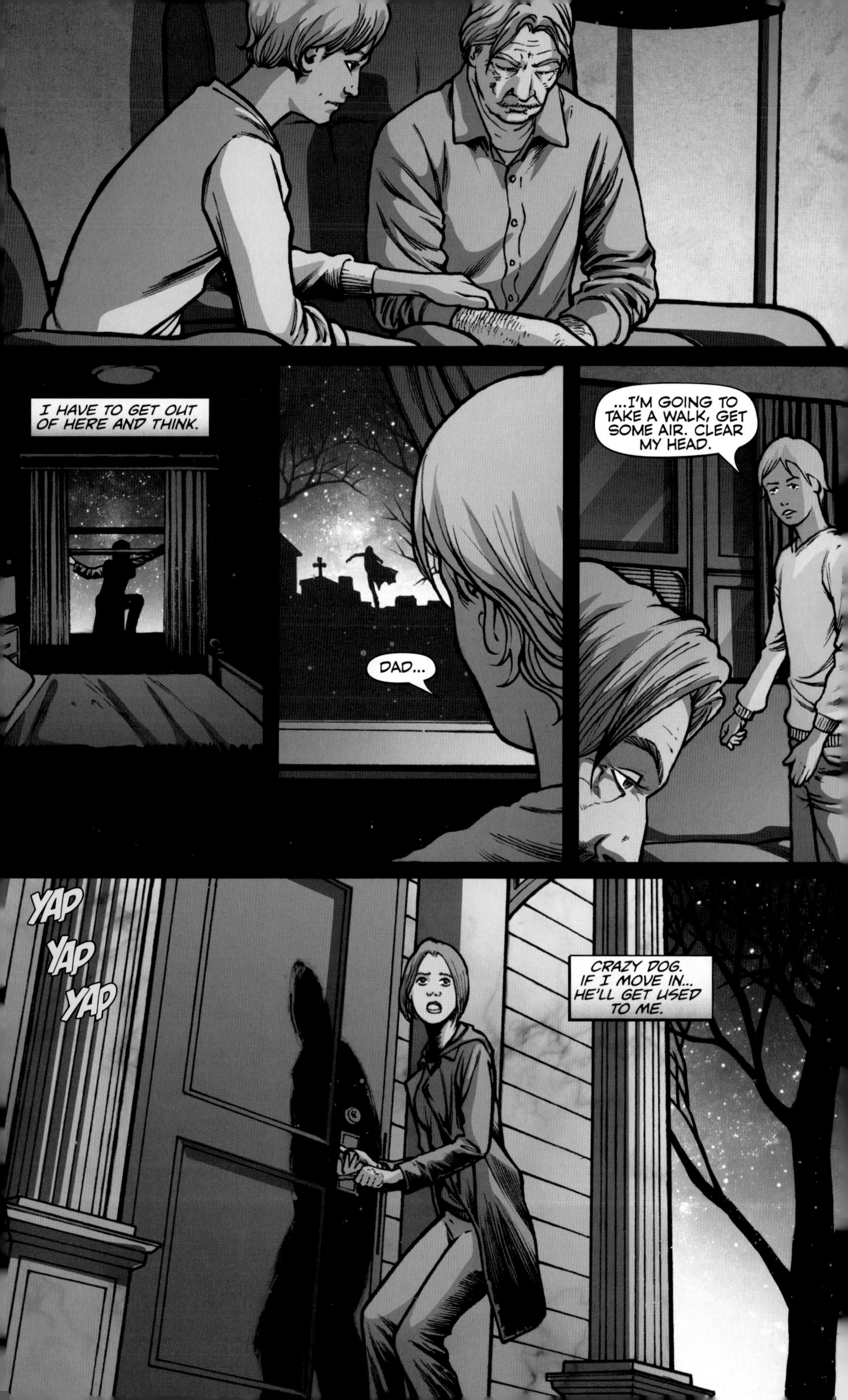
I HAVE TO GET OUT OF HERE AND THINK.
DAD...
...I'M GOING TO TAKE A WALK, GET SOME AIR. CLEAR MY HEAD.
YAP
YAP
YAP
CRAZY DOG. IF I MOVE IN... HE'LL GET USED TO ME.

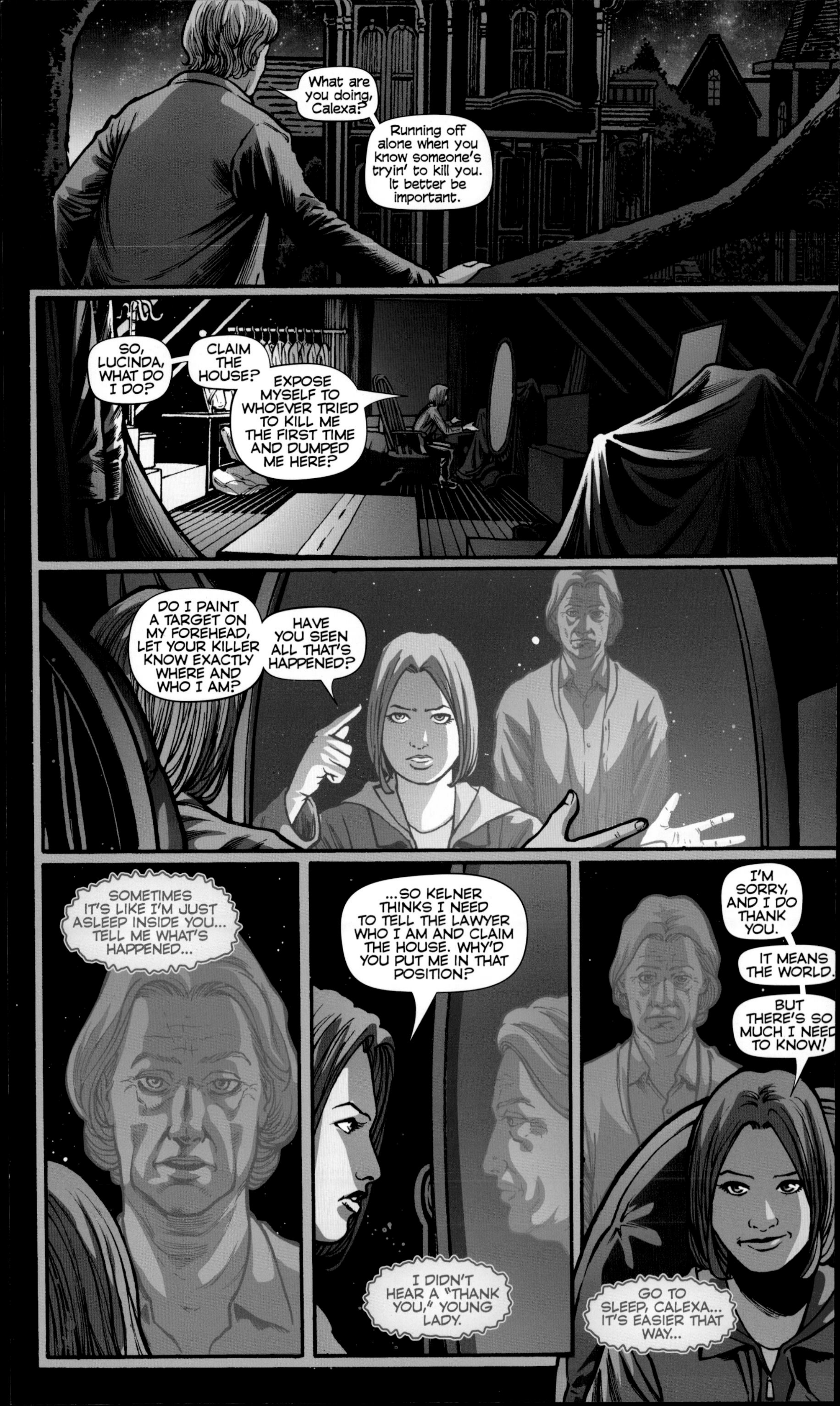
What are you doing, Calexa?
Running off alone when you know someone's tryin' to kill you. It better be important.
SO, LUCINDA, WHAT DO I DO?
CLAIM THE HOUSE?
EXPOSE MYSELF TO WHOEVER TRIED TO KILL ME THE FIRST TIME AND DUMPED ME HERE?
DO I PAINT A TARGET ON MY FOREHEAD, LET YOUR KILLER KNOW EXACTLY WHERE AND WHO I AM?
HAVE YOU SEEN ALL THAT'S HAPPENED?
SOMETIMES IT'S LIKE I'M JUST ASLEEP INSIDE YOU... TELL ME WHAT'S HAPPENED...
...SO KELNER THINKS I NEED TO TELL THE LAWYER WHO I AM AND CLAIM THE HOUSE. WHY'D YOU PUT ME IN THAT POSITION?
I DIDN'T HEAR A "THANK YOU," YOUNG LADY.
I'M SORRY, AND I DO THANK YOU.
IT MEANS THE WORLD.
BUT THERE'S SO MUCH I NEED TO KNOW!
GO TO SLEEP, CALEXA... IT'S EASIER THAT WAY...

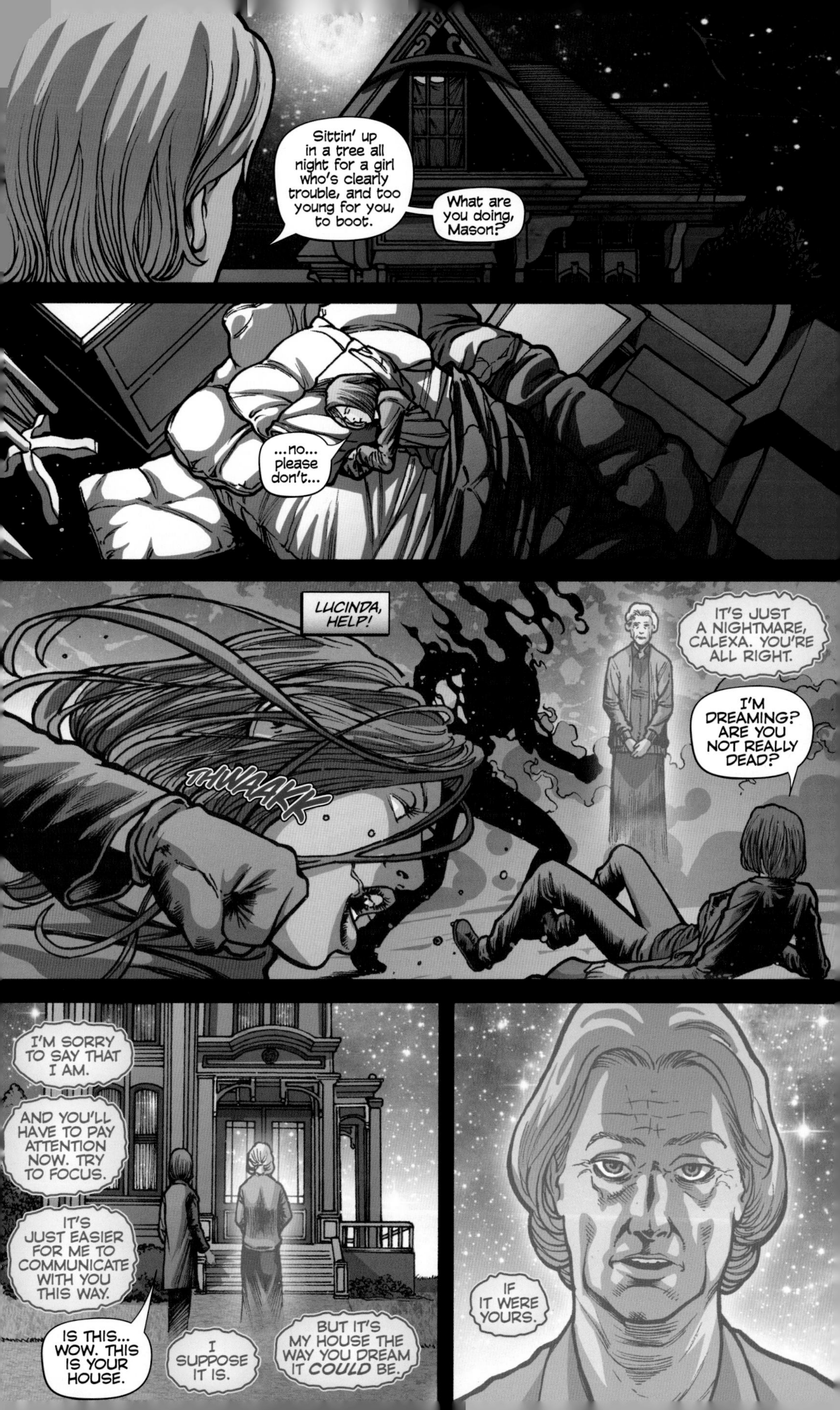
Sittin' up in a tree all night for a girl who's clearly trouble, and too young for you, to boot.
What are you doing, Mason?
...no... please don't...
LUCINDA, HELP!
THWAAKK
IT'S JUST A NIGHTMARE, CALEXA. YOU'RE ALL RIGHT.
I'M DREAMING? ARE YOU NOT REALLY DEAD?
I'M SORRY TO SAY THAT I AM.
AND YOU'LL HAVE TO PAY ATTENTION NOW. TRY TO FOCUS.
IT'S JUST EASIER FOR ME TO COMMUNICATE WITH YOU THIS WAY.
IS THIS... WOW. THIS IS YOUR HOUSE.
I SUPPOSE IT IS.
BUT IT'S MY HOUSE THE WAY YOU DREAM IT *COULD* BE.
IF IT WERE YOURS.

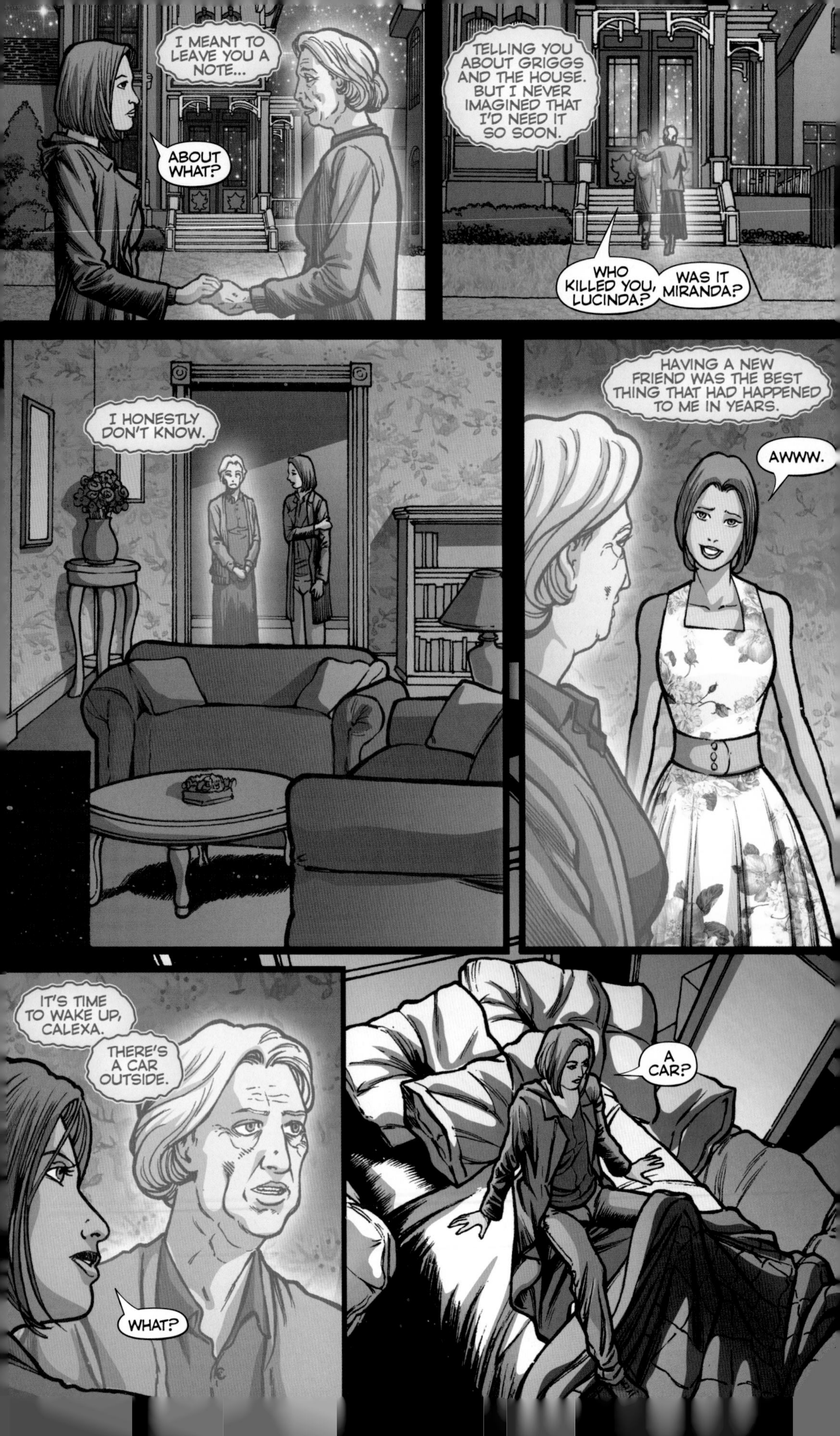
I MEANT TO LEAVE YOU A NOTE...
ABOUT WHAT?
TELLING YOU ABOUT GRIGGS AND THE HOUSE. BUT I NEVER IMAGINED THAT I'D NEED IT SO SOON.
WHO KILLED YOU, LUCINDA?
WAS IT MIRANDA?
I HONESTLY DON'T KNOW.
HAVING A NEW FRIEND WAS THE BEST THING THAT HAD HAPPENED TO ME IN YEARS.
AWWW.
IT'S TIME TO WAKE UP, CALEXA.
THERE'S A CAR OUTSIDE.
WHAT?
A CAR?

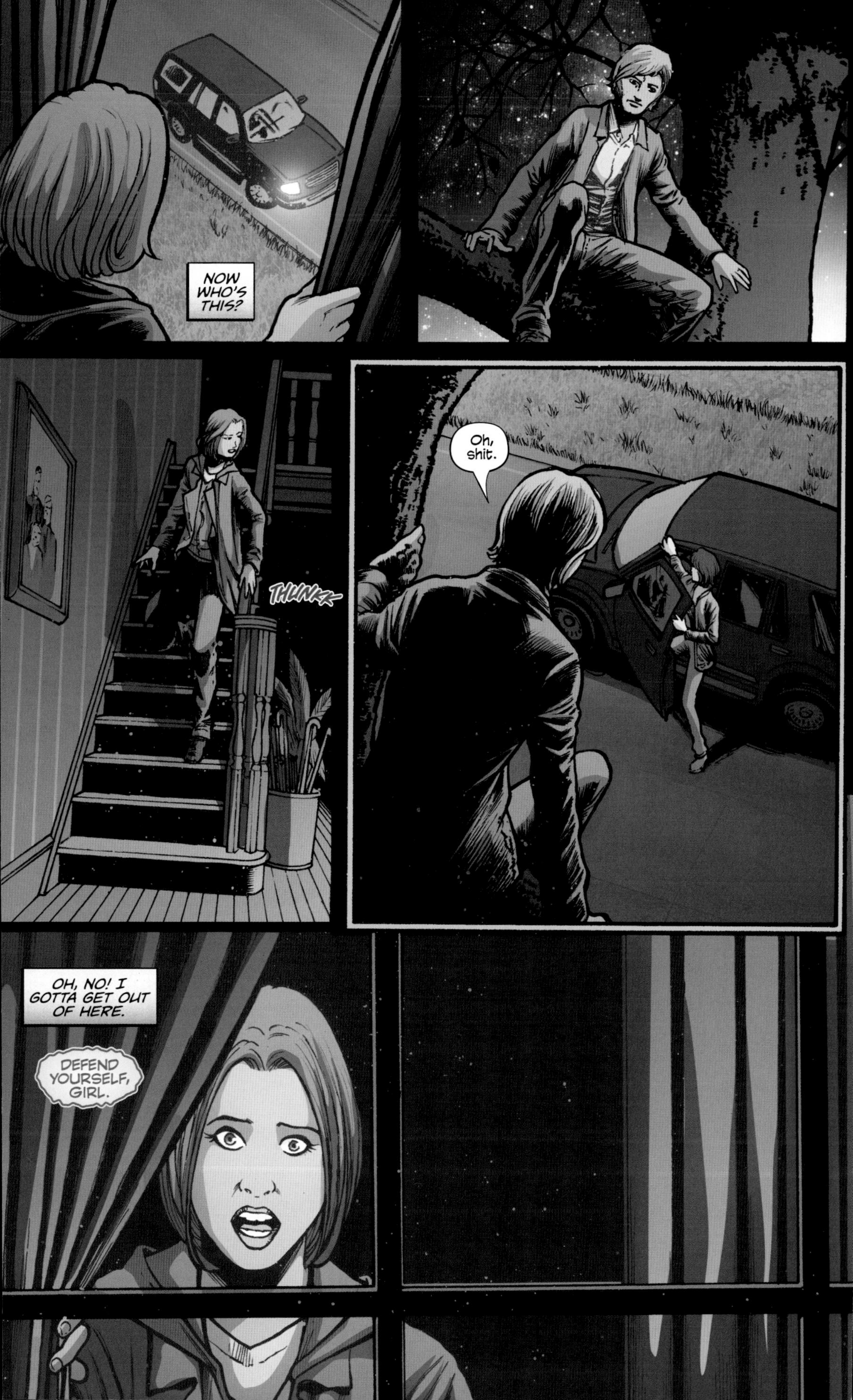
NOW WHO'S THIS?
THUNKK
Oh, shit.
OH, NO! I GOTTA GET OUT OF HERE.
DEFEND YOURSELF, GIRL.

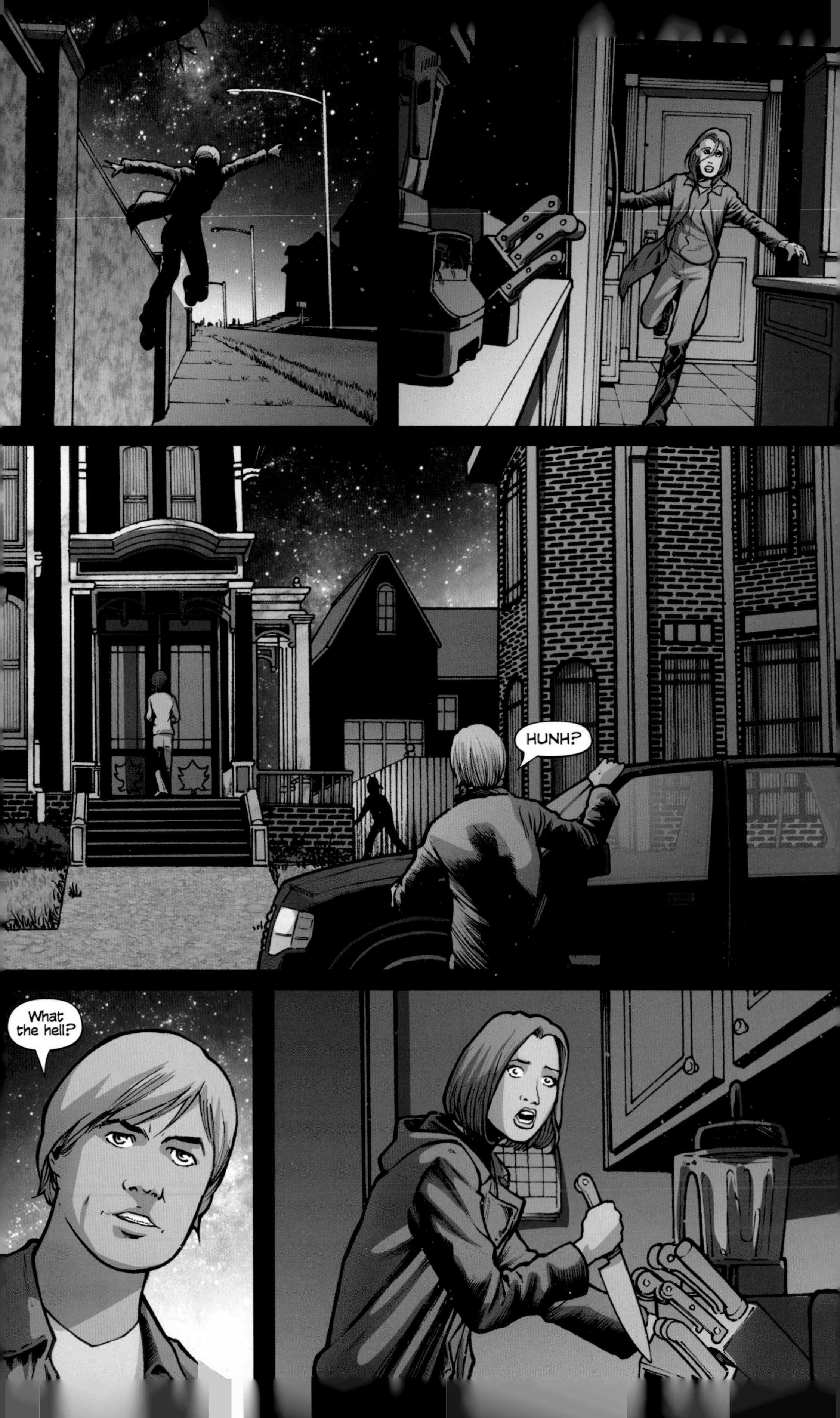
HUNH?
What the hell?

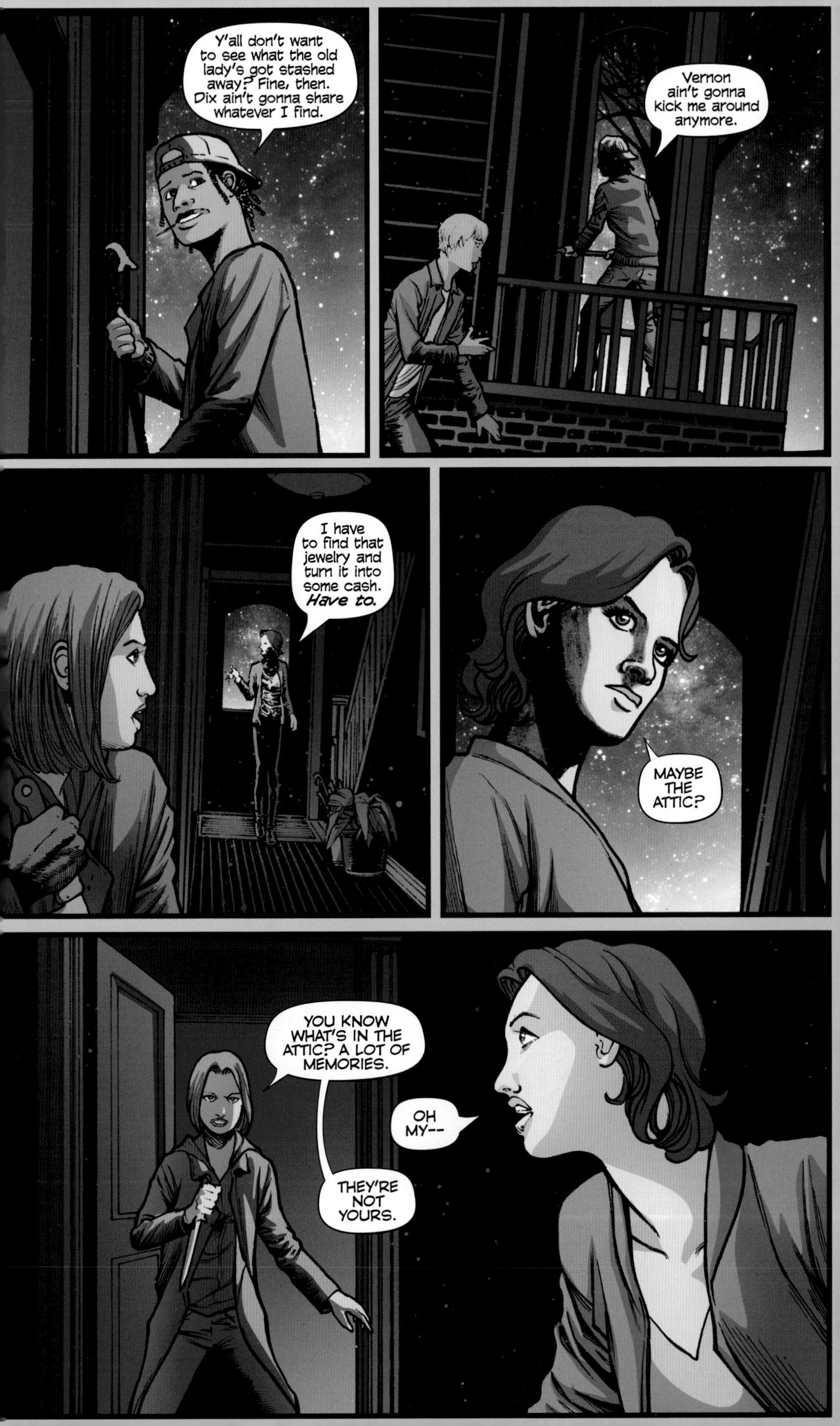
Y'all don't want to see what the old lady's got stashed away? Fine, then. Dix ain't gonna share whatever I find.
Vernon ain't gonna kick me around anymore.
I have to find that jewelry and turn it into some cash. *Have to.*
MAYBE THE ATTIC?
YOU KNOW WHAT'S IN THE ATTIC? A LOT OF MEMORIES.
OH MY--
THEY'RE NOT YOURS.

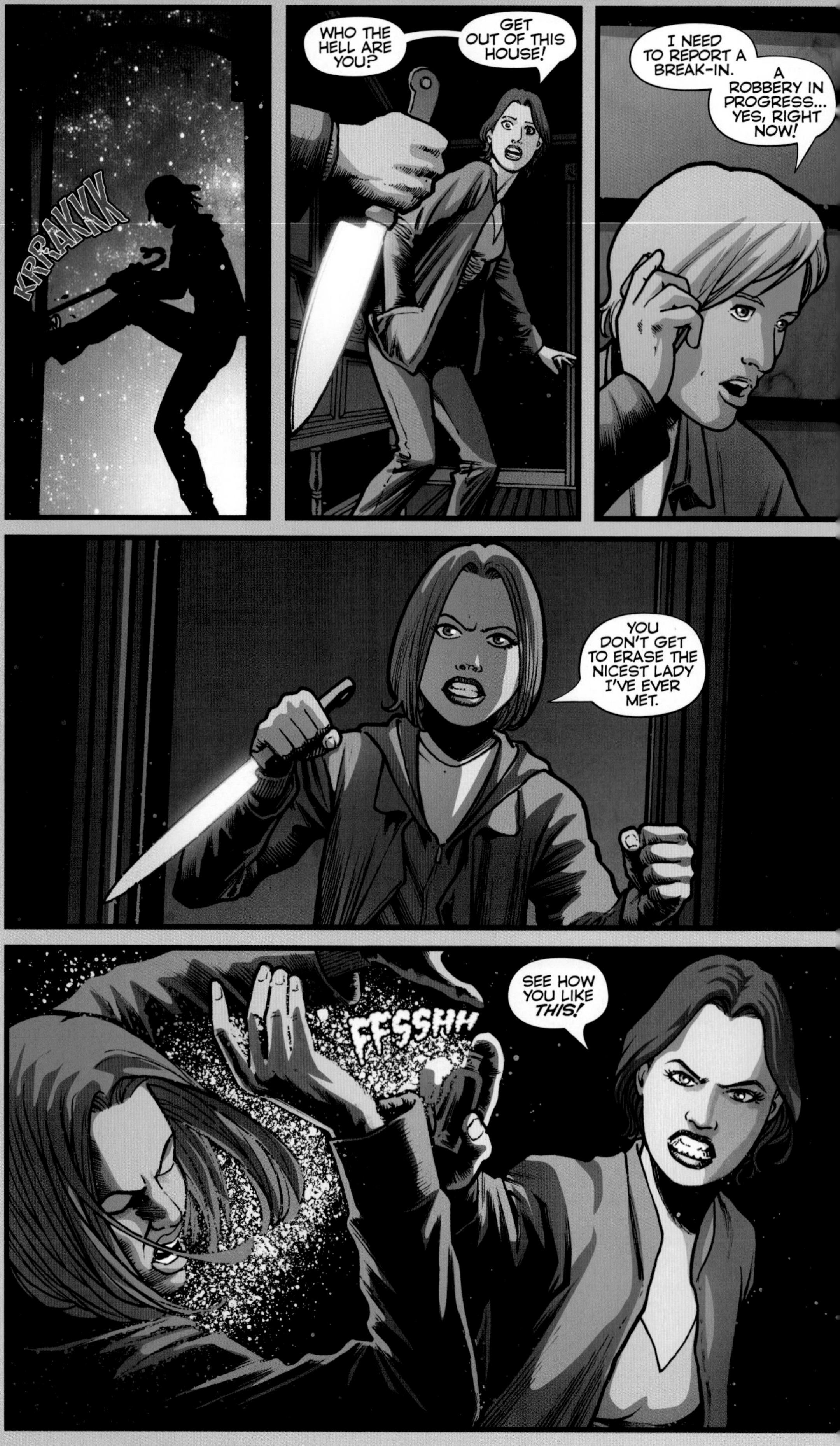
KRRAKKK
WHO THE HELL ARE YOU?
GET OUT OF THIS HOUSE!
I NEED TO REPORT A BREAK-IN.
A ROBBERY IN PROGRESS... YES, RIGHT NOW!
YOU DON'T GET TO ERASE THE NICEST LADY I'VE EVER MET.
SEE HOW YOU LIKE *THIS!*
FFSSHH

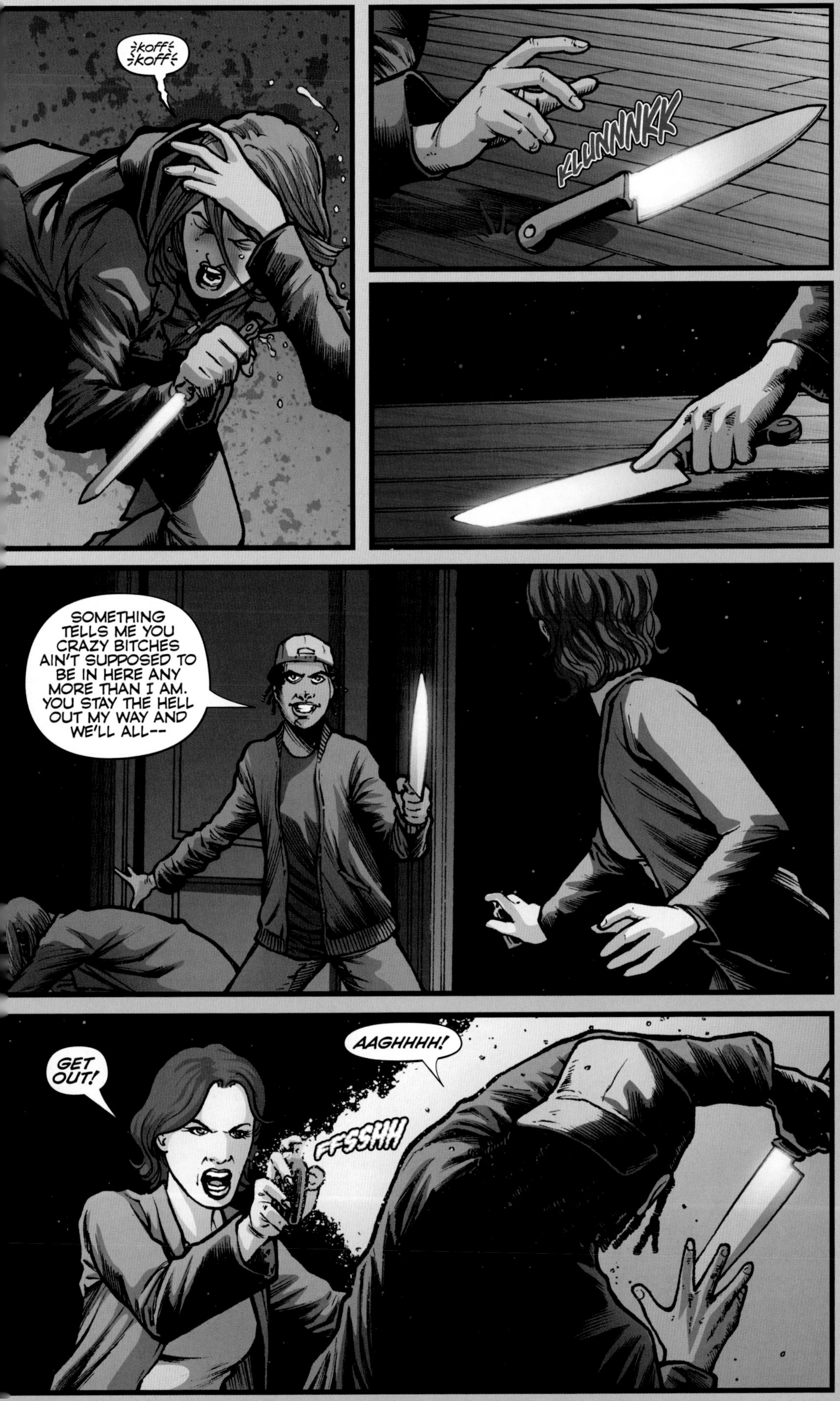
koff koff
KLUNNNKK
SOMETHING TELLS ME YOU CRAZY BITCHES AIN'T SUPPOSED TO BE IN HERE ANY MORE THAN I AM. YOU STAY THE HELL OUT MY WAY AND WE'LL ALL--
GET OUT!
FFSSHH
AAGHHHH!

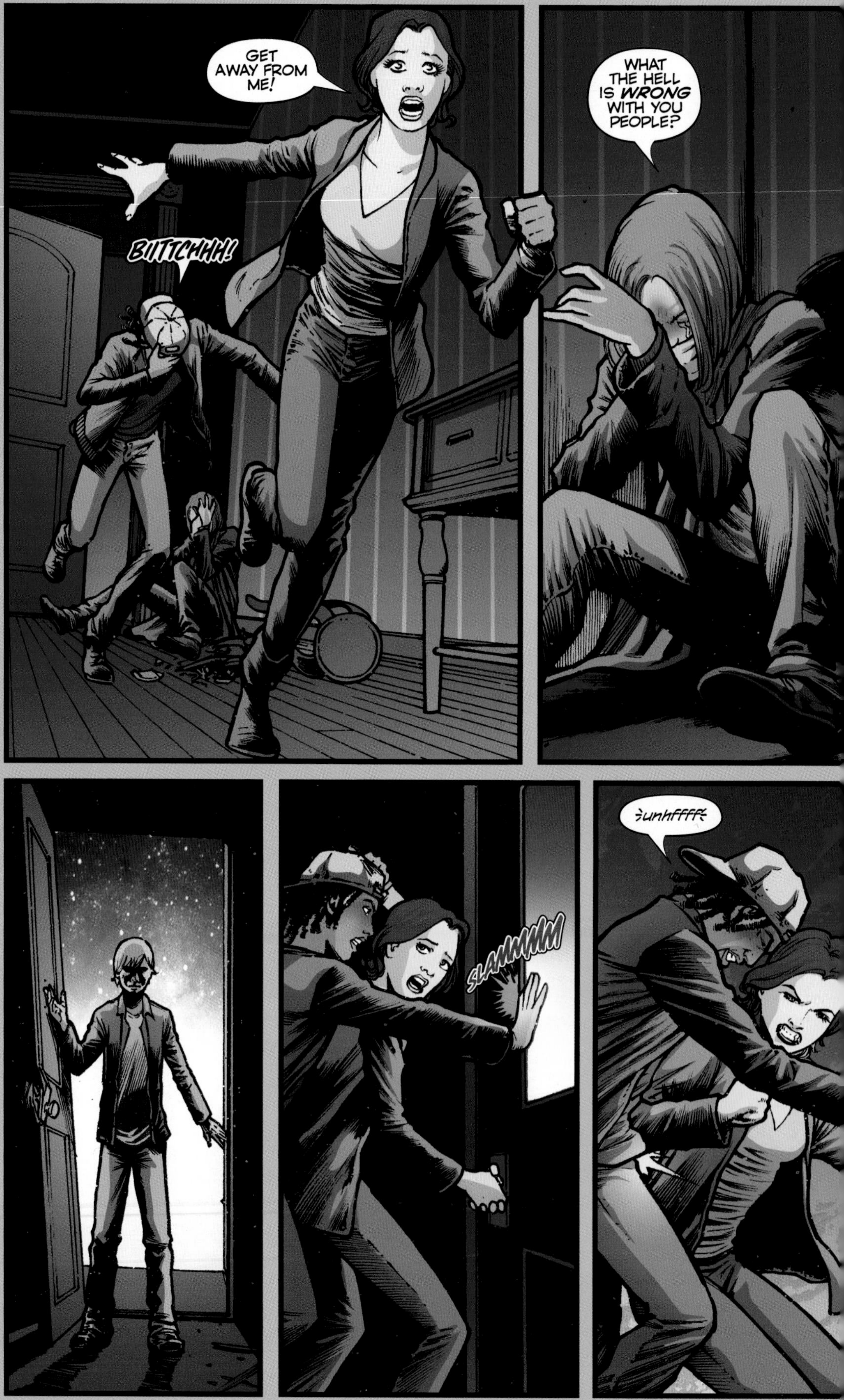

GET AWAY FROM ME!
BIITCHHH!
WHAT THE HELL IS *WRONG* WITH YOU PEOPLE?
SLAMMMMM
unhffff

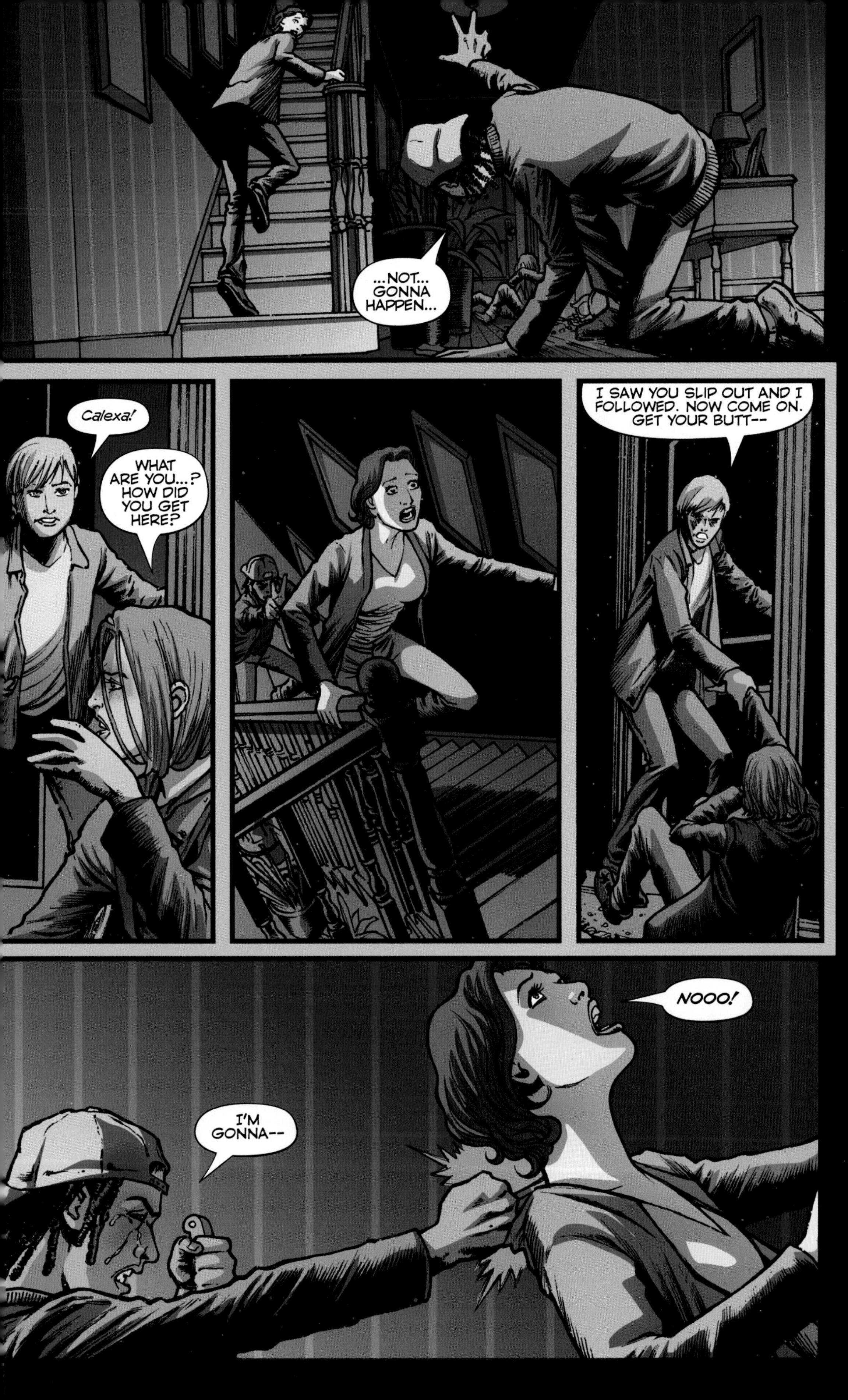
...NOT... GONNA HAPPEN...
Calexa!
WHAT ARE YOU...? HOW DID YOU GET HERE?
I SAW YOU SLIP OUT AND I FOLLOWED. NOW COME ON. GET YOUR BUTT--
NOOO!
I'M GONNA--

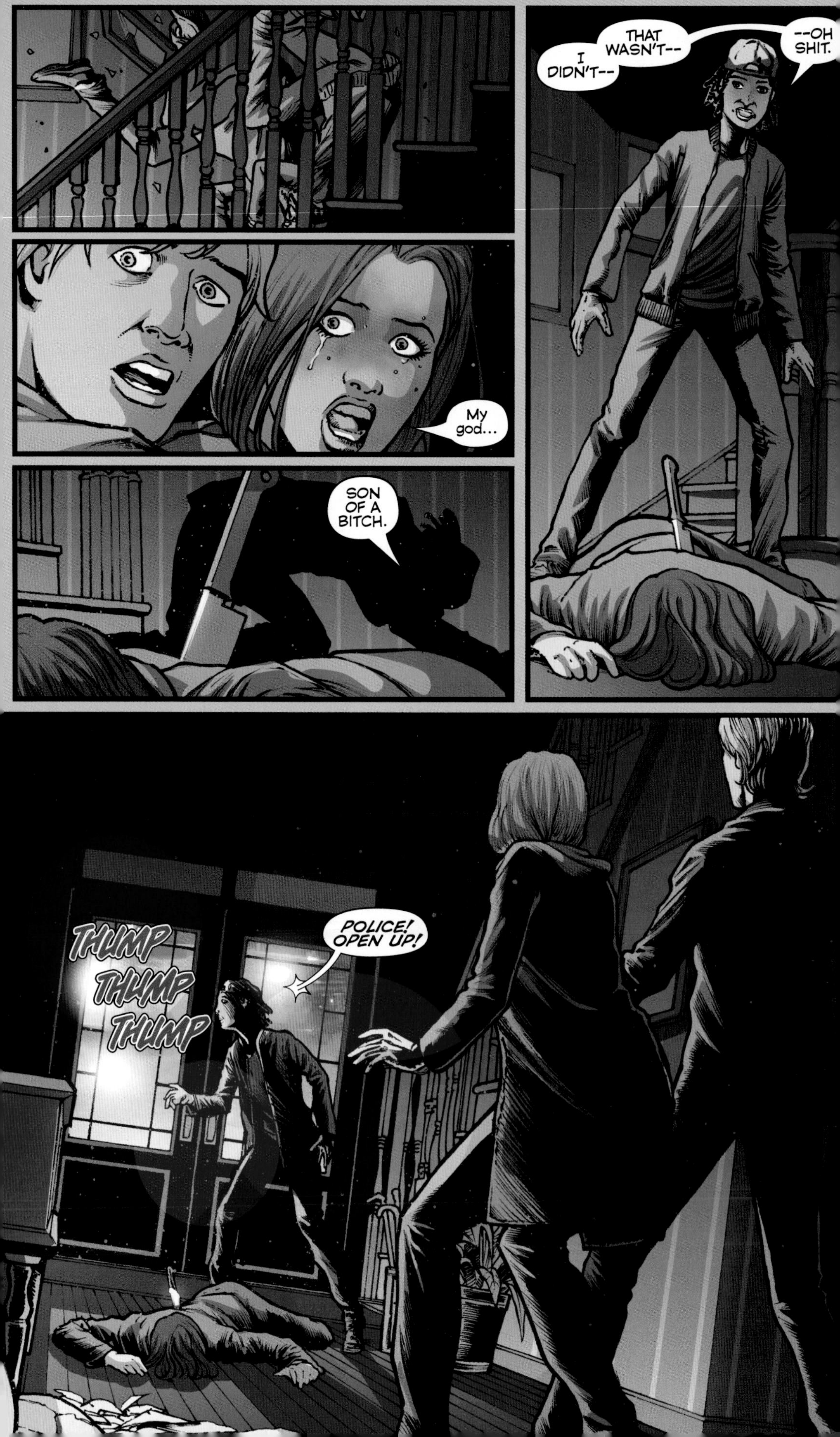
My god...
SON OF A BITCH.
I DIDN'T--
THAT WASN'T--
--OH SHIT.
THUMP
THUMP
THUMP
POLICE! OPEN UP!

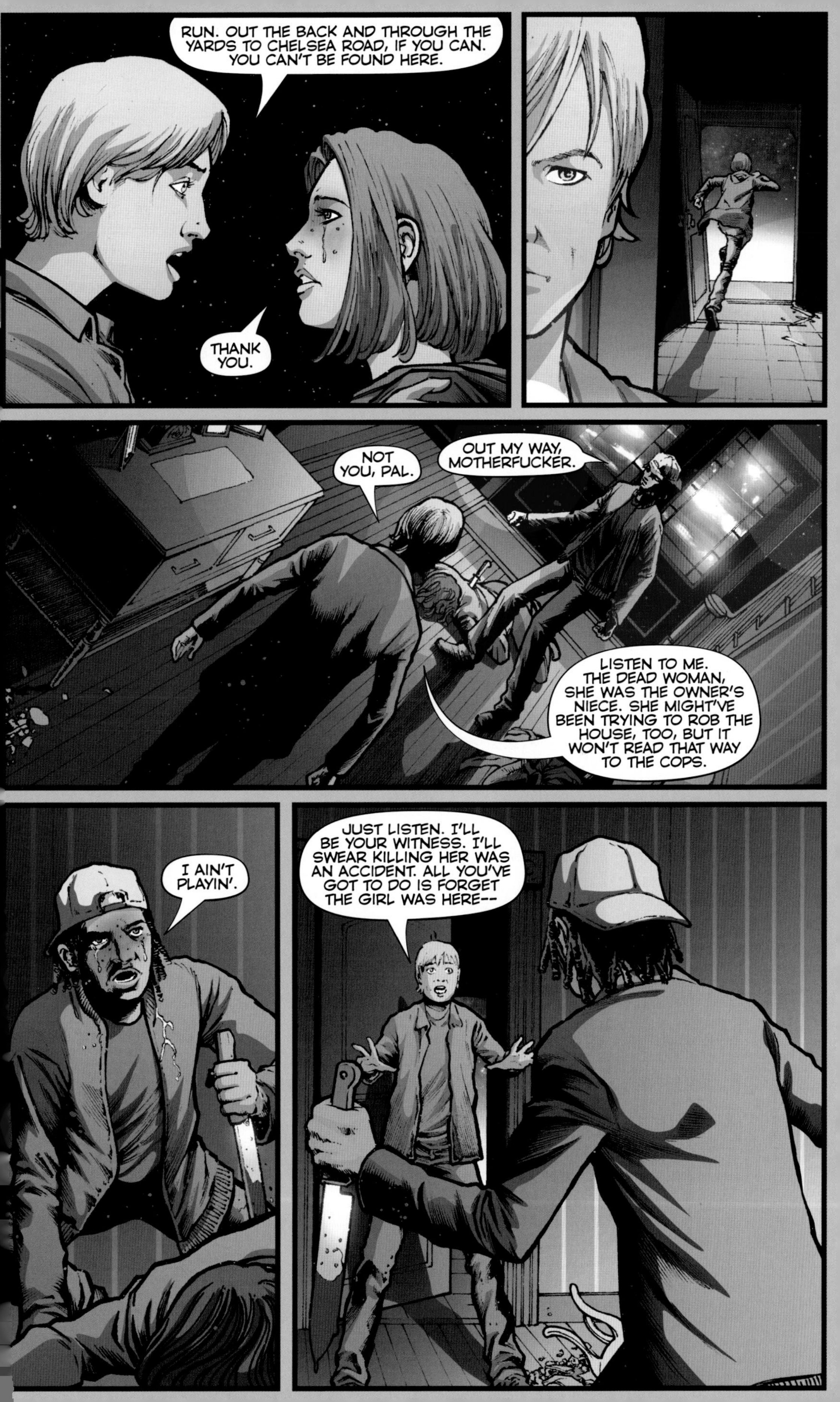
RUN. OUT THE BACK AND THROUGH THE YARDS TO CHELSEA ROAD, IF YOU CAN. YOU CAN'T BE FOUND HERE.
THANK YOU.
NOT YOU, PAL.
OUT MY WAY, MOTHERFUCKER.
LISTEN TO ME. THE DEAD WOMAN, SHE WAS THE OWNER'S NIECE. SHE MIGHT'VE BEEN TRYING TO ROB THE HOUSE, TOO, BUT IT WON'T READ THAT WAY TO THE COPS.
I AIN'T PLAYIN'.
JUST LISTEN. I'LL BE YOUR WITNESS. I'LL SWEAR KILLING HER WAS AN ACCIDENT. ALL YOU'VE GOT TO DO IS FORGET THE GIRL WAS HERE--

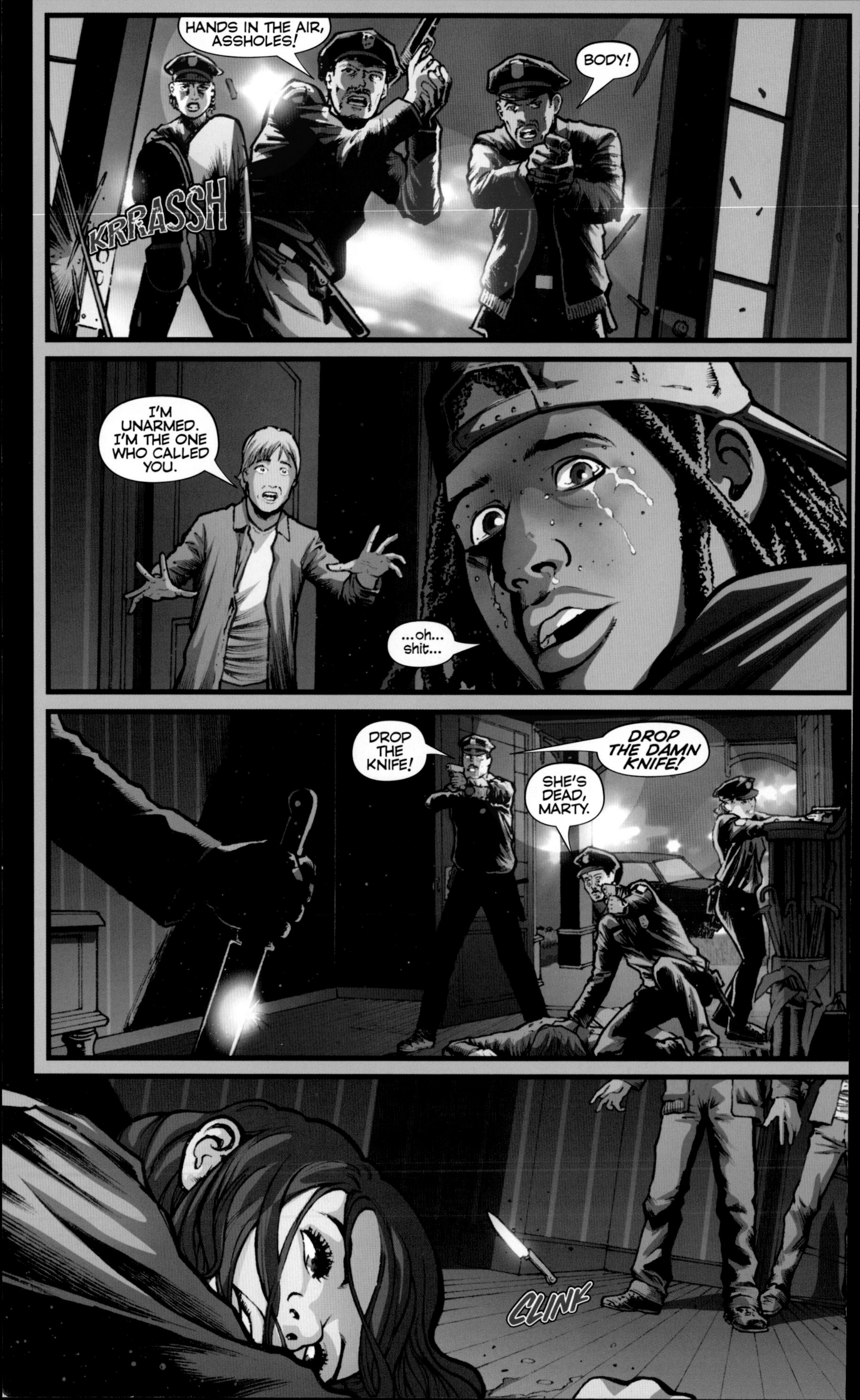
HANDS IN THE AIR, ASSHOLES!
BODY!
KRRASSH
I'M UNARMED. I'M THE ONE WHO CALLED YOU.
...oh... shit...
DROP THE KNIFE!
DROP THE DAMN KNIFE!
SHE'S DEAD, MARTY.
CLINK

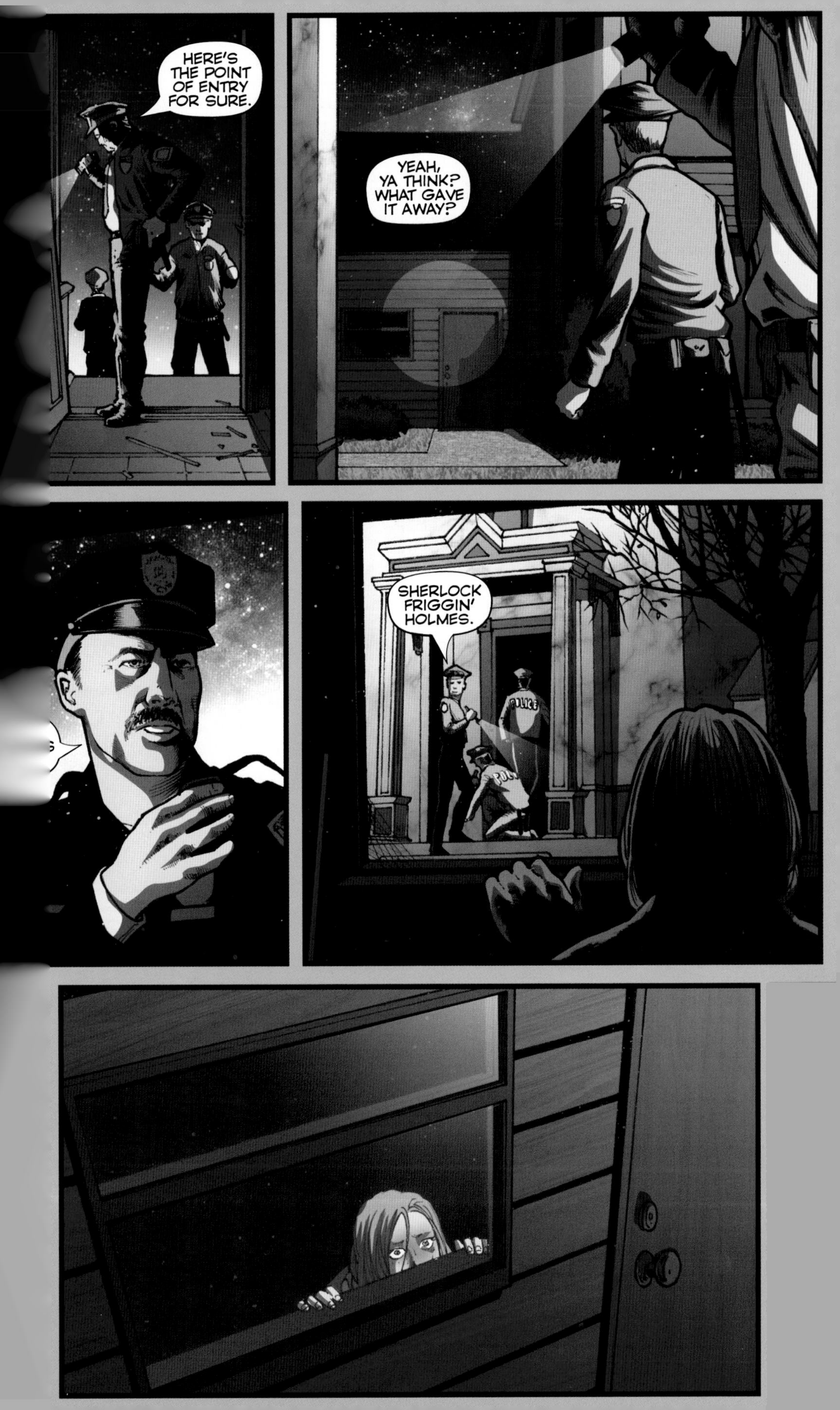
HERE'S THE POINT OF ENTRY FOR SURE.
YEAH, YA THINK? WHAT GAVE IT AWAY?
SHERLOCK FRIGGIN' HOLMES.

HOLY SHIT, DID THAT JUST HAPPEN?

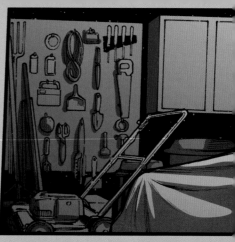

...COULDN'T SLEEP AND I WAS OUT FOR A WALK.

I SAW THE WOMAN GO IN THE FRONT DOOR, AND THEN I SPOTTED THIS GUY CREEPING THROUGH THE BACKYARDS--

IT WAS AN ACCIDENT, MAN! ASK THIS GUY!

JUST A DAMN MISUNDERSTANDING IS ALL. GO AHEAD AND ASK HIM.

WE WAS JUST ON THE STAIRS AND SHE FELL AND--

ARE YOU EVEN LISTENIN' TO ME?

HOW AM I SUPPOSED TO GET OUT OF HERE?

I WENT IN TO TRY TO WARN HER. I DIDN'T KNOW IF HE JUST WANTED TO ROB THE PLACE OR IF HE MEANT TO HURT HER.

LOOKS LIKE BOTH.

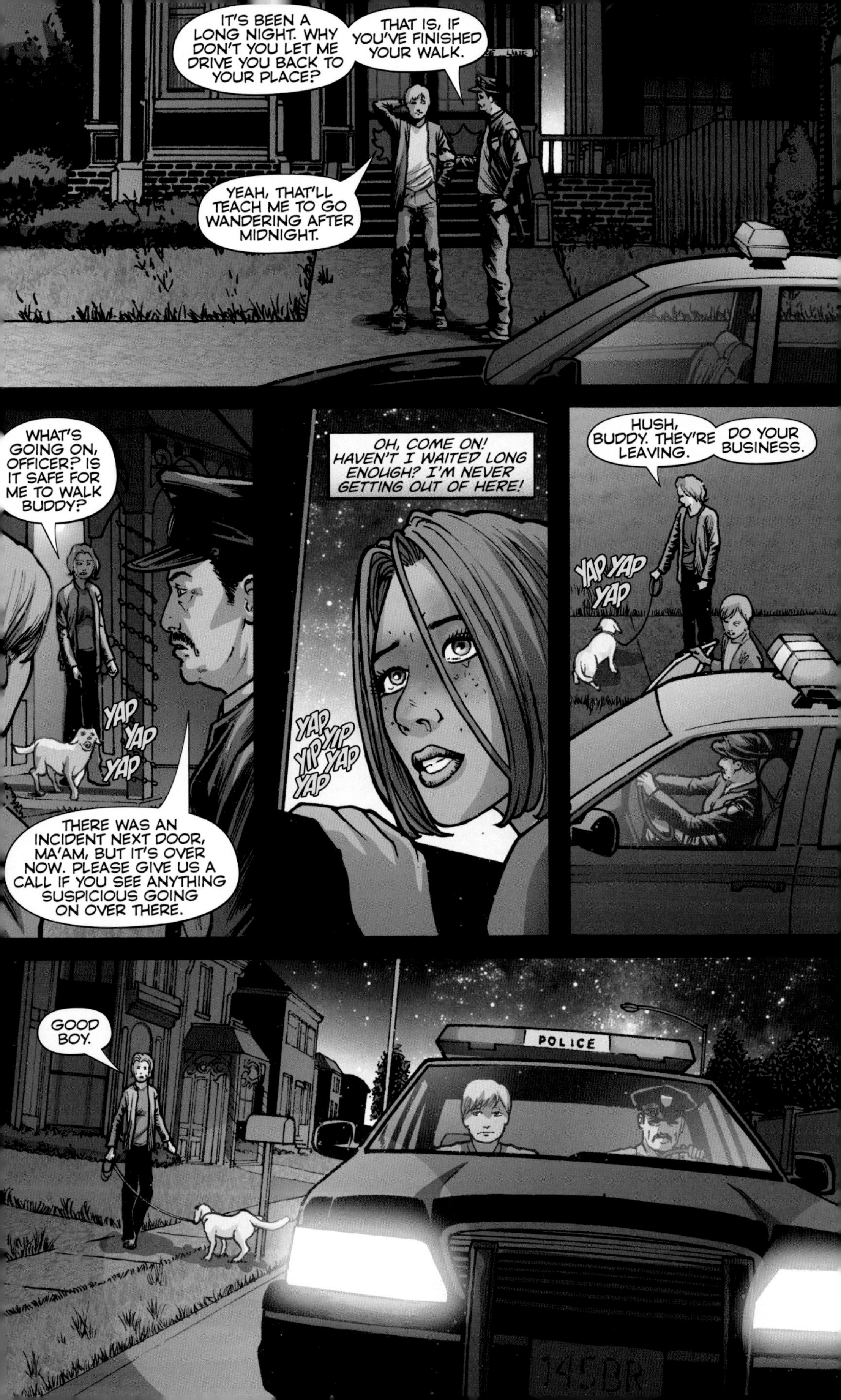
IT'S BEEN A LONG NIGHT. WHY DON'T YOU LET ME DRIVE YOU BACK TO YOUR PLACE?
THAT IS, IF YOU'VE FINISHED YOUR WALK.
YEAH, THAT'LL TEACH ME TO GO WANDERING AFTER MIDNIGHT.
WHAT'S GOING ON, OFFICER? IS IT SAFE FOR ME TO WALK BUDDY?
YAP YAP YAP
THERE WAS AN INCIDENT NEXT DOOR, MA'AM, BUT IT'S OVER NOW. PLEASE GIVE US A CALL IF YOU SEE ANYTHING SUSPICIOUS GOING ON OVER THERE.
OH, COME ON! HAVEN'T I WAITED LONG ENOUGH? I'M NEVER GETTING OUT OF HERE!
YAP YIP YIP YAP YAP
HUSH, BUDDY. THEY'RE LEAVING.
DO YOUR BUSINESS.
YAP YAP YAP
GOOD BOY.
POLICE
145BR

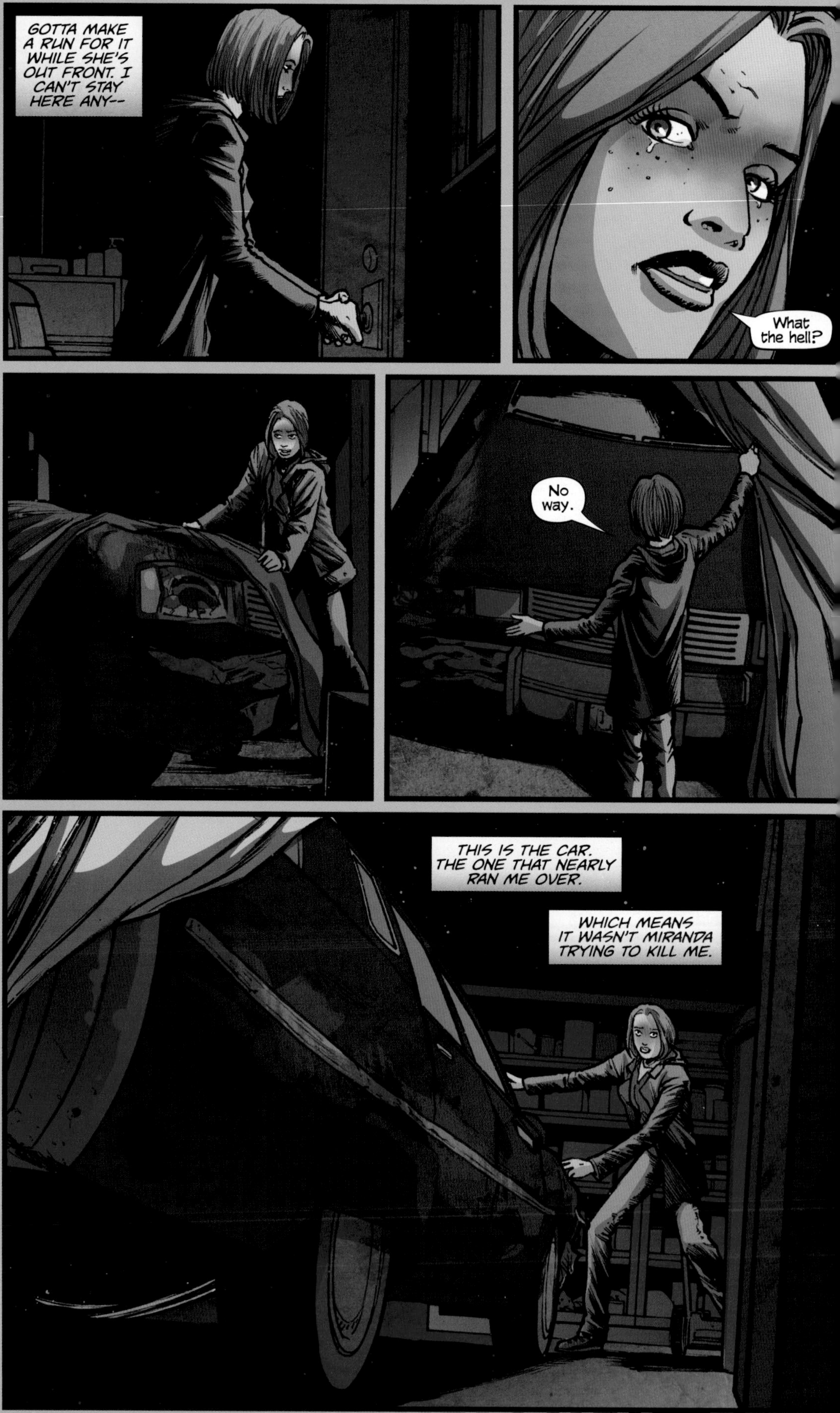

GOTTA MAKE A RUN FOR IT WHILE SHE'S OUT FRONT. I CAN'T STAY HERE ANY--
What the hell?
No way.
THIS IS THE CAR. THE ONE THAT NEARLY RAN ME OVER.
WHICH MEANS IT WASN'T MIRANDA TRYING TO KILL ME.

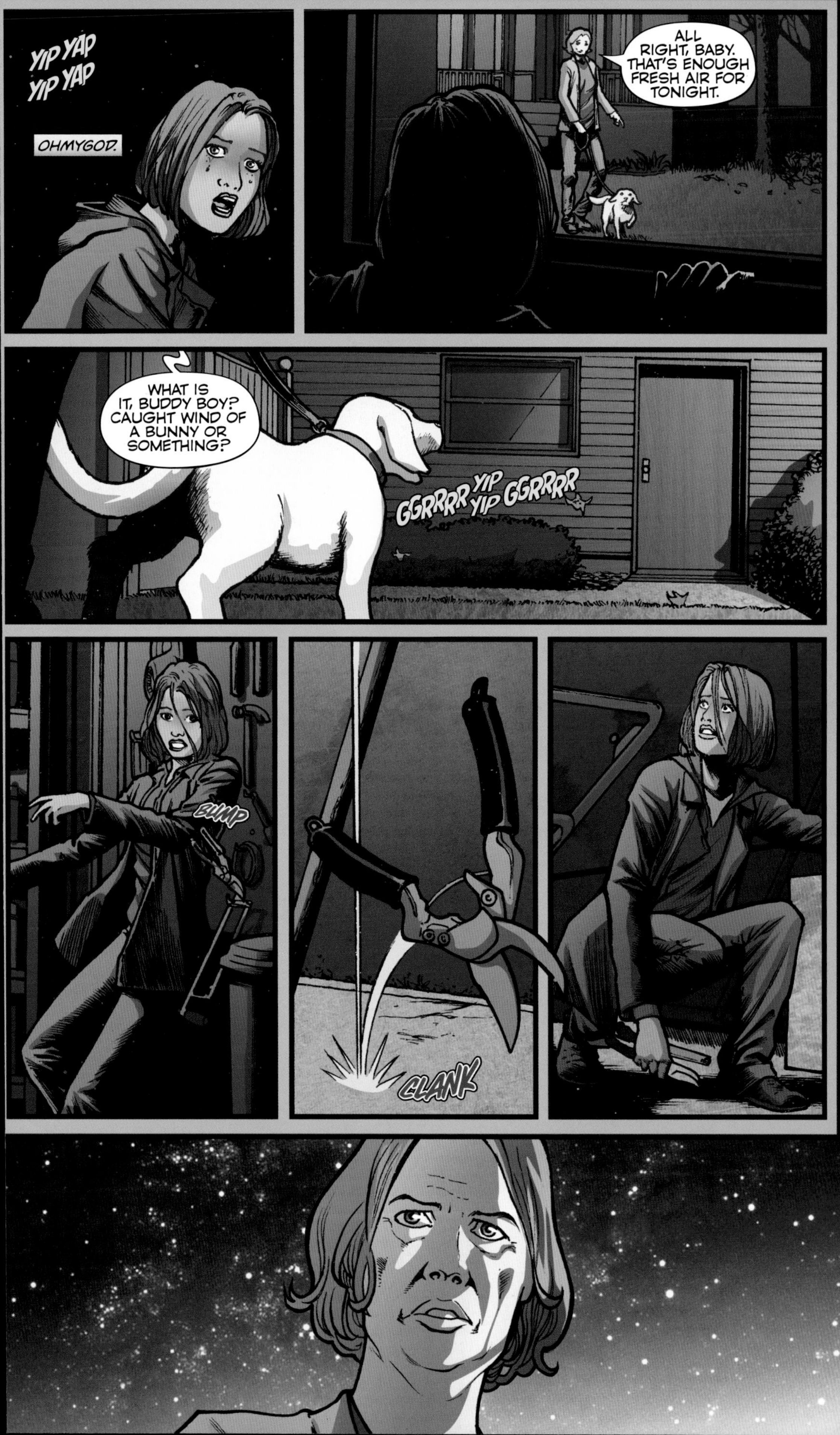
YIP YAP
YIP YAP
OHMYGOD.
ALL RIGHT, BABY. THAT'S ENOUGH FRESH AIR FOR TONIGHT.
WHAT IS IT, BUDDY BOY? CAUGHT WIND OF A BUNNY OR SOMETHING?
GGRRRR YIP YIP GGRRRR
BUMP
CLANK

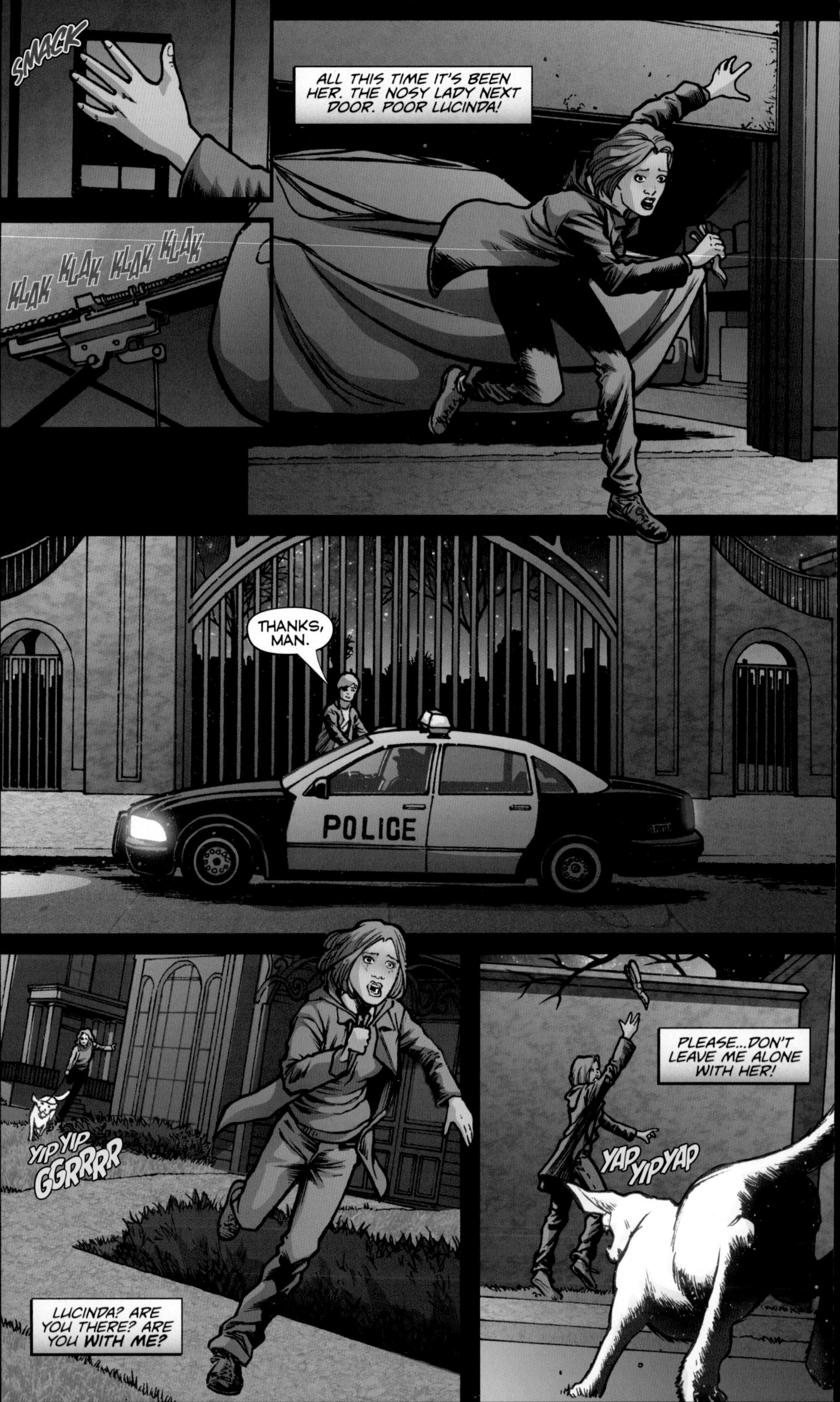
SMACK
ALL THIS TIME IT'S BEEN HER. THE NOSY LADY NEXT DOOR. POOR LUCINDA!
KLAK KLAK KLAK KLAK KLAK
THANKS, MAN.
POLICE
YIP YIP GGRRRR
LUCINDA? ARE YOU THERE? ARE YOU WITH ME?
PLEASE...DON'T LEAVE ME ALONE WITH HER!
YAP YIP YAP

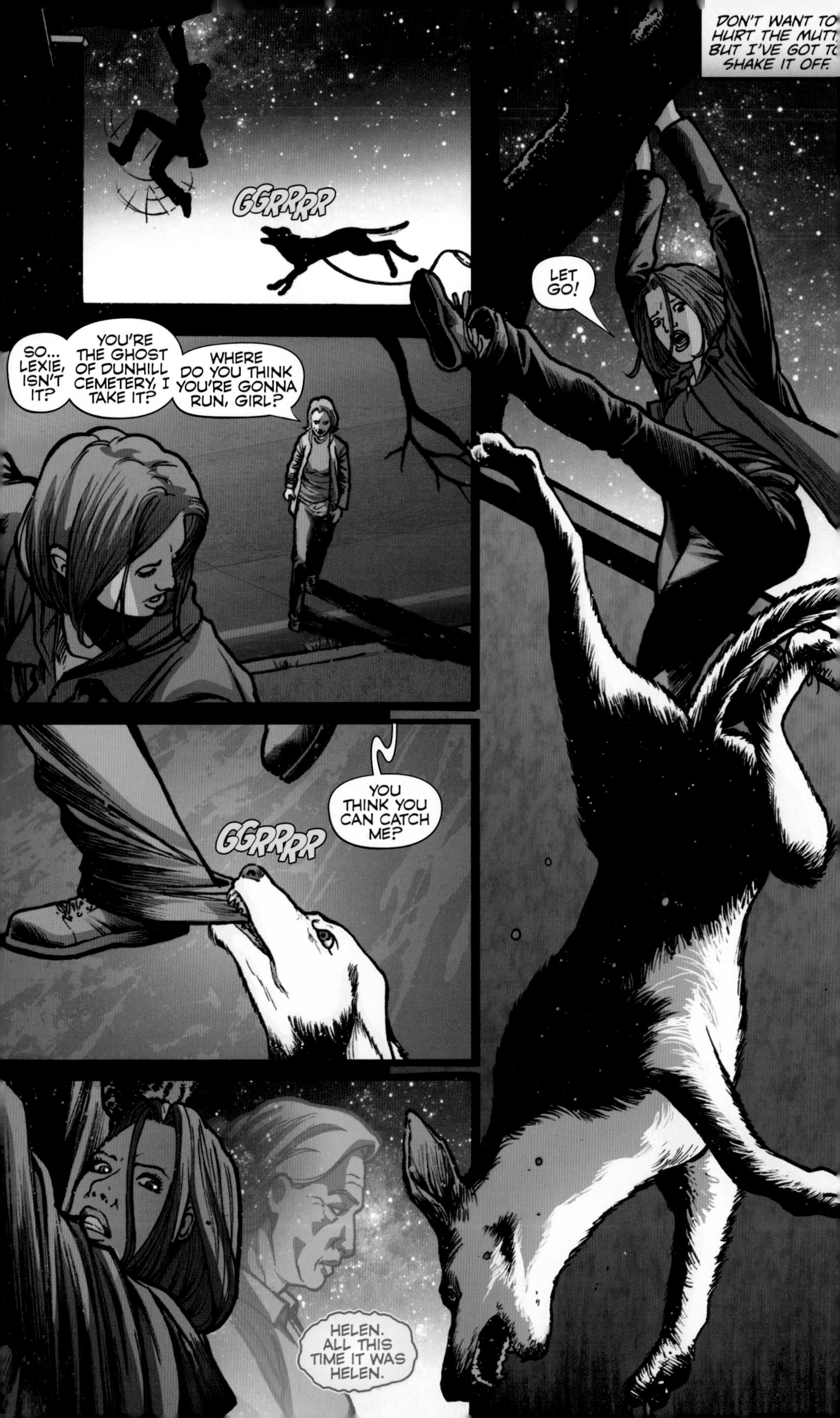
DON'T WANT TO HURT THE MUTT, BUT I'VE GOT TO SHAKE IT OFF.
GGRRRR
LET GO!
SO... LEXIE, ISN'T IT?
YOU'RE THE GHOST OF DUNHILL CEMETERY, I TAKE IT?
WHERE DO YOU THINK YOU'RE GONNA RUN, GIRL?
YOU THINK YOU CAN CATCH ME?
GGRRRR
HELEN. ALL THIS TIME IT WAS HELEN.

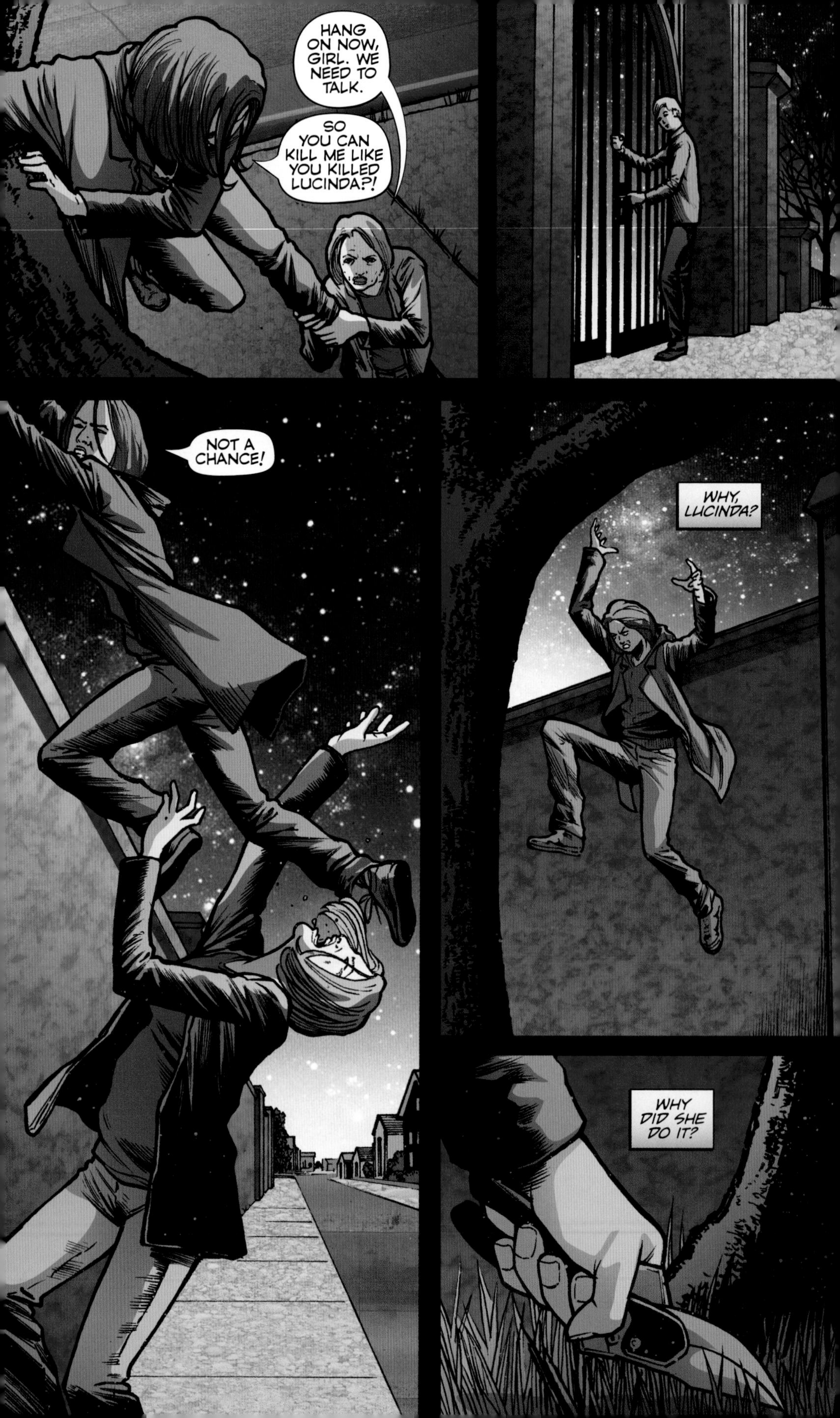
HANG ON NOW, GIRL. WE NEED TO TALK.
SO YOU CAN KILL ME LIKE YOU KILLED LUCINDA?!
NOT A CHANCE!
WHY, LUCINDA?
WHY DID SHE DO IT?

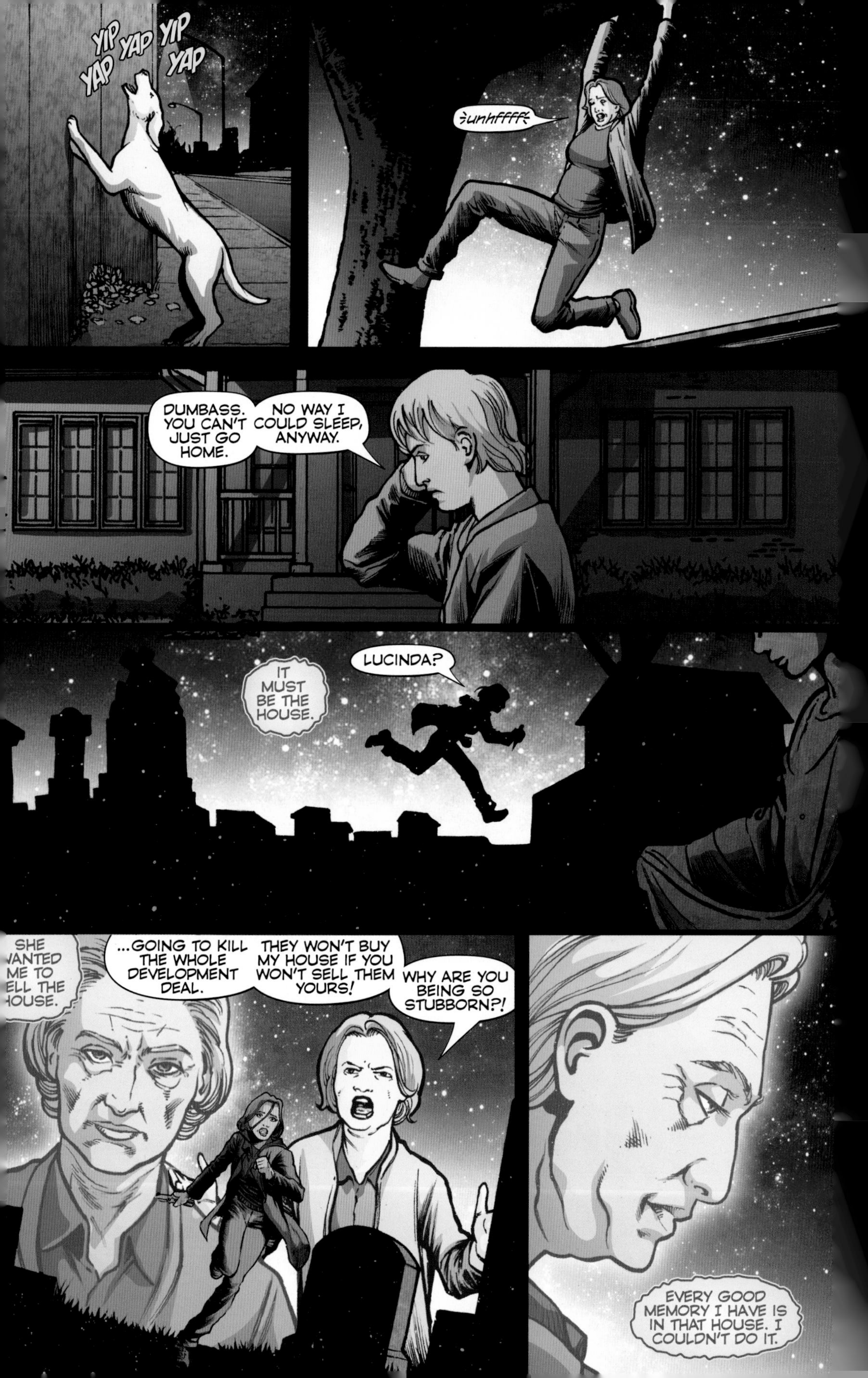
YIP YAP YAP YIP YAP
unhffff
DUMBASS. YOU CAN'T JUST GO HOME.
NO WAY I COULD SLEEP, ANYWAY.
IT MUST BE THE HOUSE.
LUCINDA?
SHE WANTED ME TO SELL THE HOUSE.
...GOING TO KILL THE WHOLE DEVELOPMENT DEAL.
THEY WON'T BUY MY HOUSE IF YOU WON'T SELL THEM YOURS!
WHY ARE YOU BEING SO STUBBORN?!
EVERY GOOD MEMORY I HAVE IS IN THAT HOUSE. I COULDN'T DO IT.

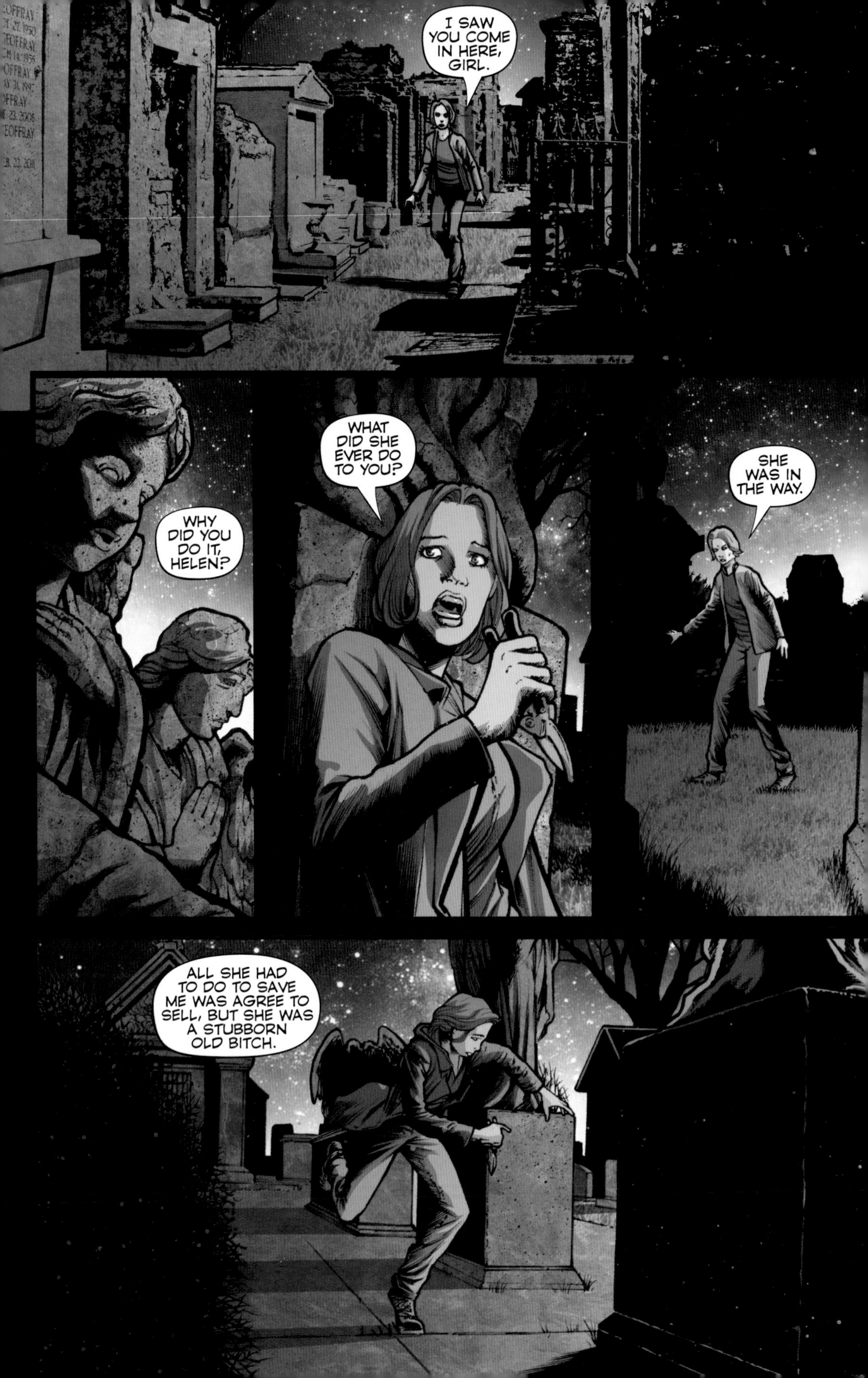
I SAW YOU COME IN HERE, GIRL.
WHY DID YOU DO IT, HELEN?
WHAT DID SHE EVER DO TO YOU?
SHE WAS IN THE WAY.
ALL SHE HAD TO DO TO SAVE ME WAS AGREE TO SELL, BUT SHE WAS A STUBBORN OLD BITCH.

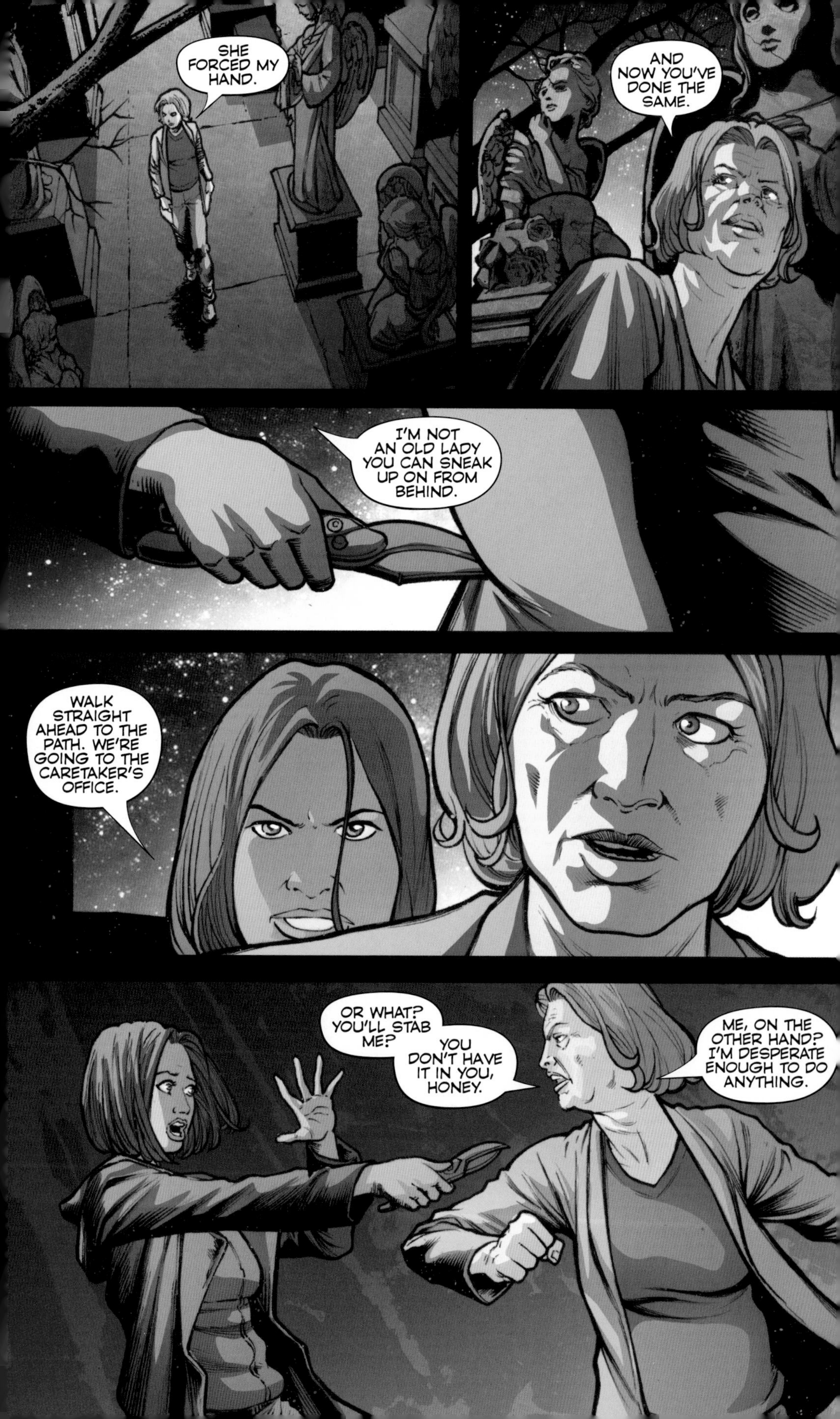
SHE FORCED MY HAND.
AND NOW YOU'VE DONE THE SAME.
I'M NOT AN OLD LADY YOU CAN SNEAK UP ON FROM BEHIND.
WALK STRAIGHT AHEAD TO THE PATH. WE'RE GOING TO THE CARETAKER'S OFFICE.
OR WHAT? YOU'LL STAB ME?
YOU DON'T HAVE IT IN YOU, HONEY.
ME, ON THE OTHER HAND? I'M DESPERATE ENOUGH TO DO ANYTHING.

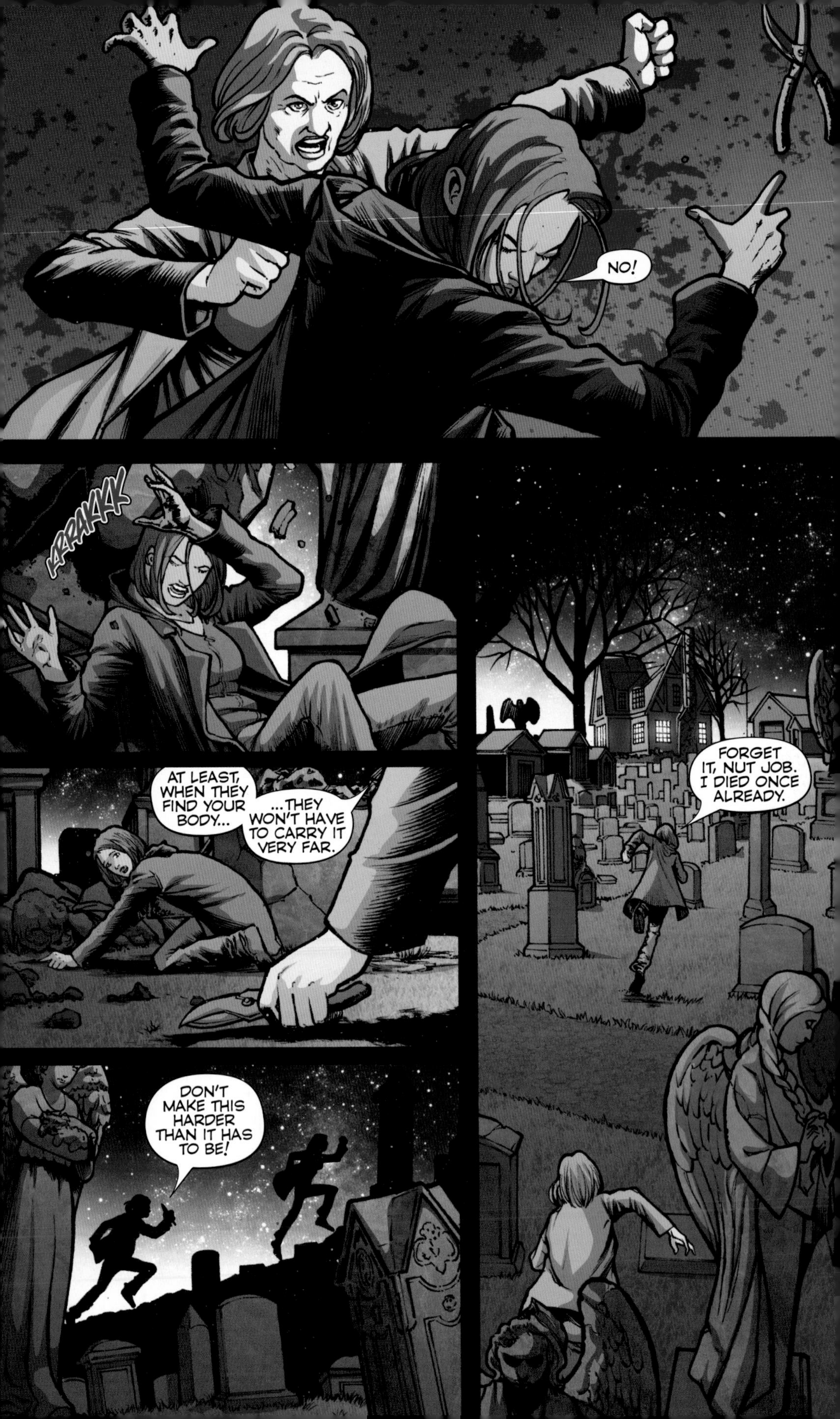
NO!
KRRAKKK
AT LEAST, WHEN THEY FIND YOUR BODY...
...THEY WON'T HAVE TO CARRY IT VERY FAR.
DON'T MAKE THIS HARDER THAN IT HAS TO BE!
FORGET IT, NUT JOB. I DIED ONCE ALREADY.

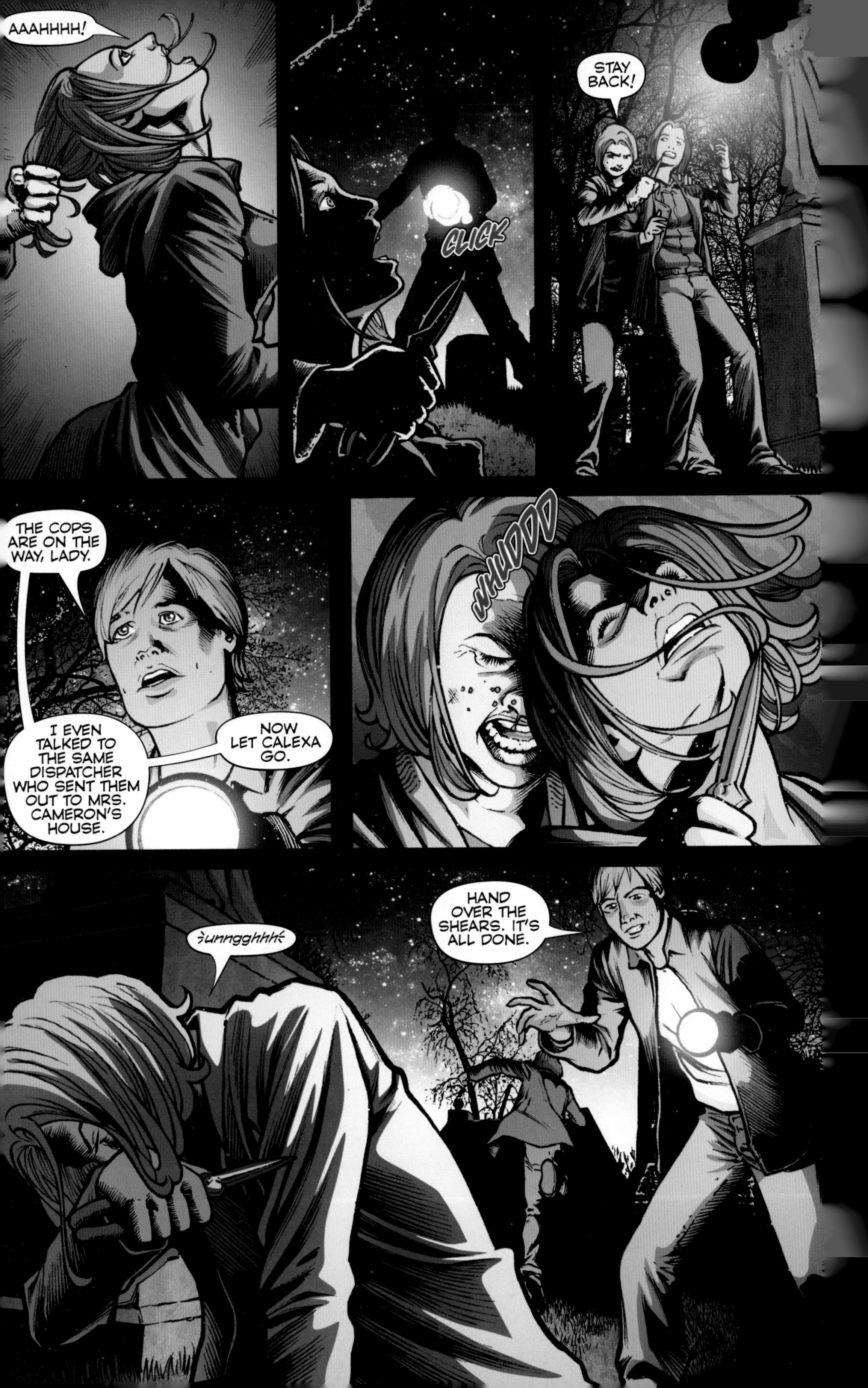
AAAHHHH!
CLICK
STAY BACK!
THE COPS ARE ON THE WAY, LADY.
I EVEN TALKED TO THE SAME DISPATCHER WHO SENT THEM OUT TO MRS. CAMERON'S HOUSE.
NOW LET CALEXA GO.
WHUDDD
unngghhh
HAND OVER THE SHEARS. IT'S ALL DONE.

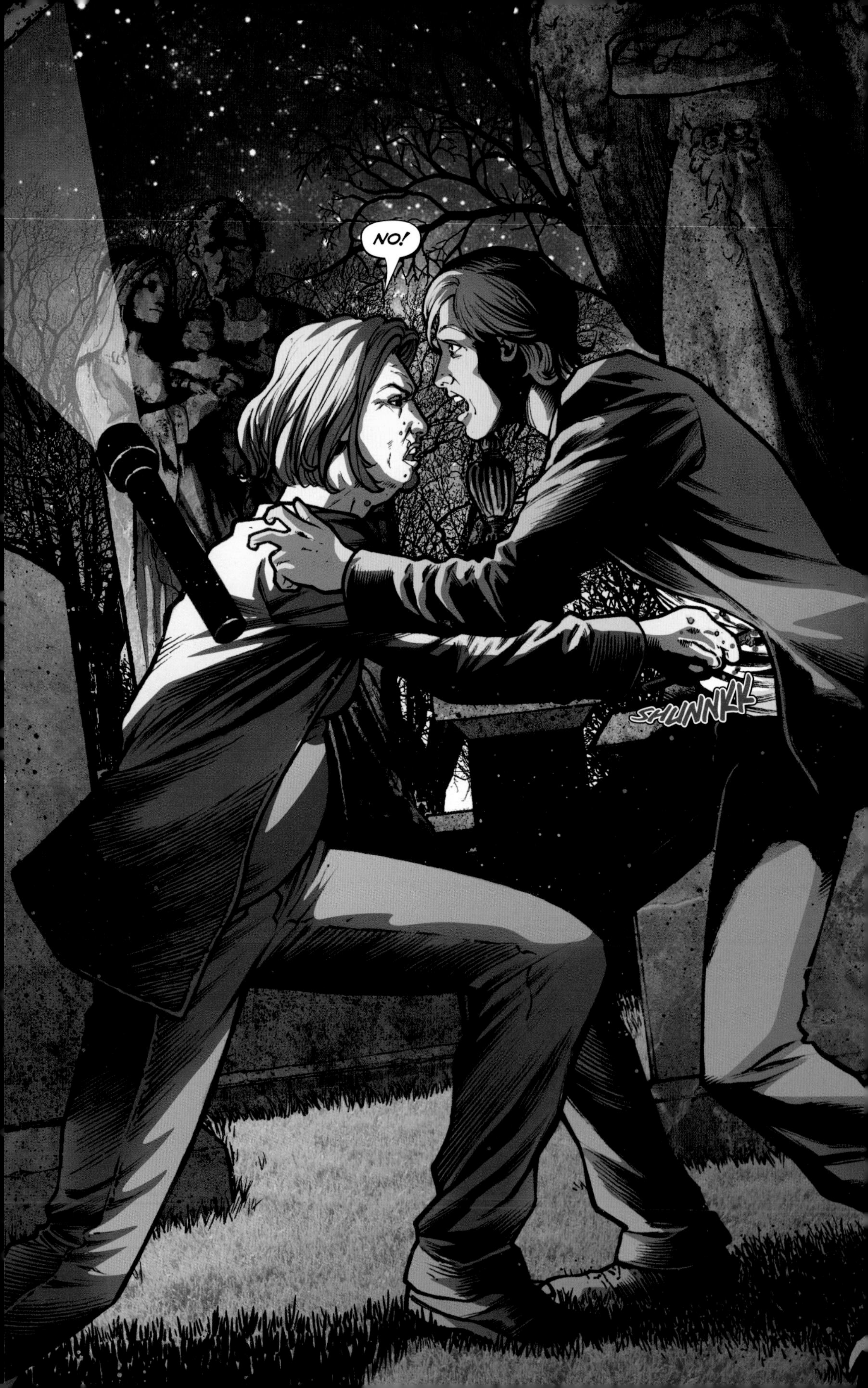
NO!
SHUNNKK

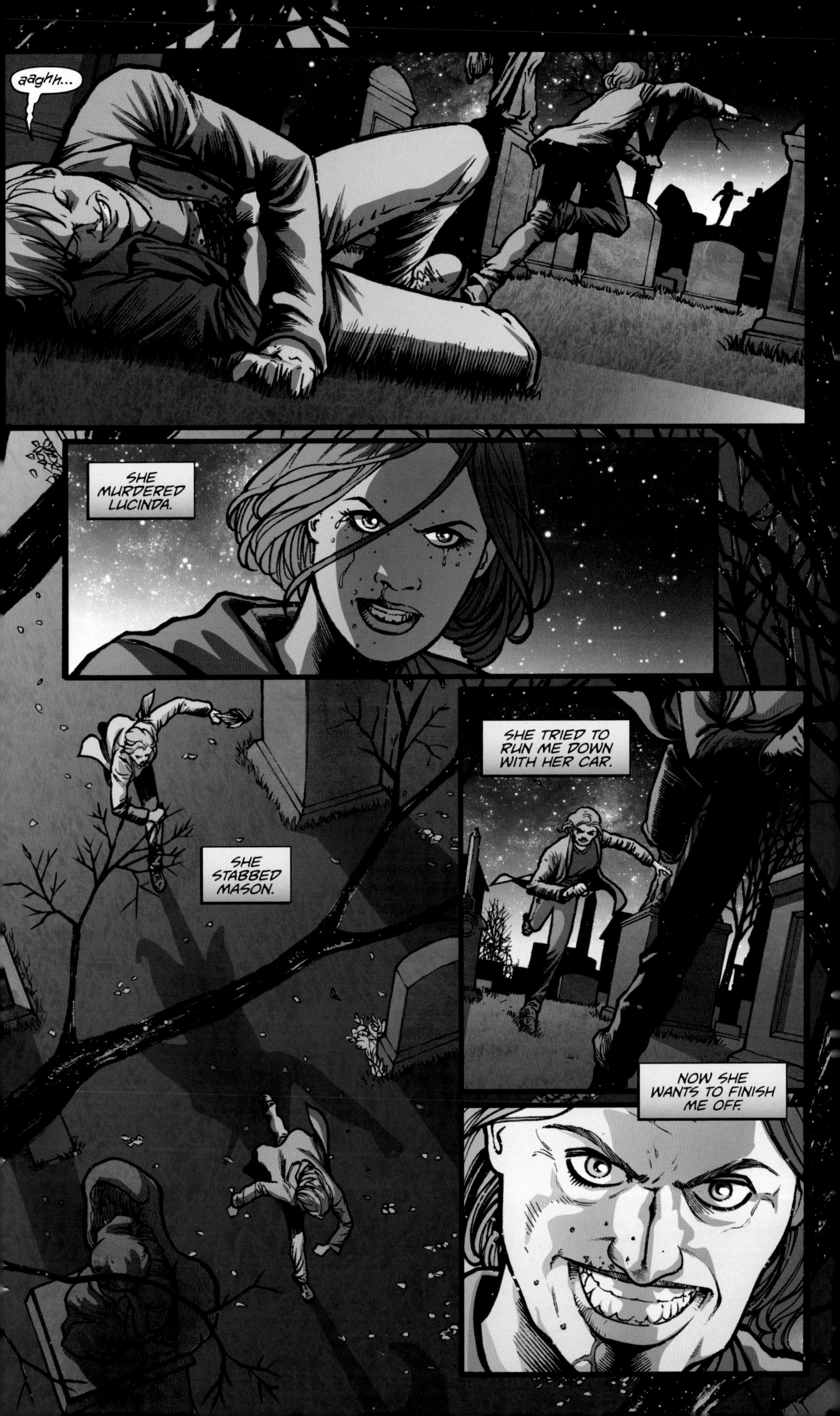
aaghh...
SHE MURDERED LUCINDA.
SHE STABBED MASON.
SHE TRIED TO RUN ME DOWN WITH HER CAR.
NOW SHE WANTS TO FINISH ME OFF.

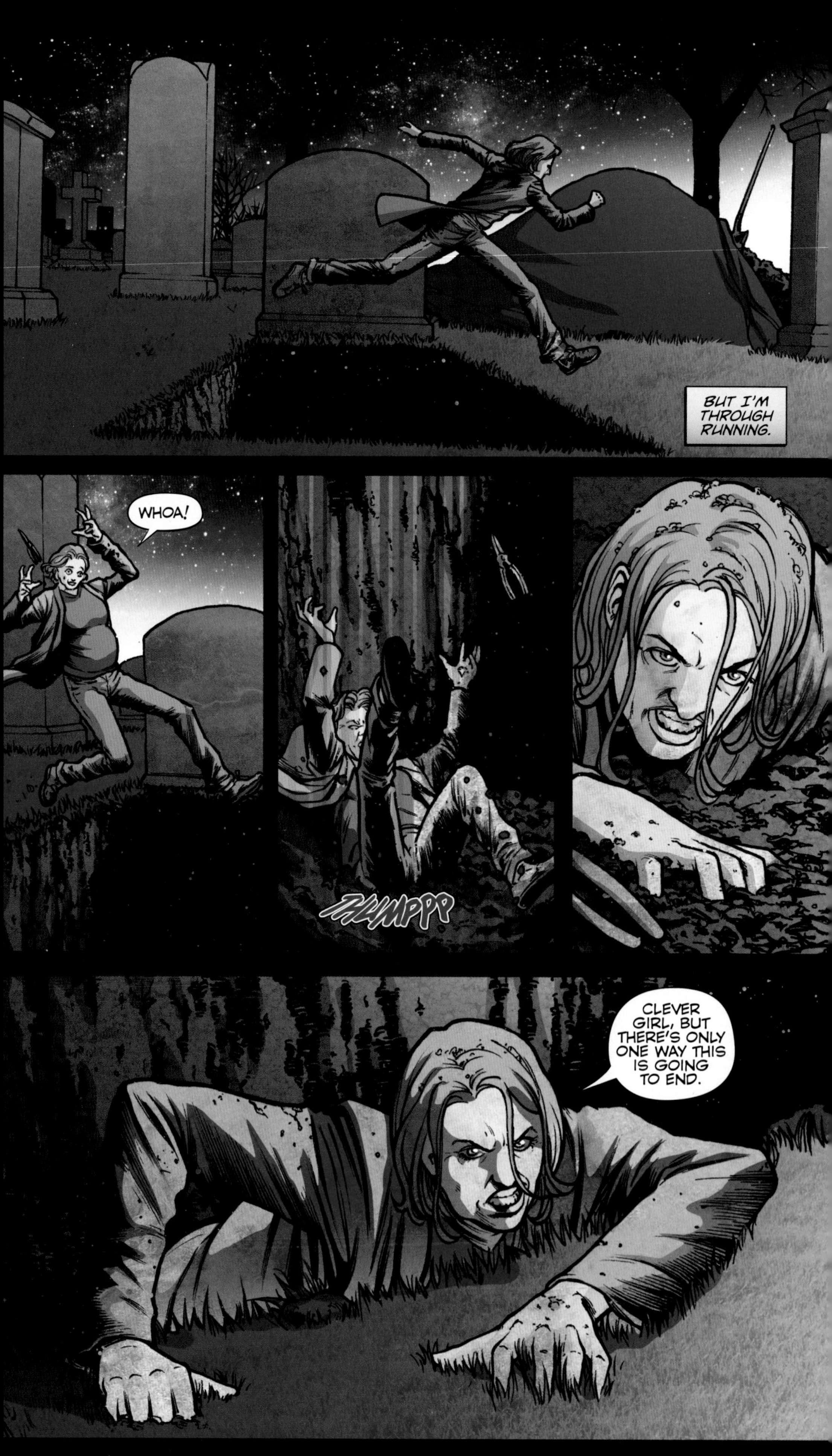

BUT I'M THROUGH RUNNING.
WHOA!
THUMPPP
CLEVER GIRL, BUT THERE'S ONLY ONE WAY THIS IS GOING TO END.

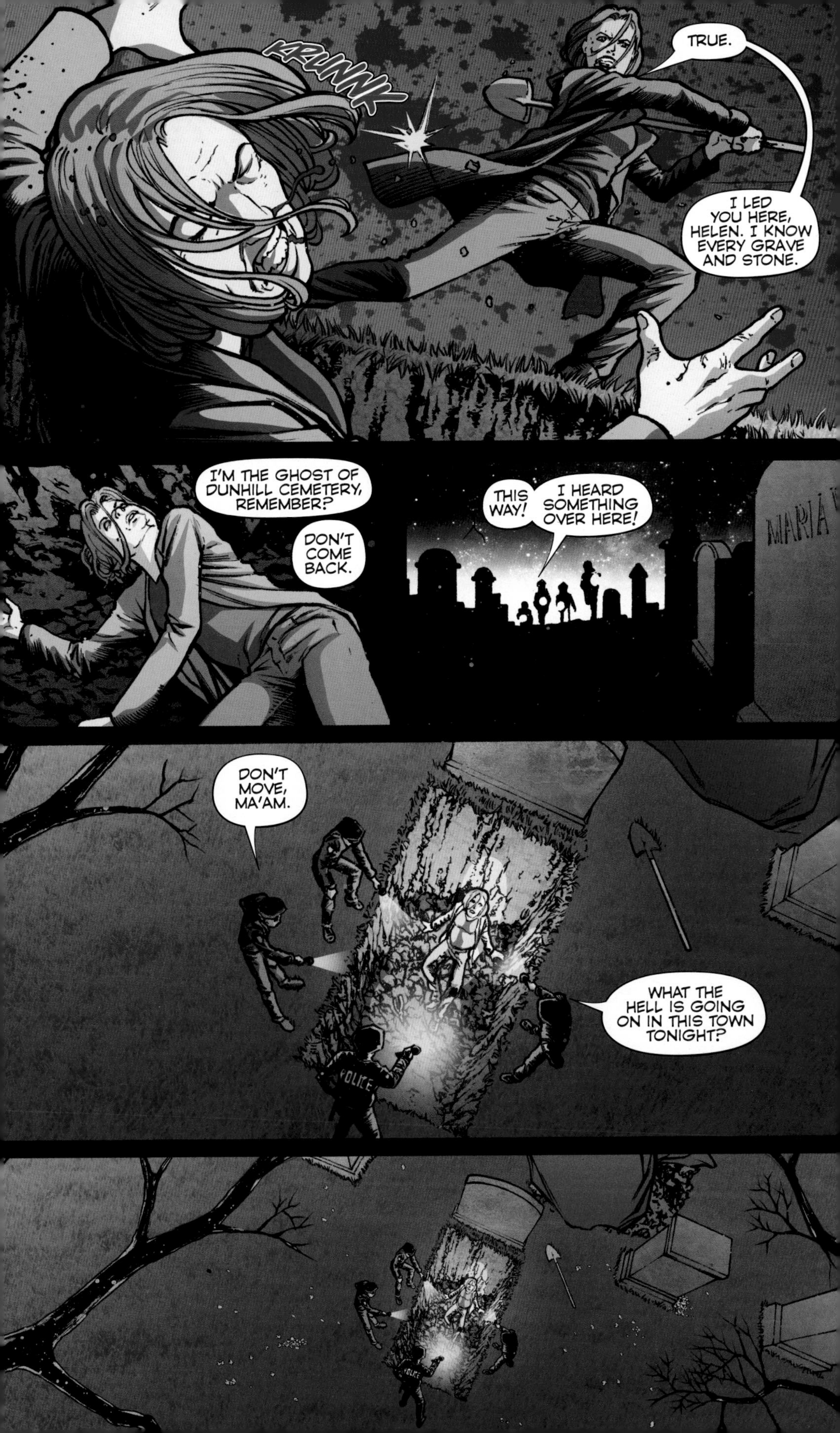
KRUNNK
TRUE.
I LED YOU HERE, HELEN. I KNOW EVERY GRAVE AND STONE.
I'M THE GHOST OF DUNHILL CEMETERY, REMEMBER?
DON'T COME BACK.
THIS WAY!
I HEARD SOMETHING OVER HERE!
MARIA
DON'T MOVE, MA'AM.
WHAT THE HELL IS GOING ON IN THIS TOWN TONIGHT?
POLICE

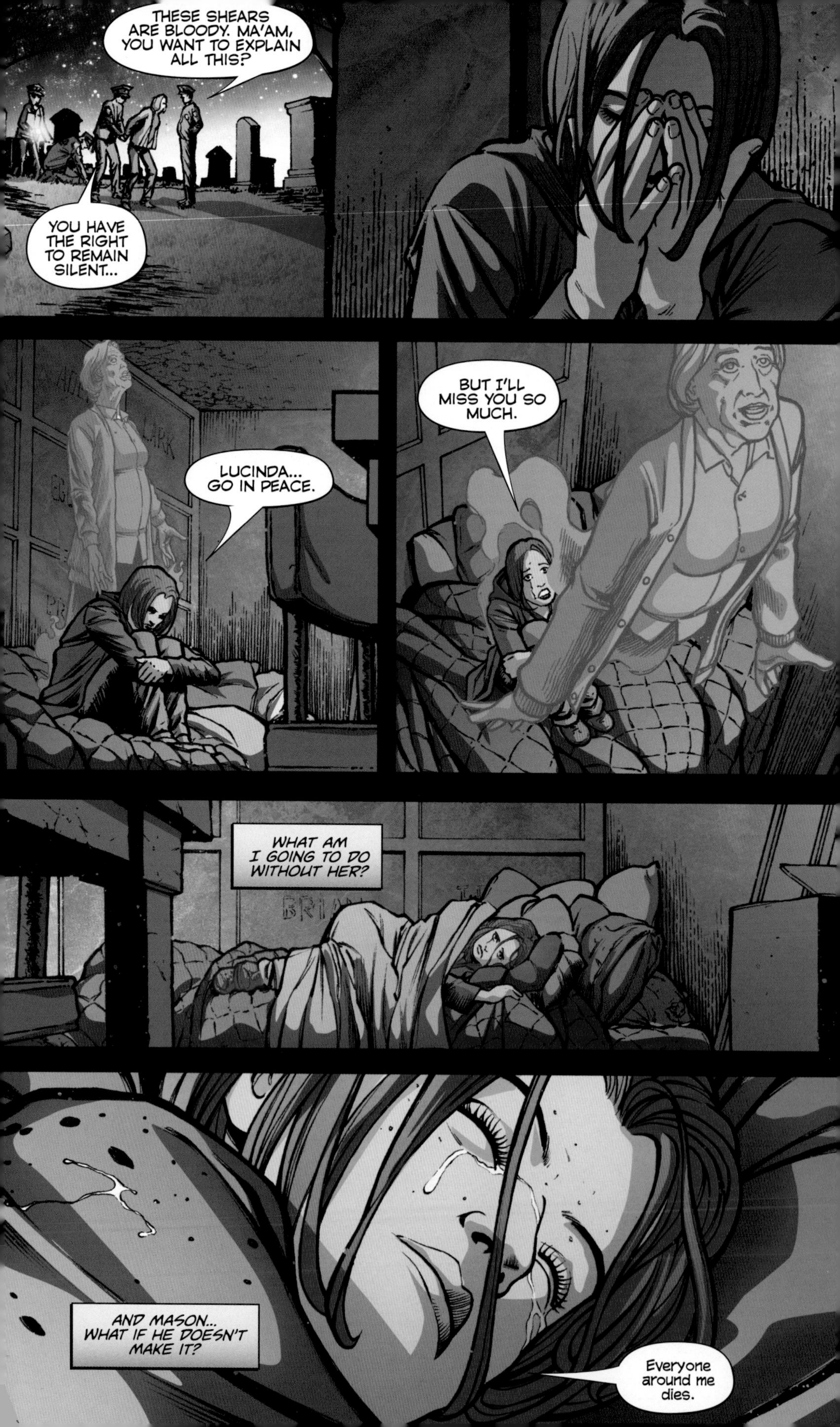
THESE SHEARS ARE BLOODY. MA'AM, YOU WANT TO EXPLAIN ALL THIS?
YOU HAVE THE RIGHT TO REMAIN SILENT...
LUCINDA... GO IN PEACE.
BUT I'LL MISS YOU SO MUCH.
WHAT AM I GOING TO DO WITHOUT HER?
AND MASON... WHAT IF HE DOESN'T MAKE IT?
Everyone around me dies.

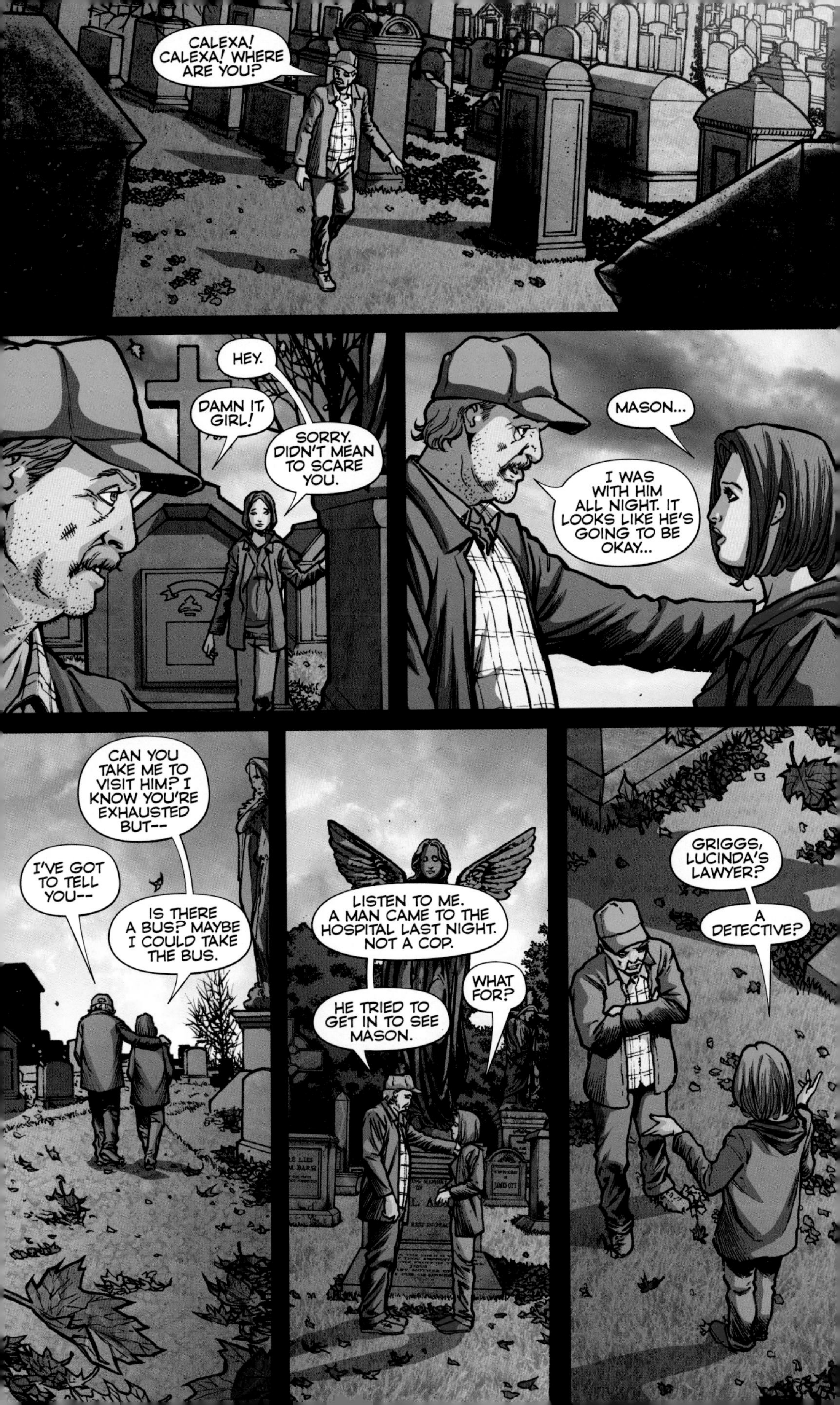
CALEXA! CALEXA! WHERE ARE YOU?
HEY.
DAMN IT, GIRL!
SORRY. DIDN'T MEAN TO SCARE YOU.
MASON...
I WAS WITH HIM ALL NIGHT. IT LOOKS LIKE HE'S GOING TO BE OKAY...
CAN YOU TAKE ME TO VISIT HIM? I KNOW YOU'RE EXHAUSTED BUT--
I'VE GOT TO TELL YOU--
IS THERE A BUS? MAYBE I COULD TAKE THE BUS.
LISTEN TO ME. A MAN CAME TO THE HOSPITAL LAST NIGHT. NOT A COP.
WHAT FOR?
HE TRIED TO GET IN TO SEE MASON.
GRIGGS, LUCINDA'S LAWYER?
A DETECTIVE?

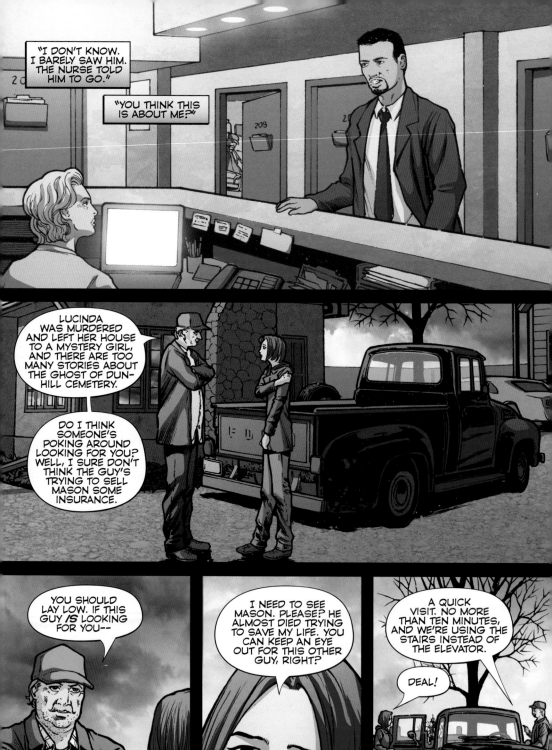

"I DON'T KNOW. I BARELY SAW HIM. THE NURSE TOLD HIM TO GO."

"YOU THINK THIS IS ABOUT ME?"

LUCINDA WAS MURDERED AND LEFT HER HOUSE TO A MYSTERY GIRL, AND THERE ARE TOO MANY STORIES ABOUT THE GHOST OF DUNHILL CEMETERY.

DO I THINK SOMEONE'S POKING AROUND LOOKING FOR YOU? WELL, I SURE DON'T THINK THE GUY'S TRYING TO SELL MASON SOME INSURANCE.

YOU SHOULD LAY LOW. IF THIS GUY *IS* LOOKING FOR YOU--

I NEED TO SEE MASON. PLEASE? HE ALMOST DIED TRYING TO SAVE MY LIFE. YOU CAN KEEP AN EYE OUT FOR THIS OTHER GUY, RIGHT?

A QUICK VISIT. NO MORE THAN TEN MINUTES, AND WE'RE USING THE STAIRS INSTEAD OF THE ELEVATOR.

DEAL!

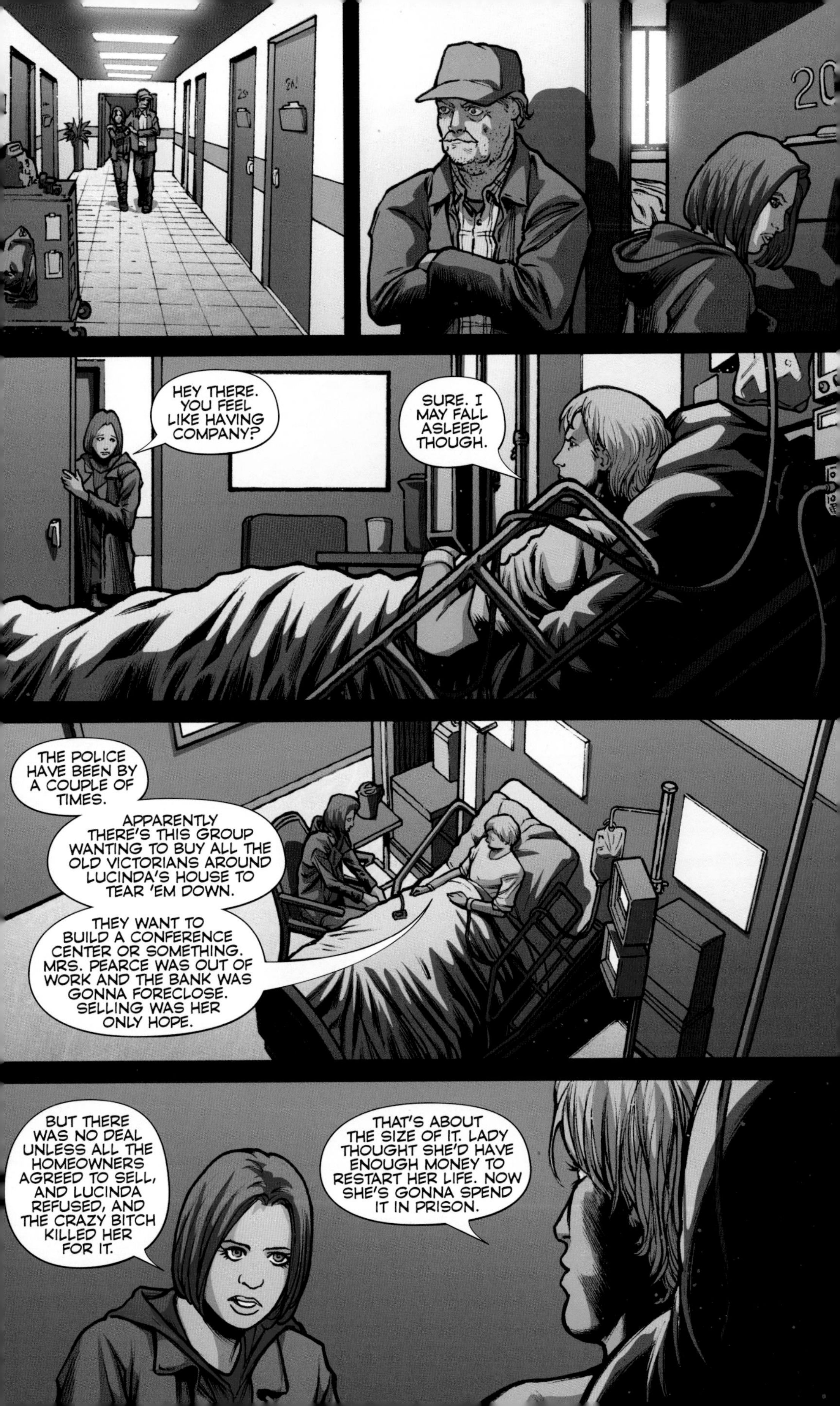

HEY THERE. YOU FEEL LIKE HAVING COMPANY?
SURE. I MAY FALL ASLEEP, THOUGH.
THE POLICE HAVE BEEN BY A COUPLE OF TIMES.
APPARENTLY THERE'S THIS GROUP WANTING TO BUY ALL THE OLD VICTORIANS AROUND LUCINDA'S HOUSE TO TEAR 'EM DOWN.
THEY WANT TO BUILD A CONFERENCE CENTER OR SOMETHING. MRS. PEARCE WAS OUT OF WORK AND THE BANK WAS GONNA FORECLOSE. SELLING WAS HER ONLY HOPE.
BUT THERE WAS NO DEAL UNLESS ALL THE HOMEOWNERS AGREED TO SELL, AND LUCINDA REFUSED, AND THE CRAZY BITCH KILLED HER FOR IT.
THAT'S ABOUT THE SIZE OF IT. LADY THOUGHT SHE'D HAVE ENOUGH MONEY TO RESTART HER LIFE. NOW SHE'S GONNA SPEND IT IN PRISON.

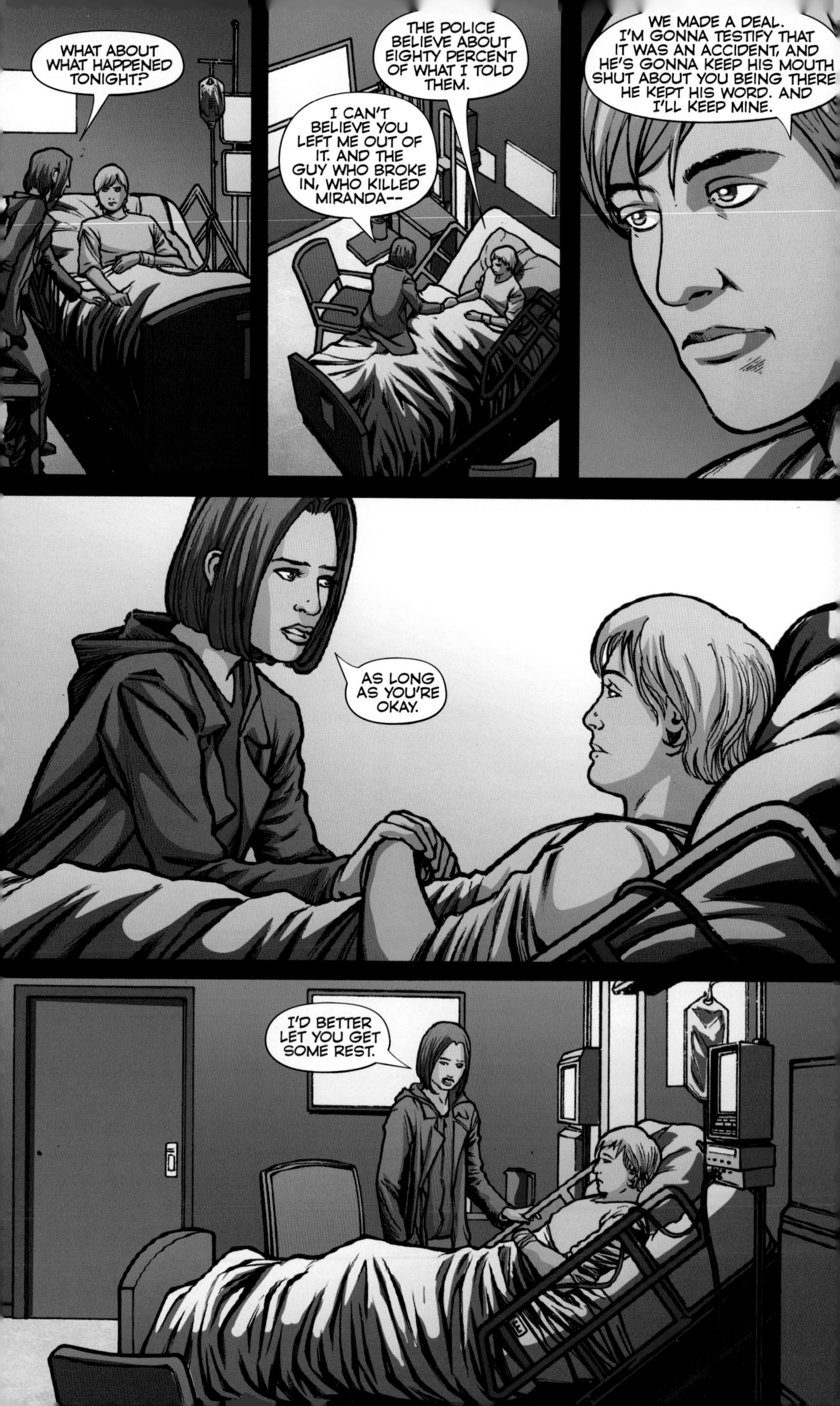
WHAT ABOUT WHAT HAPPENED TONIGHT?
THE POLICE BELIEVE ABOUT EIGHTY PERCENT OF WHAT I TOLD THEM.
I CAN'T BELIEVE YOU LEFT ME OUT OF IT. AND THE GUY WHO BROKE IN, WHO KILLED MIRANDA--
WE MADE A DEAL. I'M GONNA TESTIFY THAT IT WAS AN ACCIDENT, AND HE'S GONNA KEEP HIS MOUTH SHUT ABOUT YOU BEING THERE HE KEPT HIS WORD. AND I'LL KEEP MINE.
AS LONG AS YOU'RE OKAY.
I'D BETTER LET YOU GET SOME REST.

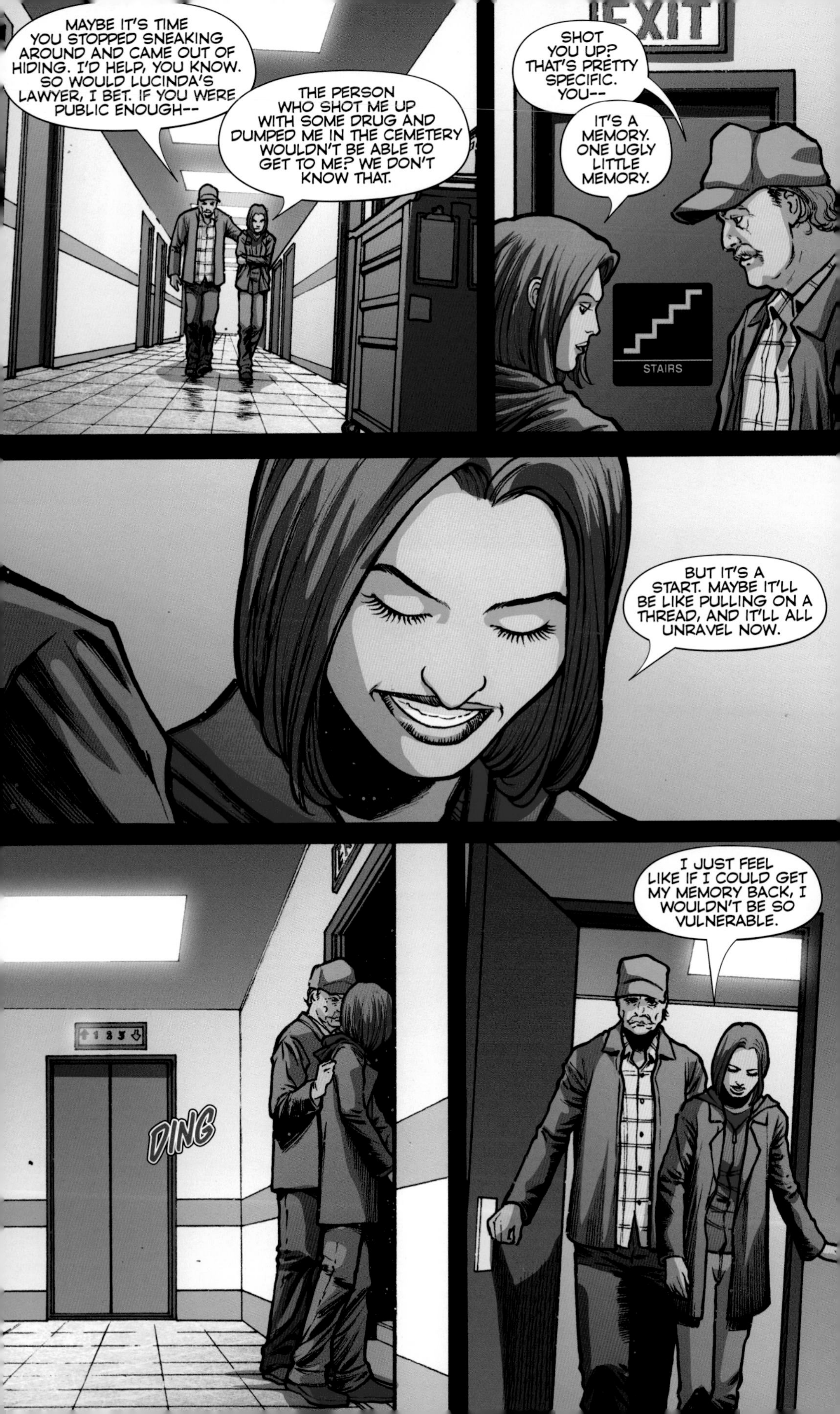

MAYBE IT'S TIME YOU STOPPED SNEAKING AROUND AND CAME OUT OF HIDING. I'D HELP, YOU KNOW. SO WOULD LUCINDA'S LAWYER, I BET. IF YOU WERE PUBLIC ENOUGH--
THE PERSON WHO SHOT ME UP WITH SOME DRUG AND DUMPED ME IN THE CEMETERY WOULDN'T BE ABLE TO GET TO ME? WE DON'T KNOW THAT.
EXIT
SHOT YOU UP? THAT'S PRETTY SPECIFIC. YOU--
IT'S A MEMORY. ONE UGLY LITTLE MEMORY.
STAIRS
BUT IT'S A START. MAYBE IT'LL BE LIKE PULLING ON A THREAD, AND IT'LL ALL UNRAVEL NOW.
DING
I JUST FEEL LIKE IF I COULD GET MY MEMORY BACK, I WOULDN'T BE SO VULNERABLE.

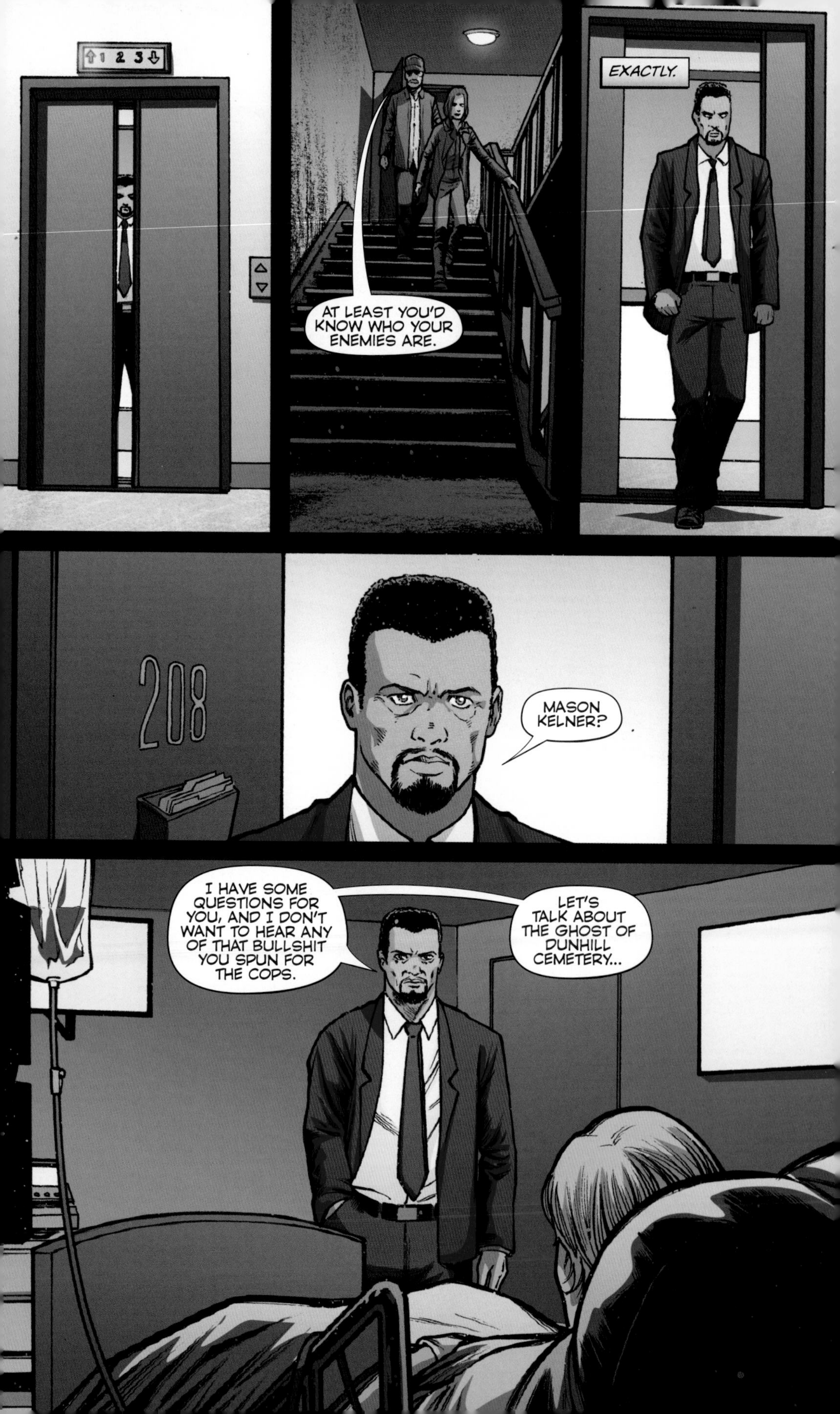

1 2 3
AT LEAST YOU'D KNOW WHO YOUR ENEMIES ARE.
EXACTLY.
208
MASON KELNER?
I HAVE SOME QUESTIONS FOR YOU, AND I DON'T WANT TO HEAR ANY OF THAT BULLSHIT YOU SPUN FOR THE COPS.
LET'S TALK ABOUT THE GHOST OF DUNHILL CEMETERY...

READ ON FOR AN EXCITING EXCERPT
FROM THE NEW MIDNIGHT, TEXAS, NOVEL

DAY SHIFT

BY CHARLAINE HARRIS

AVAILABLE NOW FROM ACE BOOKS

Five months later, Manfred Bernardo checked into Vespers, an upscale hotel on the very edge of Bonnet Park, one of the oldest and "nicest" neighborhoods in Dallas. Actually, Bonnet Park was its own little city. Manfred had thought that his clients might arrive so wired from dealing with the traffic of downtown Dallas that they might not be able to transition to a mellow séance or reading, so he'd selected Vespers first for its location, and second for its decor. The interior of Vespers combined a lot of modern lines and shades of gray with random swaths of brilliant fabric and nearly life-size sculptures of deer and lions. The deer looked startled and the lions were snarling, both reactions appropriate to finding themselves in such surroundings. Vespers played subdued techno music in the background nonstop, and all the desk staff looked as though they'd been kidnapped from a Nautica photo shoot: young, attractive, healthy, outdoorsy. They were all people who would not mind viewing their endless reflections in the other design element of Vespers—mirrors.

Manfred himself was more of an indoor kind of guy, though that was at least partly due to his occupation. Phone psychics who also had websites had to stay by the phones and the computers, so he was pale. He was also definitely not tall or pumped up. And his multiple piercings and many tattoos did not make him look hearty. But he did attract a certain kind of woman, and he did have his own brand of charm, or at least so he'd been told.

The desk clerk who checked him in and ran his credit card was not one of the women who appreciated that charm.

"And will you be wanting to make a reservation for Vespers Veneto tonight?" she asked, smiling brightly.

Though he was tempted to opt for room service, Manfred told himself that while he was in the city, he should look at as many people as he could, since there were so few in Midnight. He felt a bit starved for strangers. "Yes," he said. "That would be perfect. A reservation for one, for eight o'clock." He used the word "perfect" preemptively, hoping she would not repeat it.

"Perfect," she murmured automatically, as she entered the reservation on her keyboard. Manfred wished there were someone he could look at, to roll his eyes. Instead, he looked in the huge mirror behind the clerk, and to his utter astonishment, he *did* see someone he knew. His mouth opened to call, "Olivia!" But at that second Olivia Charity's brown eyes met his in the mirror, and she gave a tiny shake of her head.

"Did you need anything else, Mr. Bernardo?" the young clerk asked, looking at him with a bit of concern.

"No, no," he said hastily, scooping up the cardboard folder containing his plastic keycard. "Thanks," he added.

"Elevators over there," she prompted, pointing to his right. "Behind the panel of mirrors."

Of course, he grumbled to himself while he went around the large wall to find the elevator bank. When one finally whooshed open, he could see his exasperated reflection in the mirror at the back of the elevator car. He rode up in silence. Out of habit, he looked up and down the hall when he stepped out, but he didn't see any security cameras. That didn't mean they weren't there, but he found it a little surprising in a place like Vespers, whose hauteur and prices would surely attract at least some well-heeled and famous guests.

Despite the cost, Manfred had opted for a suite so he could conduct private readings in his room. If he'd been traveling for any other reason, he would have picked a cheap motel. All he needed was a bed and a functional bathroom, preferably clean. But clients always thought better of him, and therefore themselves, if they consulted him in an obviously expensive venue.

To Manfred's approval, the living room was lavish: couch, easy chair, television, bar, and microwave, with a small round dining table and two chairs that would be perfect for his readings. The bedroom was as comfortable as he'd hoped, and the bathroom was positively over-the-top. Manfred unpacked quickly and efficiently (he'd brought an all-black wardrobe for this weekend) and put his list of bookings on the round table, together with his tarot cards, his mirror, and a velvet pad on which to place objects brought to him by clients to aid him in his readings. He was not primarily a touch psychometrist, but every now and then he got a flash of clarity.

He felt keen anticipation as he viewed the layout of familiar items. In-person readings were exciting, because he had a chance to use his true gift to the best of his ability. For that reason, the sessions were not only tiring, but occasionally frightening. He'd scheduled two in the morning, three in the afternoon for Saturday, and the same for Sunday. He'd check out Monday morning and drive back to Midnight.

But this evening, he'd relax and enjoy the change of scene and the rare luxury. This was a far cry from his little house in Midnight. In the bathroom was a claw-footed tub with a showerhead added much later, and not enough room to swing a cat. He could swing a good-sized lynx in this tiled wonder, with its multiple showerheads and double sinks. "Time to shower, change, and have a great dinner," he said happily. He'd put the glimpse of Olivia Charity out of his mind.

Manfred felt far more urbane when he went downstairs. Though he knew it was probably not the fancy-restaurant thing to do, he took his e-reader with him. He wasn't fond of staring off into space, and he was in the middle of a book about the Fox sisters, who'd founded Spiritualism. He'd also brought his cell phone.

A table-for-one diner is often in a less-than-stellar position, but Veneto wasn't busy that night. Manfred had a whole horseshoe-shaped booth to himself, his back to an identical booth facing the opposite direction. Thanks to the ubiquitous mirrors, he found he had a good view of the room and almost everyone in it. After he'd ordered, Manfred decided he could see almost too much. In his black suit, he looked like a crow in a daisy field; the other diners were in light summer colors, as befitted June.

Then in a mirror high on the wall opposite him, he spotted one other person in black, a woman. She was seated directly behind him in the booth with another woman and a man. Though Manfred got out his e-reader and turned it on, he glanced up several times because her head and shoulders seemed familiar. After the third or fourth time Manfred checked out the woman, he realized he was looking at Olivia Charity again. He'd never seen Olivia so groomed before, and he was astonished at how sophisticated and gorgeous she looked.

In Midnight, Olivia wore jeans and T-shirts and boots, very little makeup or jewelry. The Dallas version of Olivia was wearing a lot of eye makeup. Her hair was put up perfectly in a roll at the nape of her neck. Her black dress was sleeveless and sleek. She was wearing a necklace formed to look like overlapping leaves. Manfred decided it was made of jade, though he was not knowledgeable about gems.

From his position, Manfred could only glimpse Olivia's face from time to time. But her companions seemed engrossed in her conversation, so he felt free to watch them. They were both in their late fifties or even early sixties, he decided, but were definitely what you would call "well preserved."

The woman was blond by courtesy, but not glaringly so. She looked like a tennis player. Her jewelry glittered.

The man had a lot of gray hair, well styled and cut, and he was wearing a suit that Manfred suspected was very expensive.

They're not talking about playing tennis, Manfred told himself. To a casual observer, the man and woman might appear to be having a pleasant conversation with Olivia, but Manfred was a keen observer by nature and trade. The couple both had the slight knowingness to their smiles, the wink-wink, nudge-nudge consciousness that told him they were talking about sexual things in a public place.

Manfred was through with his meal by the time the three finished their conversation. The couple left together. In the mirror Manfred saw the woman fish something from her tiny purse and slide it over to Olivia's hand. A keycard. *Huh, I didn't expect that,* he thought. He'd always speculated about his mysterious neighbor, who had an apartment in the basement of the pawnshop next door to Manfred in Midnight.

Manfred had met Olivia during the previous year at the same time he'd met Bobo's other tenant, Lemuel Bridger. No one had ever given him much background on his neighbors, because people in Midnight weren't prone to gossiping about one another, as a rule. But gradually, Manfred had come to understand that Olivia had a mysterious job that took her out of town from time to time. And he'd observed that Olivia sometimes returned to Midnight the worse for wear. Amid other possibilities, he had considered the idea that Olivia might be a prostitute. But as he'd gotten to know her, something about the way she handled herself made him discard the idea.

Despite the way her dinner with the older couple had played out, he couldn't believe it now. *What's she up to?* he asked himself. He glanced down at his watch. After seven minutes, Olivia rose and left the restaurant. She walked right by him, but she didn't acknowledge him by so much as a twitch of an eyebrow.

Manfred left the restaurant maybe three minutes later, but he did not see Olivia at the elevator bank as he'd half expected. In fact, he didn't see her again that night. He woke once in the early morning, aware of some hubbub down the hall from his third-floor room; but it subsided, and he slept another hour.

When he stepped out of his room to go down to the hotel's coffee shop for breakfast, the police were wheeling a body in a bag out of a room closer to the elevators than his. Manfred thought, *Oh, shit. What did Olivia do?*

E